SOUL DRIVER
OCEAN COLOUR SCENE

1995-1999

A PHOTOGRAPHIC JOURNAL OF A MODERN ROCK'N'ROLL BAND

Tony Briggs / Ian Snowball
Foreword by Damon Minchella

54321 COUNTDOWN

First published 2014.

A Countdown Publishing paperback.

First published in Great Britain in 2014 by
Countdown Publishing Limited,
58 Bury Mead Road, Hitchin, Hertfordshire SG5 1RT.
www.countdownbooks.com

1st Edition.

© 2014 Tony Briggs / Ian Snowball.

The right of Tony Briggs / Ian Snowball to be identified
as the author of this work has been asserted by him in
accordance with the Copyright Designs and Patents Act 1988.

All rights reserved. No part of this publication may be
reproduced, stored in a retrievable system or transmitted
in any form or by any means, electronic, mechanical,
photocopying, recording or otherwise without the prior
permission of the copyright owner.

ISBN 978 0 9928304 27

A CIP catalogue record for this book
is available from the British Library.

Photography © 2014 Tony Briggs.
www.tonybriggs.com

Designed by
Hand Creative,
Suite B, 21A Bucklersbury, Hitchin, Hertfordshire SG5 1BG.
www.handcreative.com

Printed and bound in the UK by
Serendipity Print Limited
14 Sandringham, Brighton BN3 6XD.
Telephone: 01273 241417
www.serendipityprint.co.uk
james@serendipityprint.co.uk

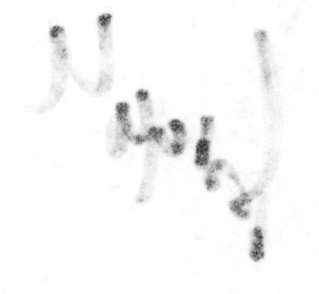

This book is dedicated to Sean Bye

FOREWORD
DAMON MINCHELLA

The period between the first album and Moseley Shoals had its down times. Looking back it's easy to think why didn't we split up and get proper jobs, but at that age and at that time we were just pleased to get off of the record label. It was a nightmare. We did the album three times. At first they wanted us to be the Stone Roses, then they wanted us to be Nirvana and then they just wanted a pop band - and we just weren't any of those things. Back then we were only alright anyway, we hadn't found our way and we were nowhere near as good as we became. So when we asked to leave the label in 1993 they said 'yes please, bye!' Then between '93 and '95 we had twenty four months in which we wrote all of Moseley Shoals and maybe two thirds of Marchin' Already (and most of all the B-sides). We must have written around 120 songs. Also during that period we learned how to do it and engineer it ourselves, and how to write songs and how to play properly.

When Steve came back after working on Wildwood with Paul he had loads of great records and we started spending lots of time hanging out with Paul and he would say 'try this or try that'. Then I joined Paul's band and started playing with Steve White and I learnt loads playing with him.

We grew up as a band and before Moseley Shoals me and Steve started playing with Weller on the Stanley Road tour, and Oscar and Simon would be the support. We played across UK and Europe and because of this Simon and Oscar really learned to play on their own too.

Looking back now we must have been so stupid and pig-headed to think it was going to happen for us. We had been signed to one of the biggest labels in the world but it had been a complete disaster. No one in the band had any money and we were scraping our coppers together to pay the rent on the studio we were using. This studio in Birmingham only had a one bar electric heater but we making this really beautiful music and we just believed it was going to happen for us. That's why, when MCA came along, we weren't going to take any nonsense. We told them that we didn't want a big advance, instead we wanted a small advance, total control and we would do exactly what we wanted to do.

By this time we knew we had become good and during those twenty four months between leaving Fontana and joining MCA, because we had nothing, we became ready. And the Moseley Shoals and Marchin' Already songs were written.

INTRODUCTION
IAN SNOWBALL

**OCEAN COLOUR SCENE:
ELECTRIC BALLROOM, CAMDEN
27TH FEBRUARY 2013**

The last of three sell-out nights at the Electric Ballroom and it's a packed house. A mixture of teenagers, twenty, thirty and forty-somethings all mingled together. The support act have been gone fifteen minutes and then the evocative Hammond organ sound of Green Onions begins alerting all that OCS are just seconds away from entering the stage.

There's a roar and applause and the audience shuffles forward. Beer is spilt but no one minds. Cradock is wearing a light grey suit with white shoes. His guitar tech hands him his instrument and he slings the strap across his shoulders. Harrison is making himself comfortable on his throne and Fowler holds his acoustic, he is ready and is dressed casually in jeans and a crew-neck shirt.

The first few songs are all from the album Pictures, which the band are promoting. The songs sound great live. OCS always sound great live. A few more songs on and a few older classics are thrown in and the audience are 'into it'. There is jumping and pushing and squeezing, smiles and blurry eyes all around. The sweat is pouring. At one point Fowler hovers his microphone, still attached to its stand, above the heads of the people nearest the front. We sing along. Fowler grins.

From here on it's classic OCS that includes the Riverboat Song and Profit in Peace. People sing along and wave their arms in the air. Memories of more youthful days when the band played alongside the 90's big hitters, Oasis and Paul Weller, and at much bigger venues like Knebworth abound. Good memories. But this gig is good too. Just what the doctor ordered.

Ocean Colour Scene complete their set but the audience want more. I spot two familiar faces in the crowd, Nathan and Shooting Suzie, I grab her 'Take a photo of me and my pals Bazza and Dan'. She does. It's fitting because the three of us have been to several OCS gigs together over the years. A few hundred people begin chanting the chorus from Day We Caught the Train and a few moments later Fowler re-appears. More cheers because we know he is going to perform Robin Hood. As always it's a pleasure to hear and to sing along 'Life's so simple'.

The rest of the band join Fowler and play a couple more songs, of course The Day We Caught the Train is one of them, and then their work is done. The audience satisfied. The band line up at the front of the stage, wrap their arms around each other and bow gracefully, each move meaningful and honest. It's a touching end to the night. OCS had just done it again and are about to prepare themselves for their celebrations of 25 years of magic carpet days.

8

I'VE TAKEN VERY FEW PICTURES OF CHRIS CRADDOCK, HE WOULD NEVER POSE FOR ANY, BUT THE FIRST ONE OF HIM AND THE BOYS ON THE BANK OF REGENT'S CANAL IS MY FAVOURITE. I REMEMBER IT WAS A FREEZING DAY IN LATE NOVEMBER 1995. I GOT WHAT WAS TO BECOME THE CUSTOMARY TWO MINUTES BEFORE THEY ALL FUCKED OFF IN DIFFERENT DIRECTIONS. **TONY BRIGGS**

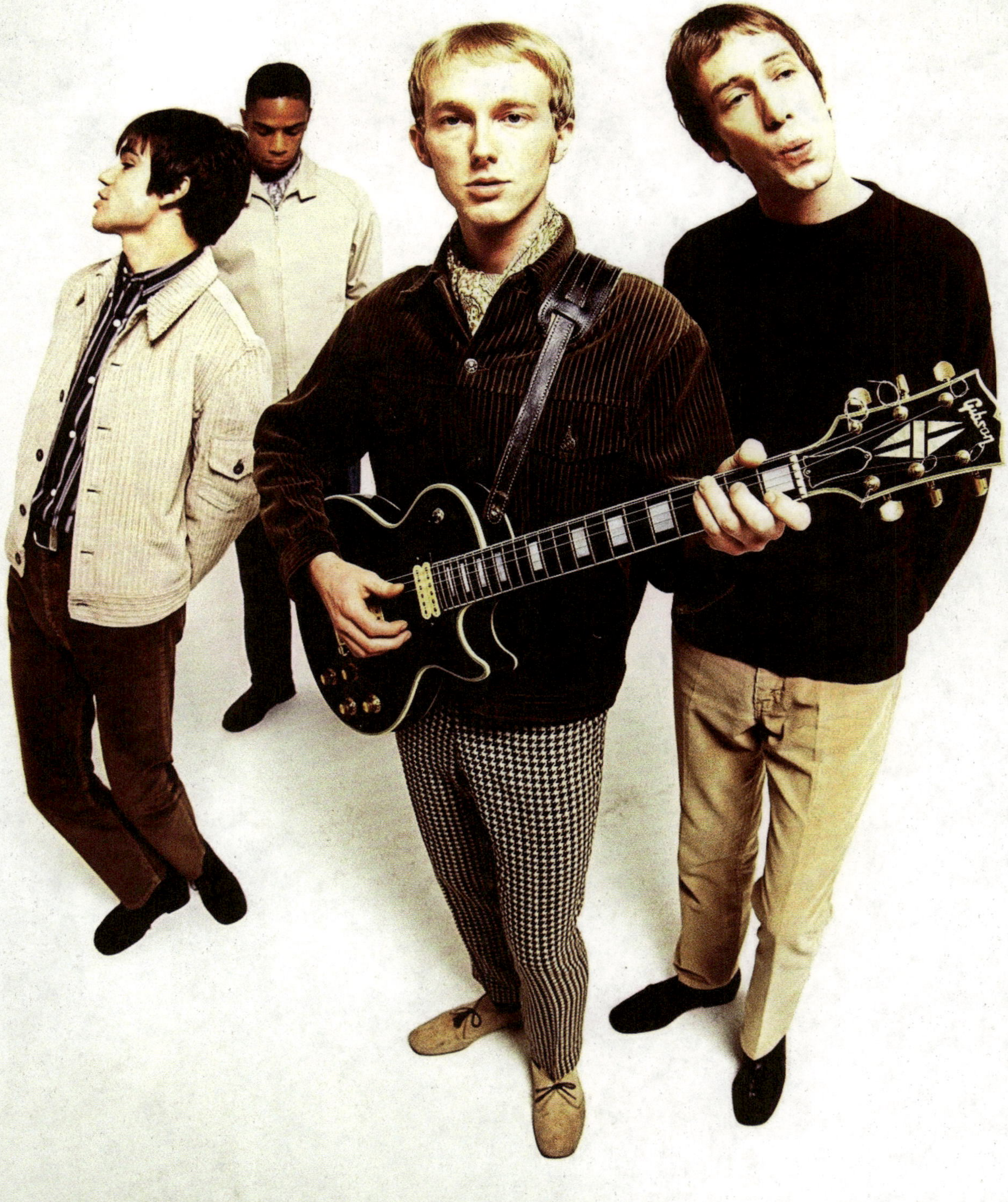
Gibson

11

MY FAVOURITE RECORD FROM THAT PERIOD WAS YOU'VE GOT IT BAD. THE USE OF THE MEDALS ON THE SLEEVE WAS A NOD TO ALL THAT STUFF THAT PETE TOWNSHEND USED TO DO WITH THE WHO. THE MEDALS ACTUALLY BELONGED TO STEVE'S GRANDDAD. **TONY BRIGGS**

13

14

15

FROM THE FIRST SHOOT AT HOLBORN STUDIOS MY PHOTOS WERE USED ON THE FIRST FOUR SINGLE COVERS AND INSIDE THE MOSELEY SHOALS ALBUM. **TONY BRIGGS**

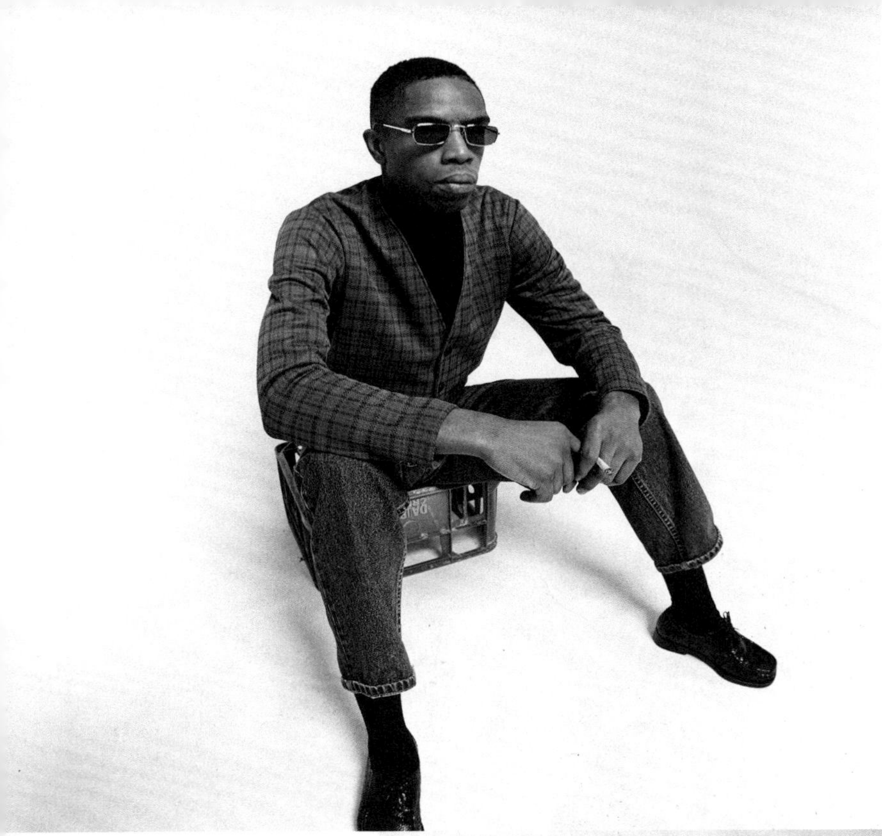

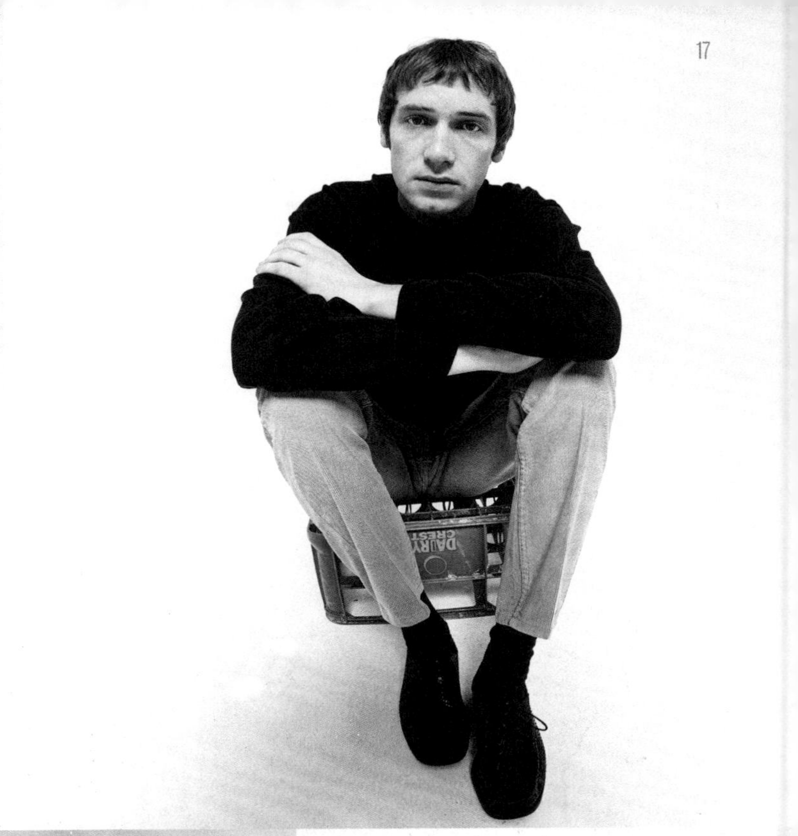

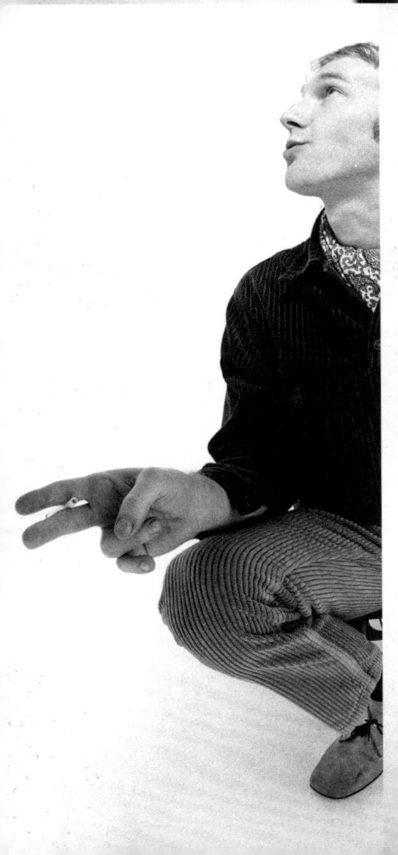

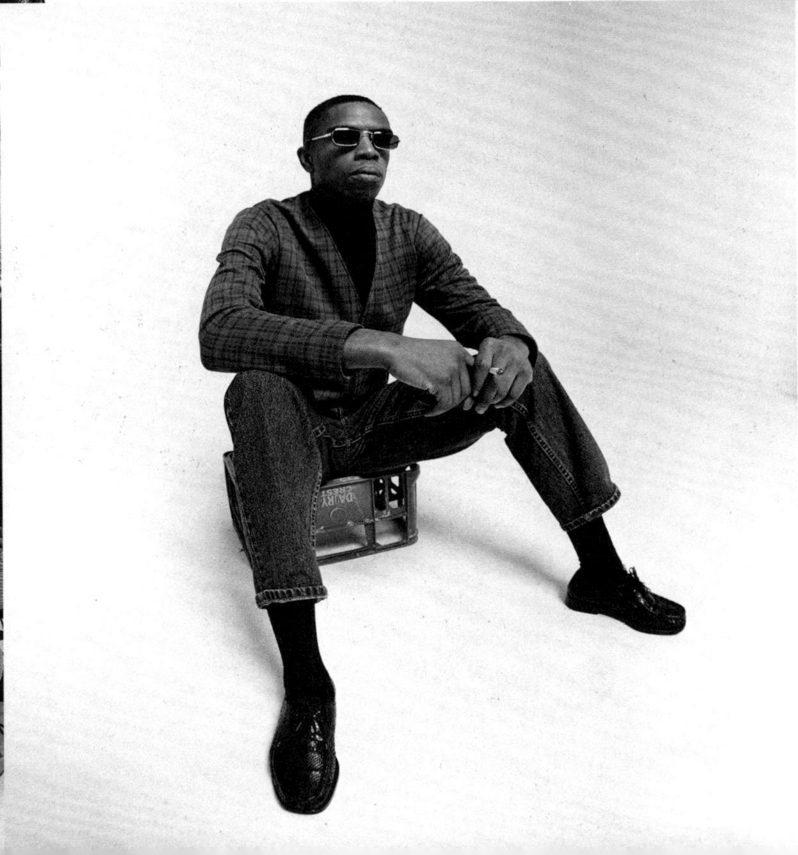

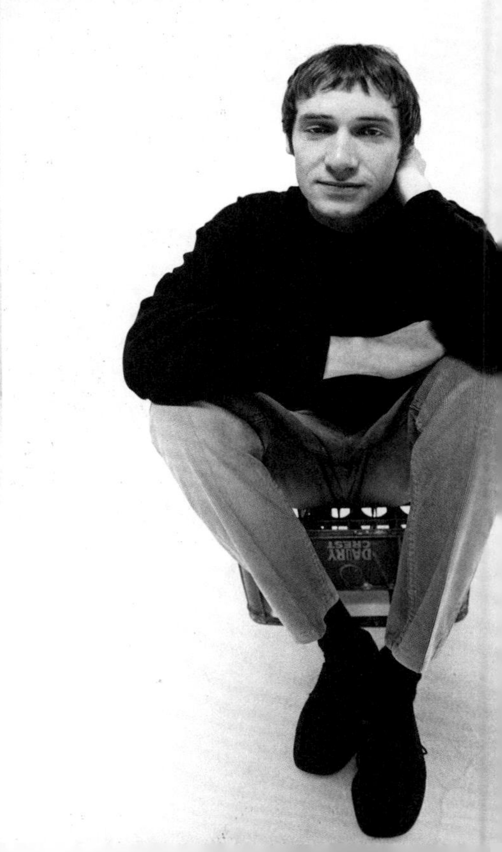

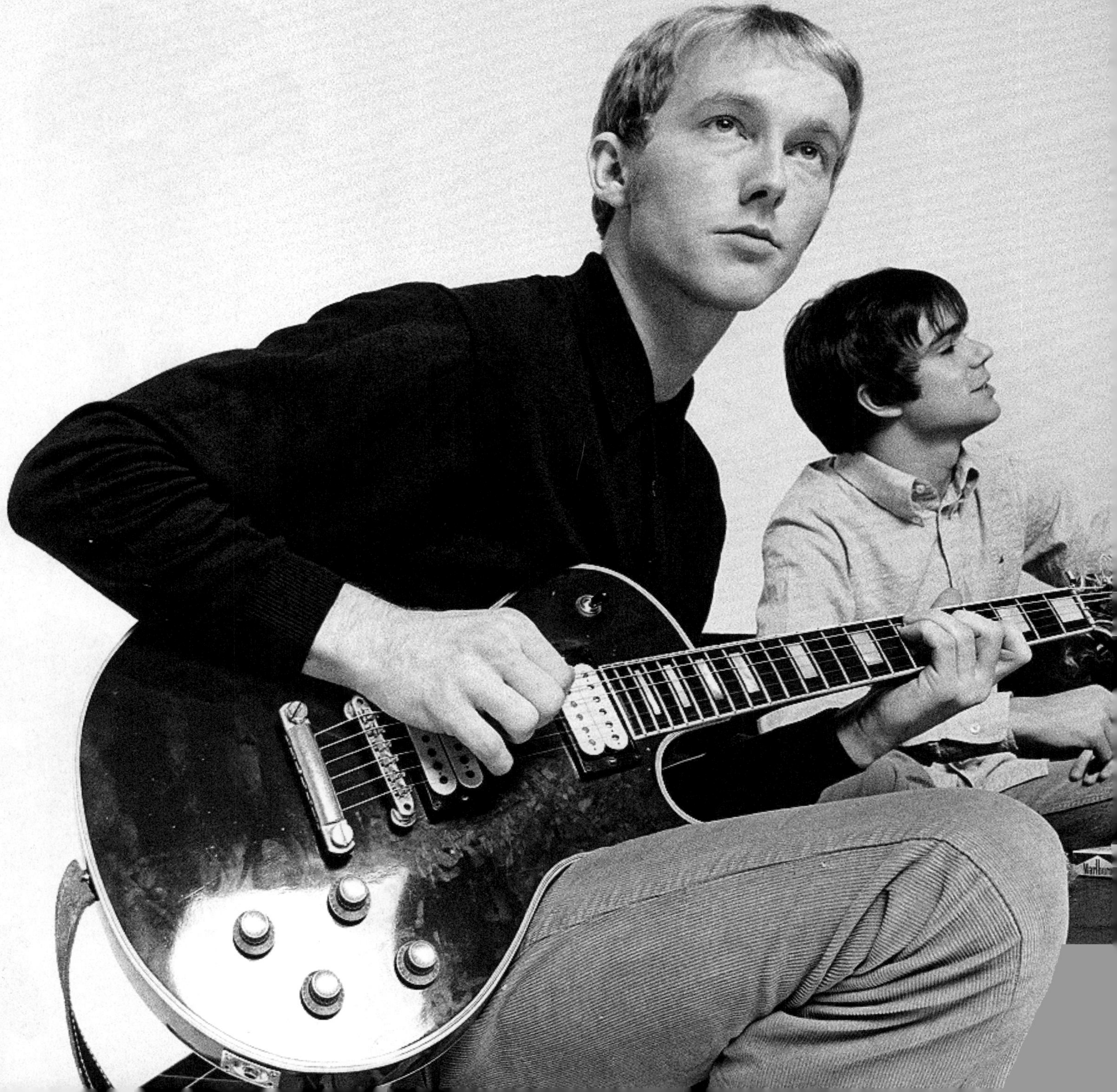

I'VE MET OCS A FEW TIMES, DOWN AT THE STUDIOS AND AT GIGS WITH BRIGGSY. I'VE SEEN THEM LIVE MANY TIMES AND WITH WELLER, I KNOW THEY DEDICATED THEIR TRACK SOUL DRIVER TO PAUL SO IT'S A GREAT NAME FOR THE BOOK. **BILLY McCARTNEY, HOLBORN STUDIOS**

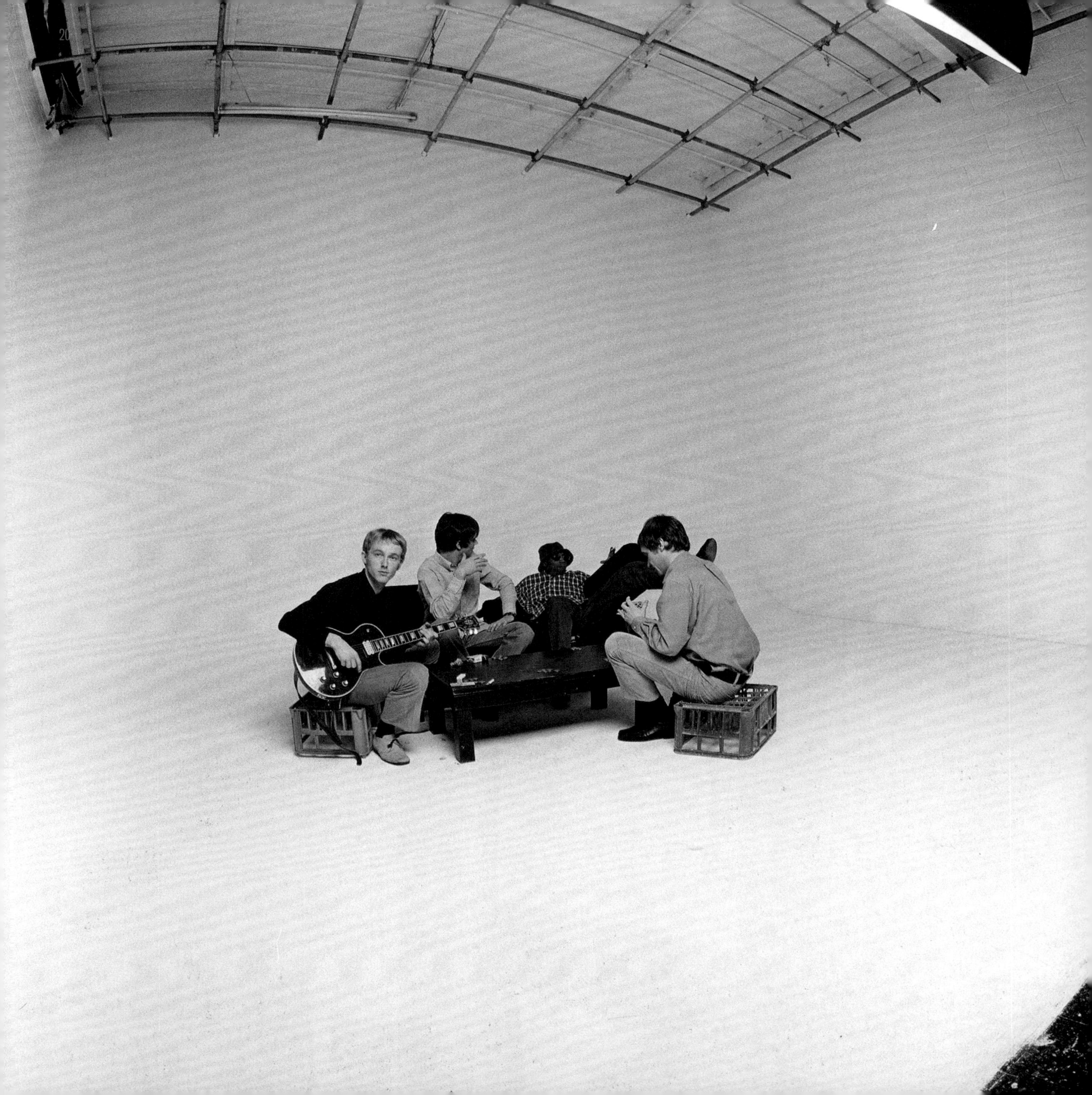

21

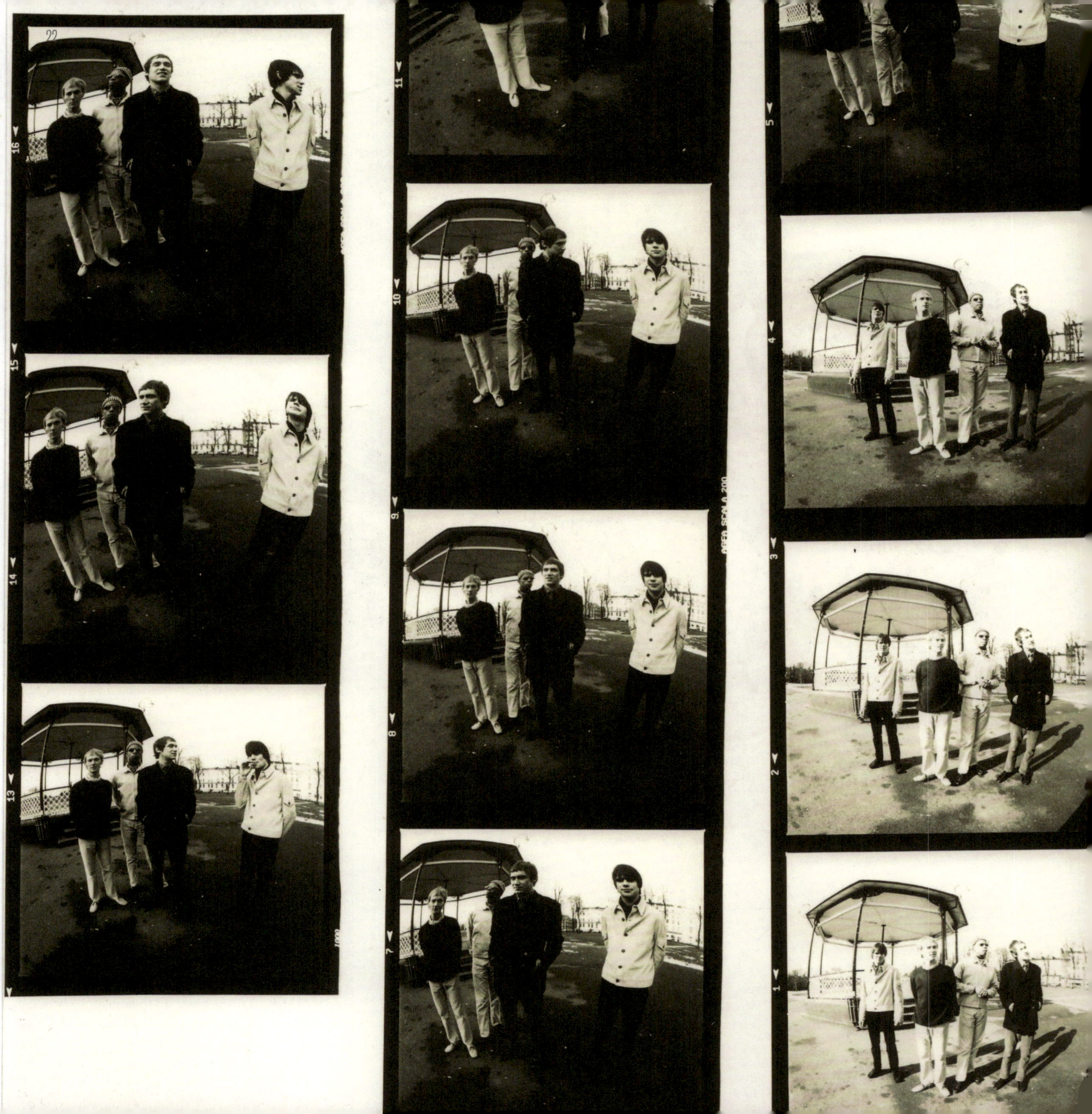

23

24

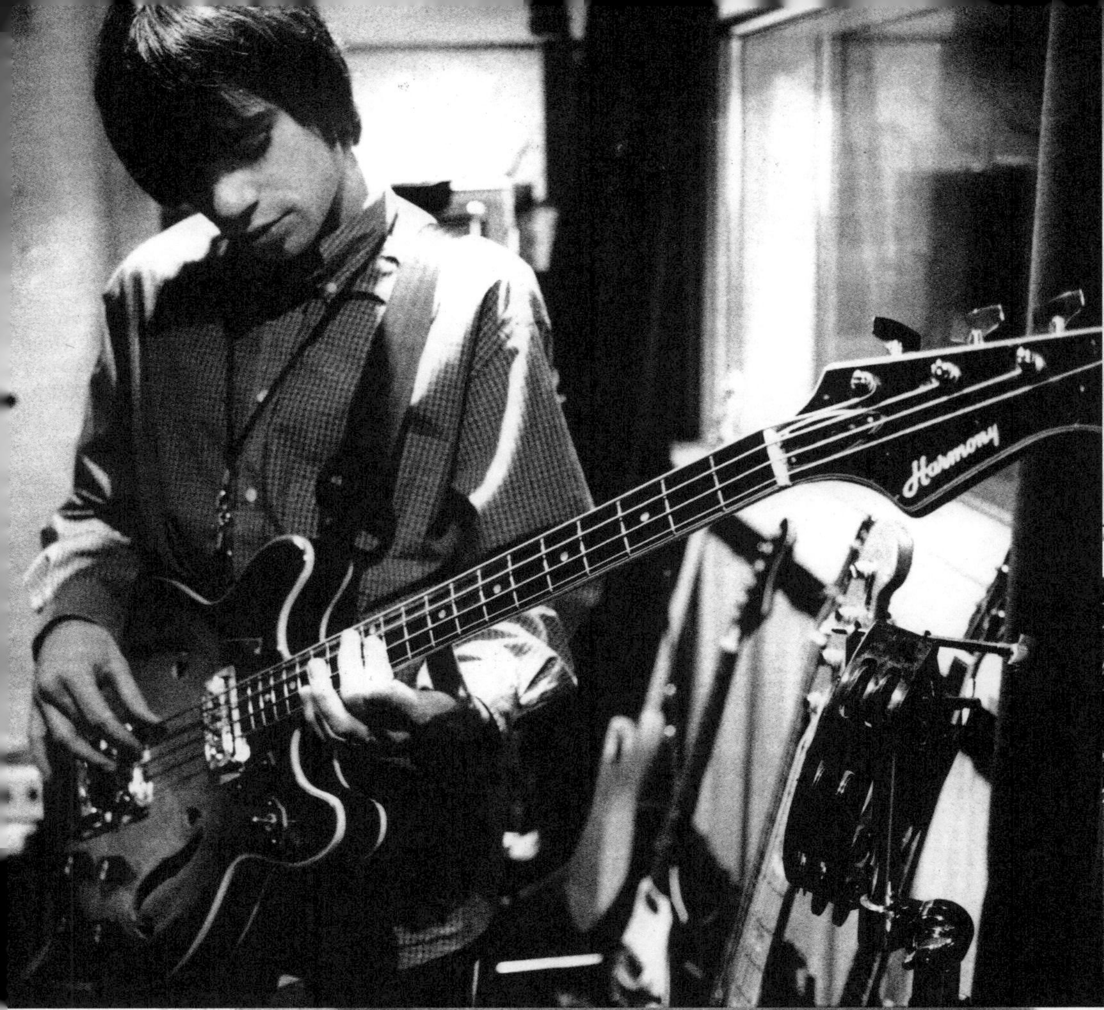
Harmony

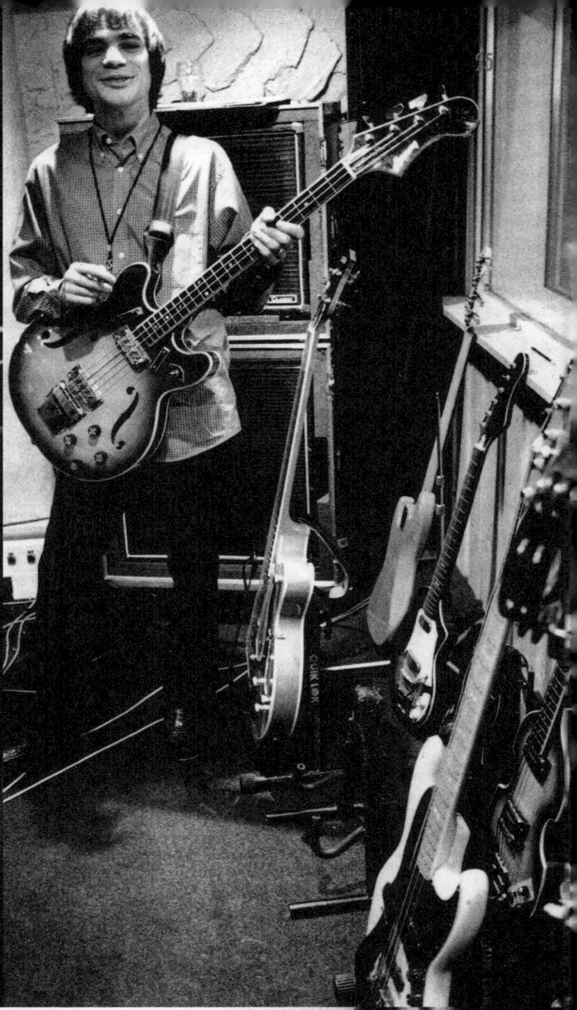

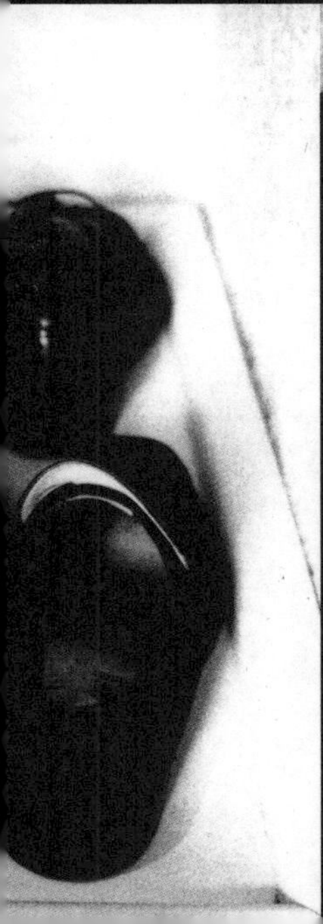

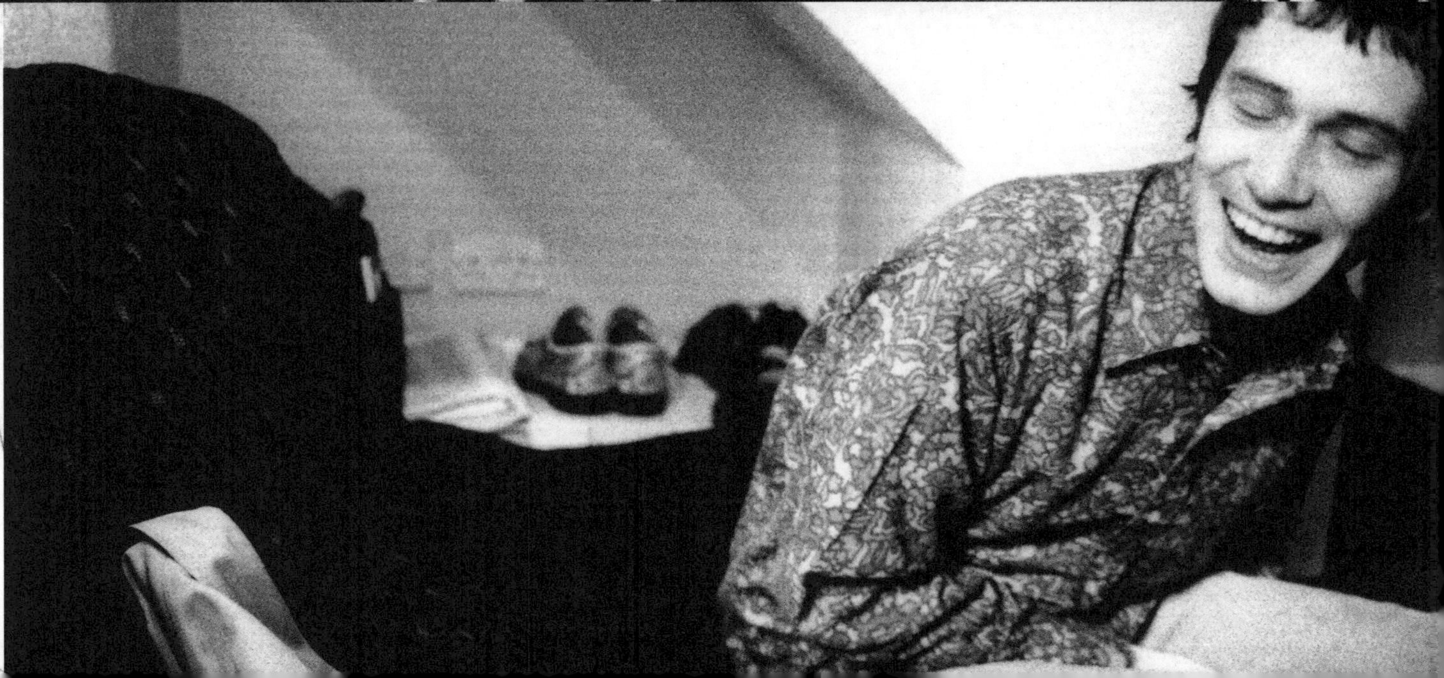

GEZ AND I WENT TO MEET THE BAND UP AT WOODBINE STUDIOS IN LEAMINGTON SPA. I THINK IT WAS WHERE THEY FINISHED THE MOSELEY SHOALS ALBUM. THE PICTURES I SHOT THAT DAY WERE USED ON THE MOSELEY ALBUM SLEEVE. THE BUILDING ON THE ALBUM'S FRONT COVER LOOKS IMPRESSIVE BUT IT WAS ACTUALLY A REALLY TINY OLD WATER BOARD BUILDING IN A PARK WE STUMBLED ACROSS. WE HAD SPENT ALL OF THE MORNING IN THE STUDIO AND THEN WE ALL WENT FOR A WALK TO GET SOME CHIPS. **TONY BRIGGS**

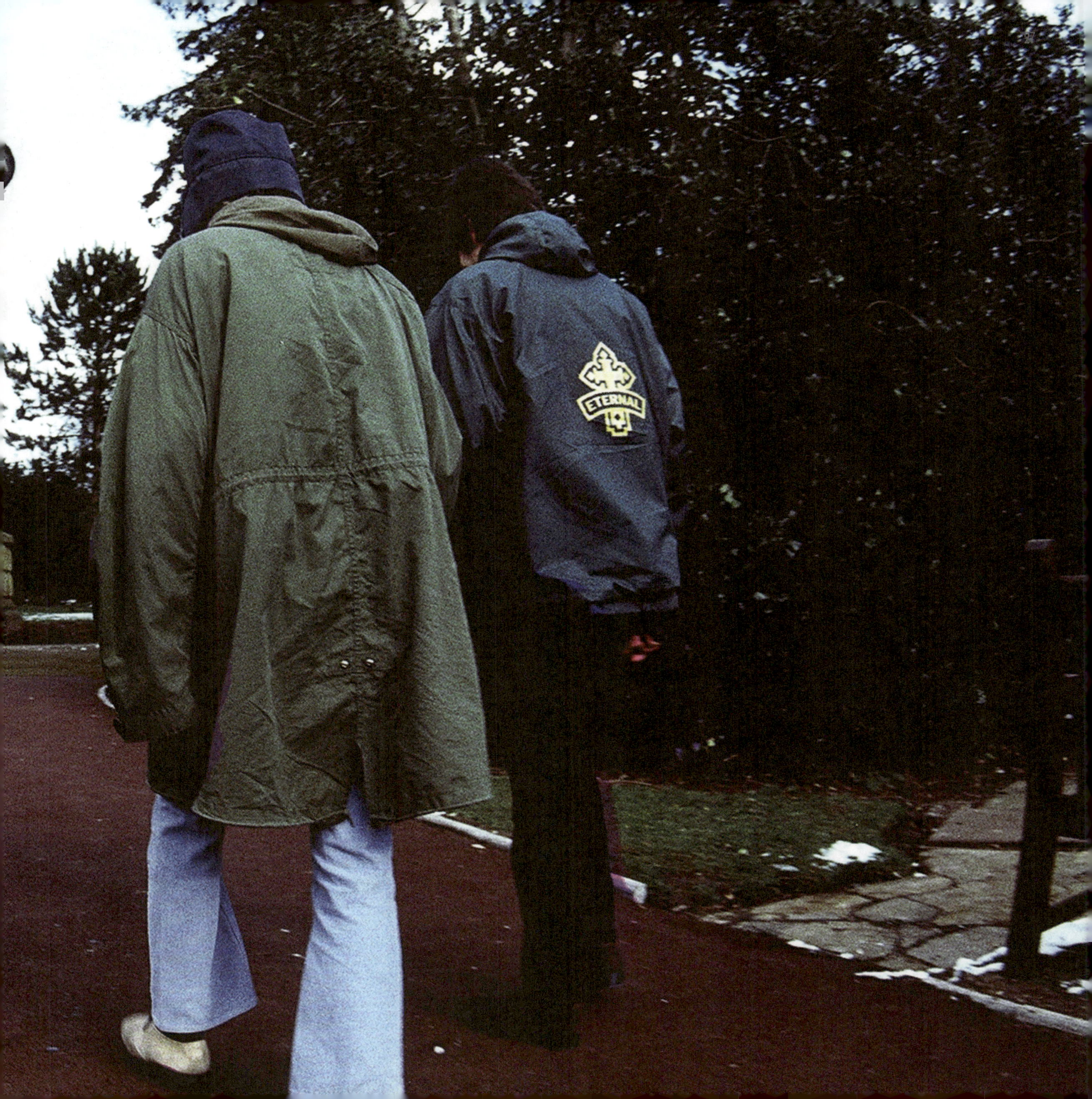
ETERNAL

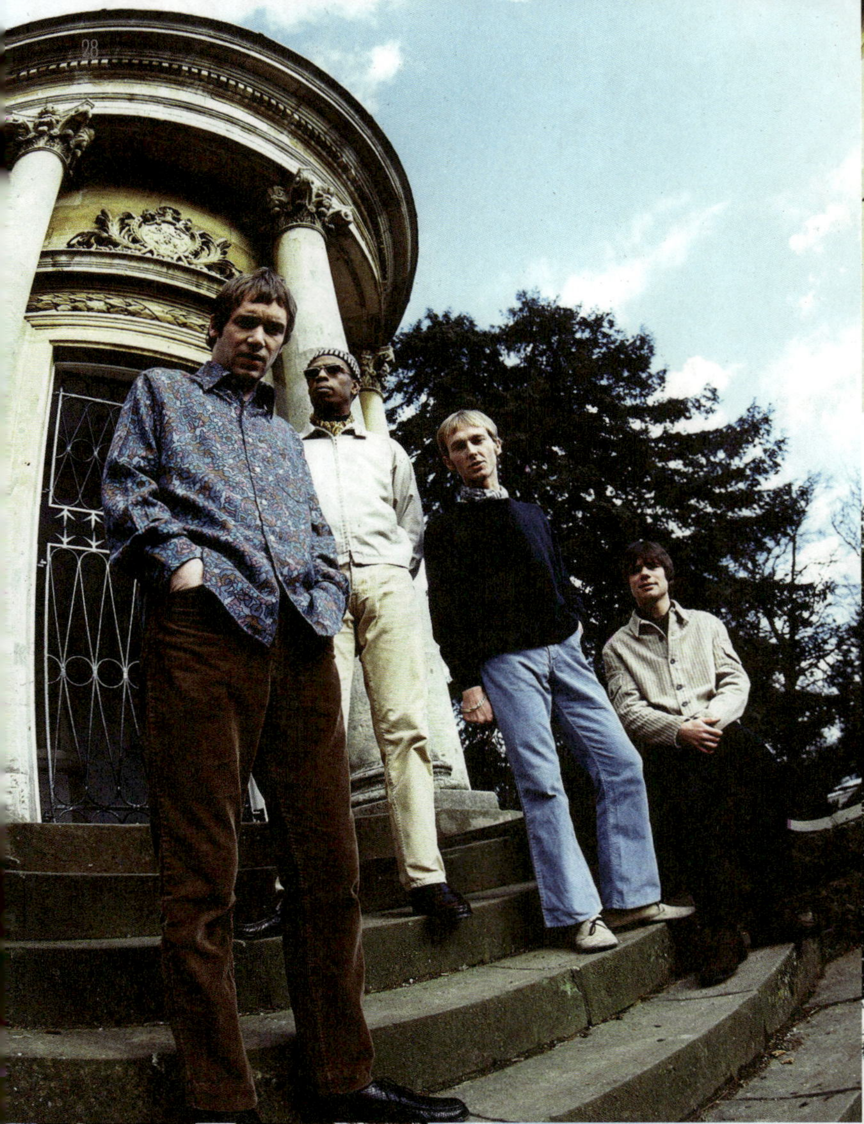

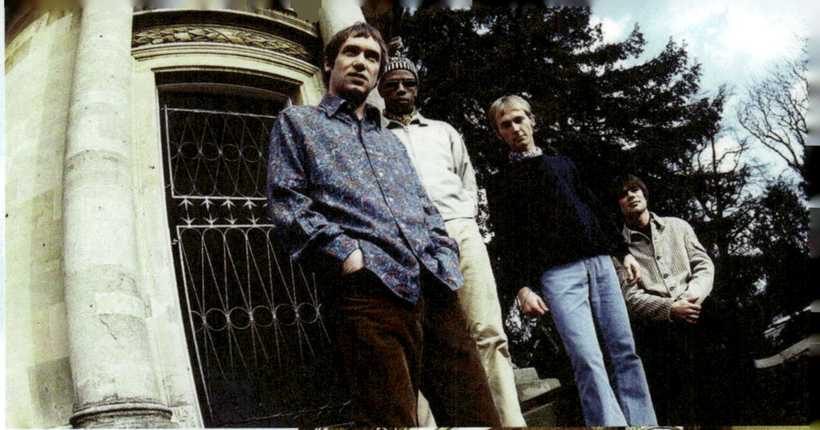

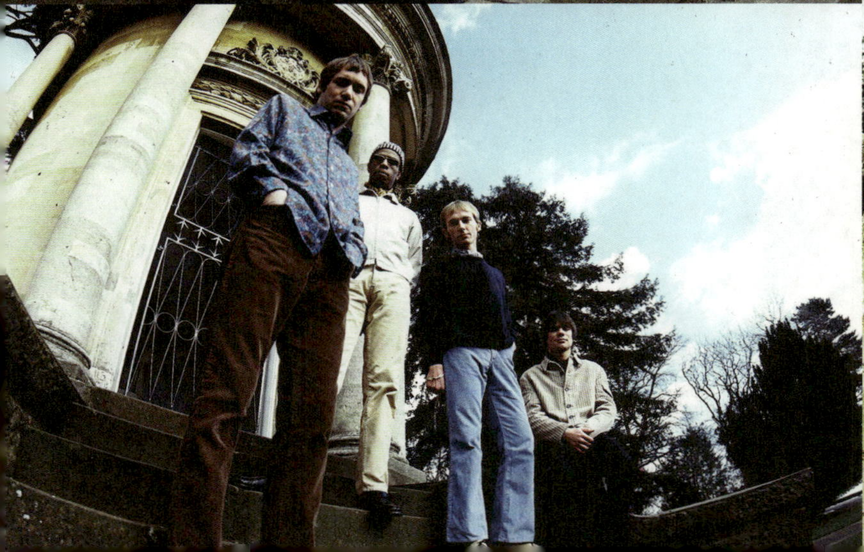

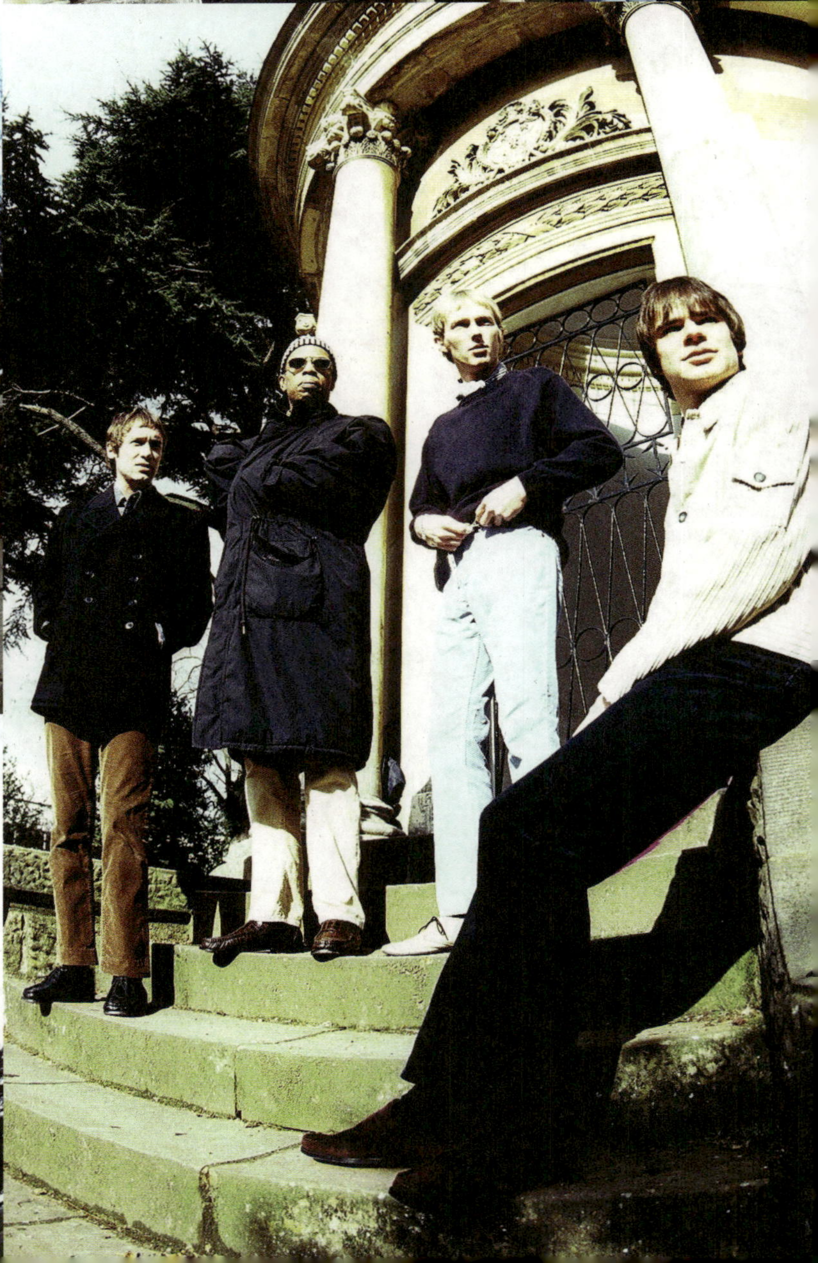

WHEN I WAS TAKING THE SHOTS I REMEMBER WE ALL HEARD THIS KID SHOUTING. IT WAS COMING FROM THE LAKE AND WE COULD SEE SOME KID SPLASHING AROUND. HE WAS SHIT SCARED AND THE WATER WAS PAST HIS WAIST. IT WAS ME THAT HAD TO WADE IN AND SAVE THE KID. I WAS SOAKED UP TO MY WAIST, CAMERA DANGLING FROM MY NECK AND THEY WERE ALL JUST TAKING THE PISS. THERE WAS ONE PICTURE THAT STEVE REALLY LIKED BUT HE REFUSED TO SIGN IT OFF BECAUSE HE HAD ONE HAND TUCKED IN HIS POCKET AND SAID IT LOOKED LIKE HE WAS PLAYING WITH HIMSELF. THE FINAL PICTURE IS CROPPED SO YOU CAN ONLY SEE THEM FROM THE WAIST DOWN. **TONY BRIGGS**

THE FRONT COVER, FOUR FACES LOOKING OUT FROM UNDER THE VICTORIAN MONUMENT SHOT IN JEPHSON GARDENS, LEAMINGTON SPA. THE ALBUM WAS FLYING OUT THE SHOPS. THE RECORD BOASTED FOUR SMASH SINGLES AND JOSTLED FOR THE NUMBER ONE SPOT THROUGHOUT 1996. SPENDING OVER A YEAR IN THE CHART, SELLING OVER 1.3 MILLION COPIES, INCLUDING AN INCREDIBLE SIX MONTH TENURE AT NUMBER TWO. **DANIEL RACHEL**

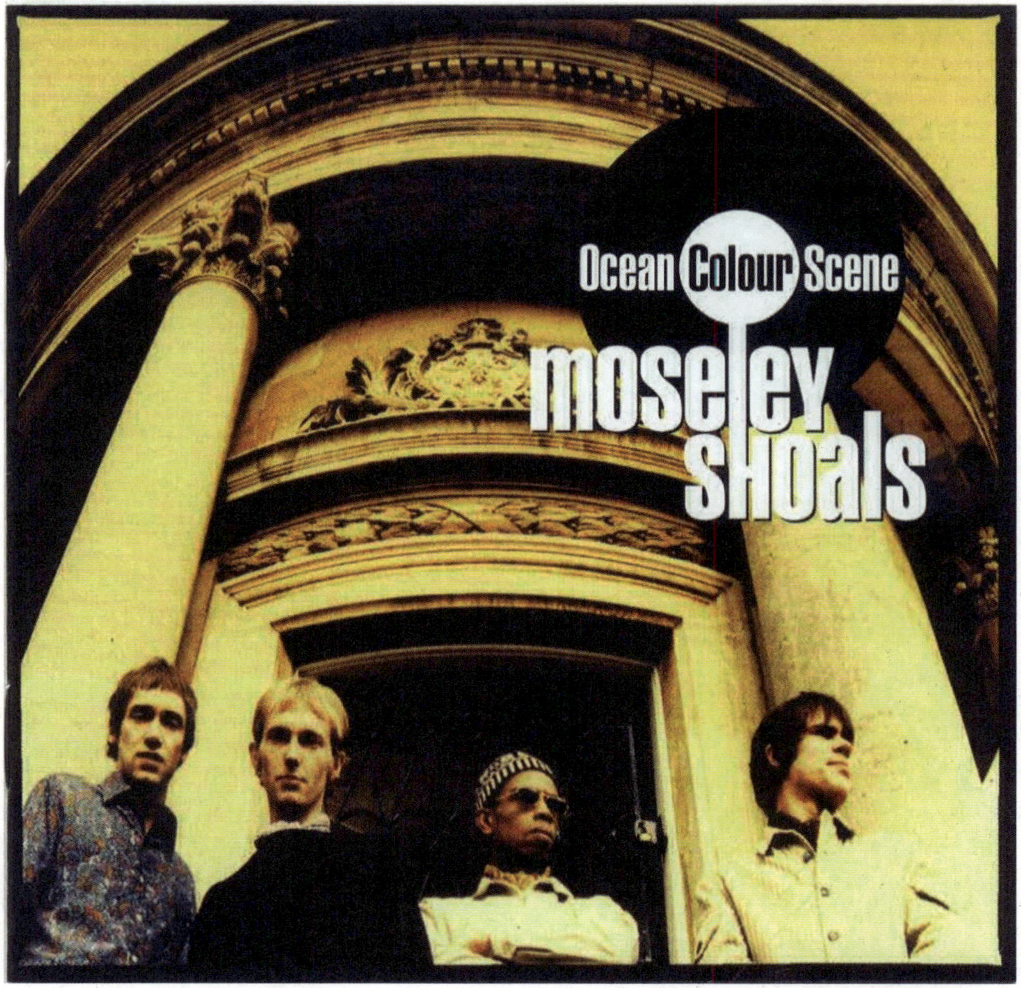

Steve

Simon

Oscar

Damon

32

33

34

BY THE TIME OF THAT HOLBORN STUDIO SESSION IN '95 THE BAND WERE REALLY STARTING TO PICK UP SOME MOMENTUM. I REMEMBER CHRIS EVANS USED THE RIVERBOAT SONG ON HIS TFI PROGRAM AND PLAYED THEM REGULARLY ON HIS RADIO SHOW. CHRIS EVANS REALLY GOT BEHIND THEM WHEN A LOT OF THE MUSIC PRESS DIDN'T. I REMEMBER HIM SAYING TO NOEL GALLAGHER THEY WERE THE ONLY BAND WORTH WATCHING IN 1996. **TONY BRIGGS**

36

"WE FELT AN ENORMOUS WAVE OF CONFIDENCE BECAUSE WE KNEW WHATEVER WE DID WAS GOING TO BE WELL RECEIVED" **SIMON FOWLER**

38

THE GROUP SHOTS OF THE BAND TRYING NEW MERC SHIRTS AKA THE SMALL FACES STUDIO SHOTS WERE SHOT AT THE CUSTARD FACTORY, AS THEY SAY IMMITATION IS THE GREATEST FORM OF FLATTERY. **TONY BRIGGS**

merc
www.merc.com

40

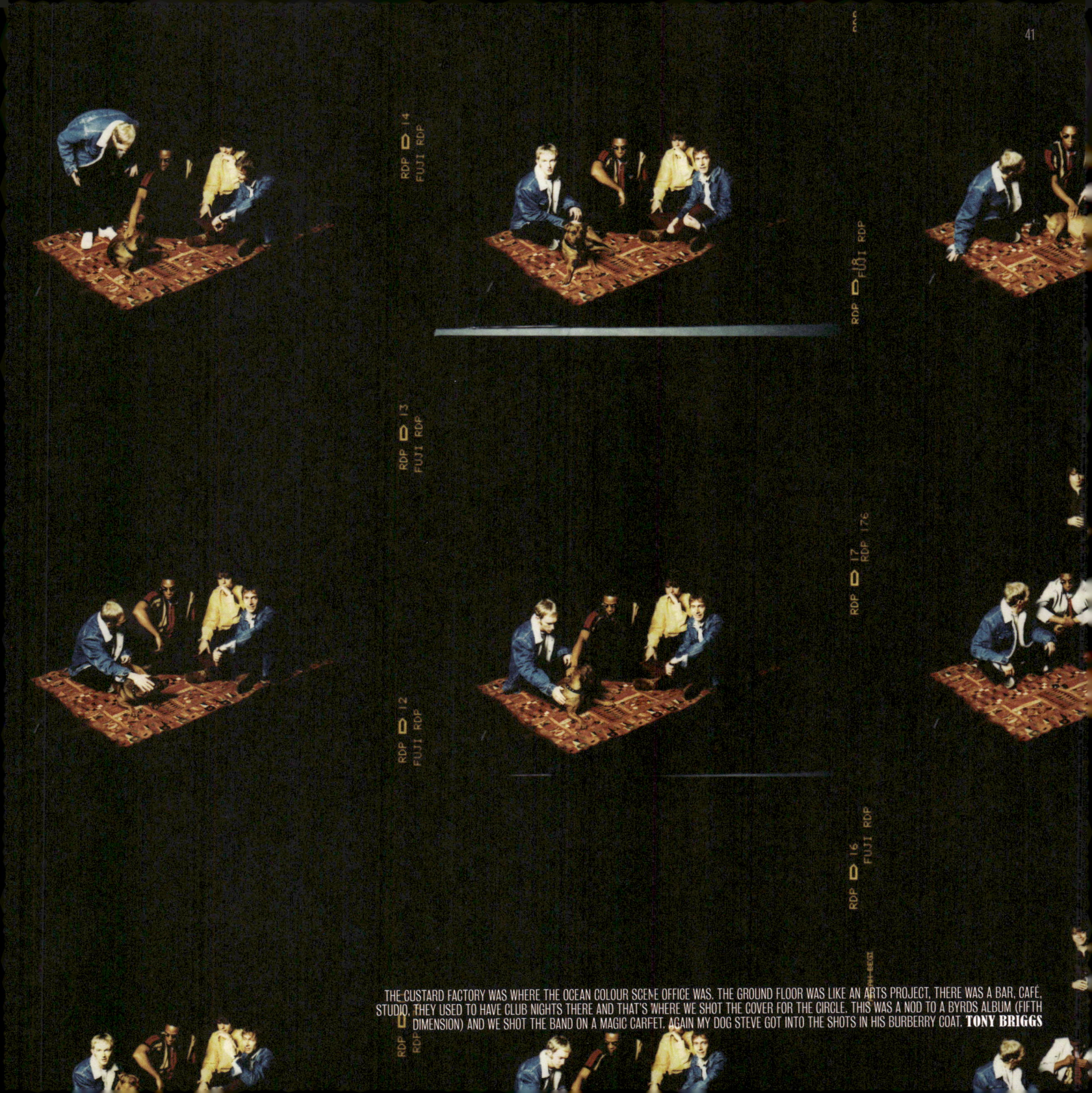

THE CUSTARD FACTORY WAS WHERE THE OCEAN COLOUR SCENE OFFICE WAS. THE GROUND FLOOR WAS LIKE AN ARTS PROJECT, THERE WAS A BAR, CAFÉ, STUDIO, THEY USED TO HAVE CLUB NIGHTS THERE AND THAT'S WHERE WE SHOT THE COVER FOR THE CIRCLE. THIS WAS A NOD TO A BYRDS ALBUM (FIFTH DIMENSION) AND WE SHOT THE BAND ON A MAGIC CARPET. AGAIN MY DOG STEVE GOT INTO THE SHOTS IN HIS BURBERRY COAT. **TONY BRIGGS**

DO YOU NOT GET NERVOUS STEPPING OUT IN FRONT OF 125,000 PEOPLE?
IT'S ALRIGHT, THERE'S FOUR OF US
SIMON FOWLER

43

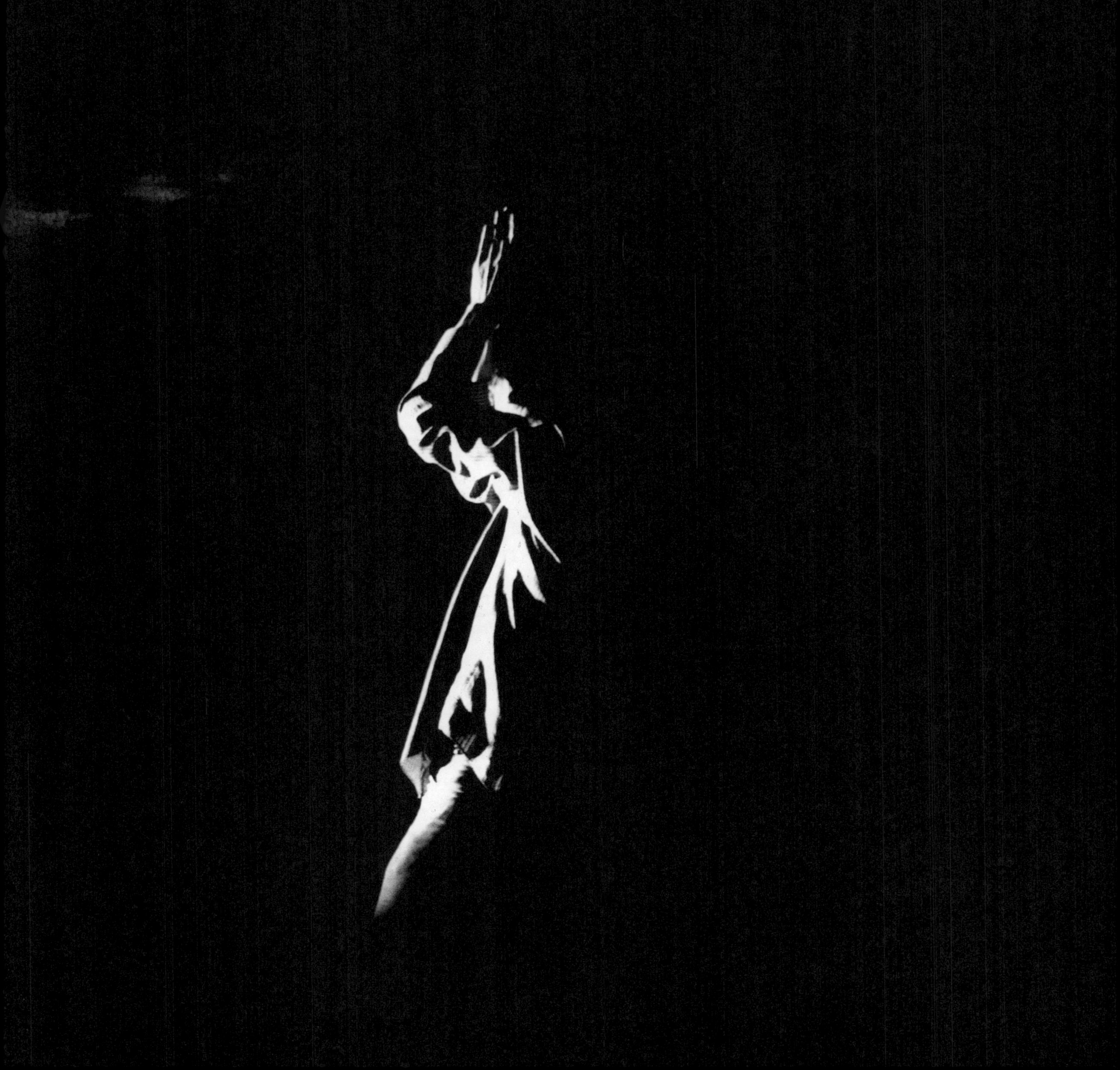

45

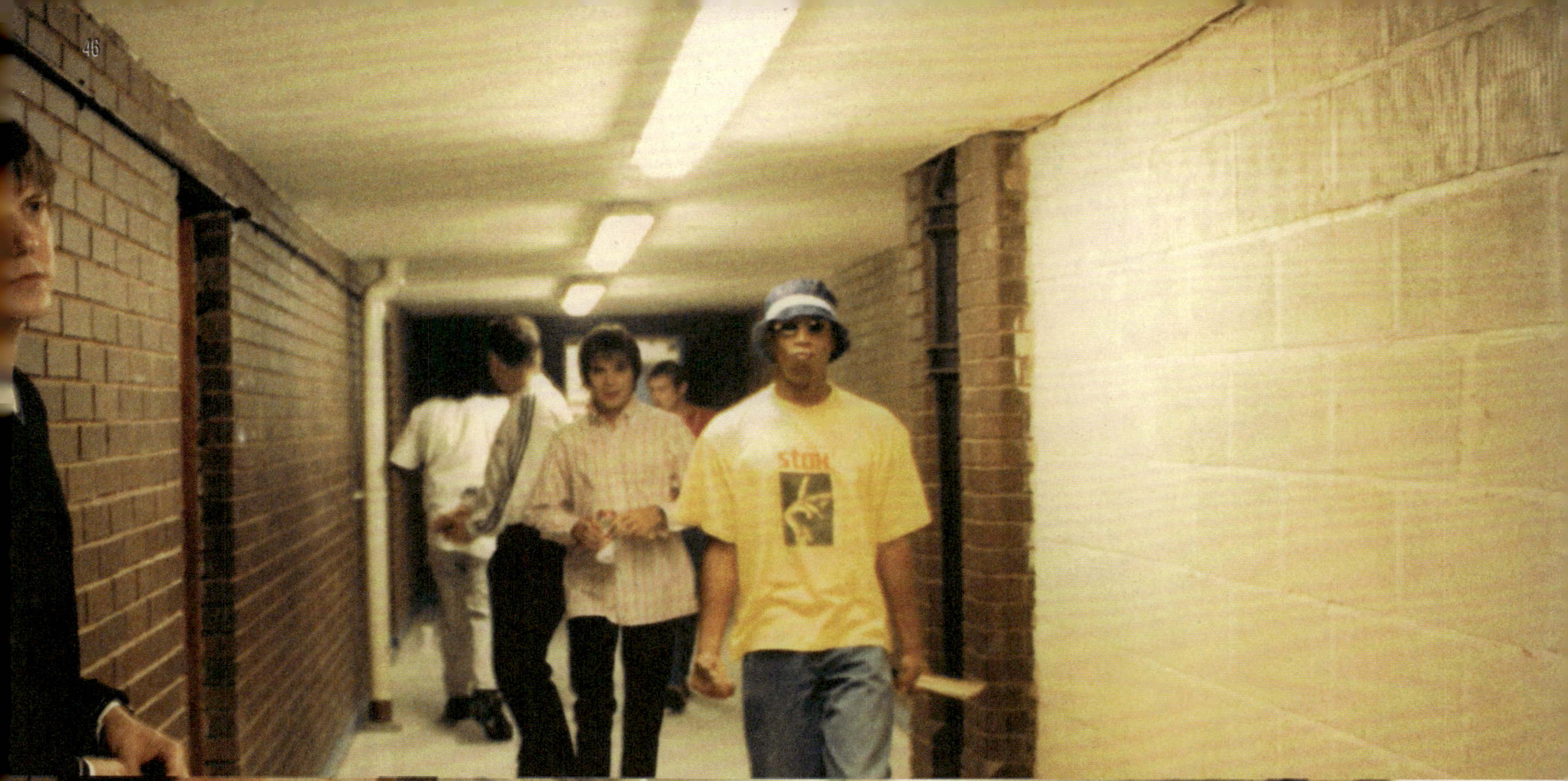

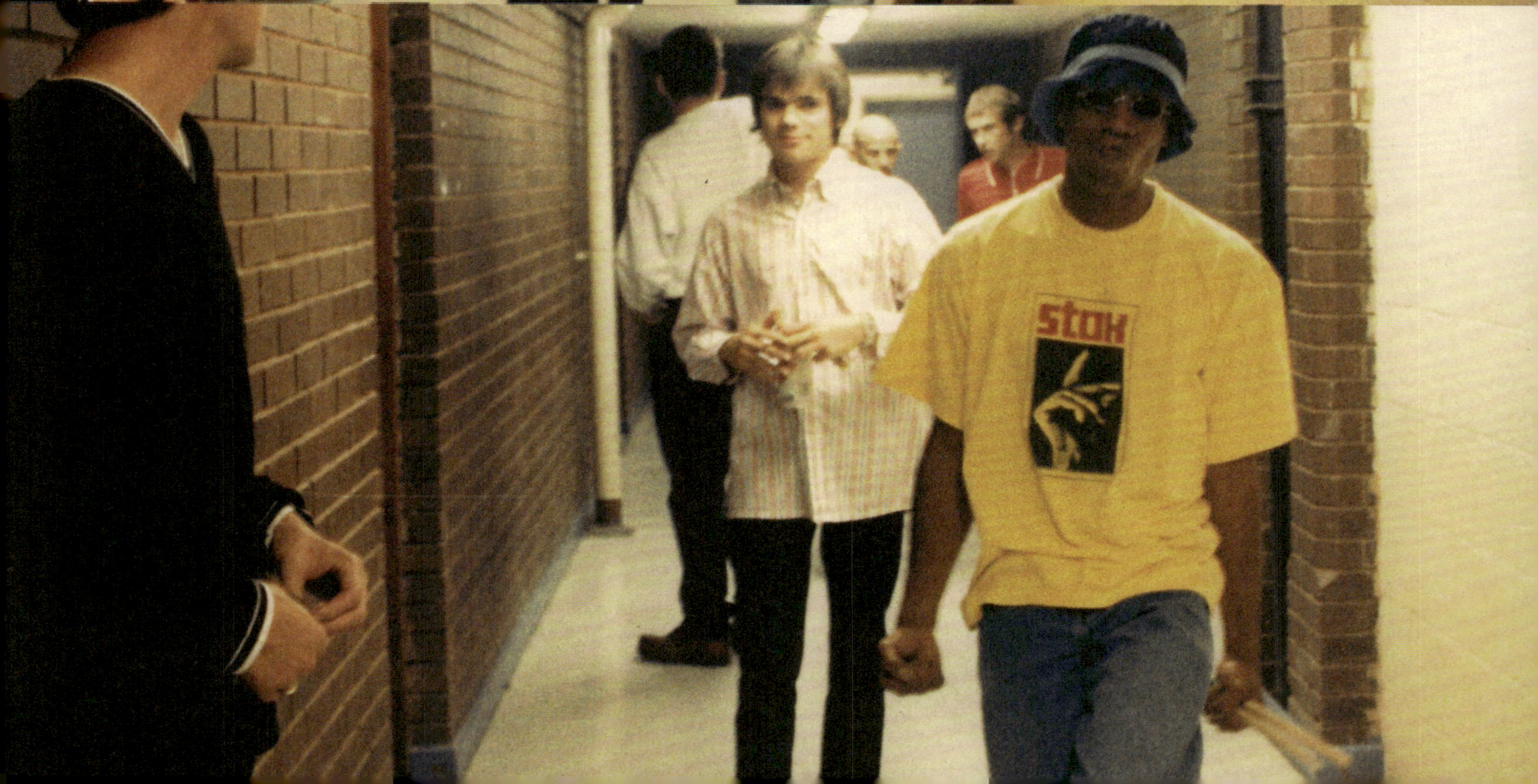

(BACKSTAGE AT ASTON VILLA)

THE EMOTIVE SWELL OF BETTER DAY, THE GROUP'S THIRD SINGLE FROM THE ALBUM AND LAST OF SIX CONSECUTIVE SINGLES TO MAKE THE TOP 10, WAS PURE AUTOBIOGRAPHY, WITH THE CHARACTER SONNY IN THE SONY BEING SIMON FOWLER, DAVEY AND MINNIE BEING DAMON MINCHELLA, STEVIE BEING STEVE CRADOCK AND HARRY BEING OSCAR HARRISON.

48

I REMEMBER RICO RODRIGUEZ PLAYING
TROMBONE WITH THEM. WE WERE IN CARLISLE,
RICO WAS LITERALLY A LIVING LEGEND AND
A LOVELY GENTLE OLD FELLA. THEN STEVE WAS
TYPICALLY RUDE ONE NIGHT, HE SAID SOME
SHIT ABOUT HIM BEING OUT OF TIME
OR SOMETHING. RICO SAID NOTHING, JUST
GENTLY PACKED UP HIS BONE AND LEFT.
DIDN'T ASK FOR ANY MONEY, NO FUSS, JUST
DISAPPEARED AND WE NEVER SAW HIM AGAIN.
TOO OLD FOR ALL THAT SHIT I THOUGHT... HA.
TONY BRIGGS

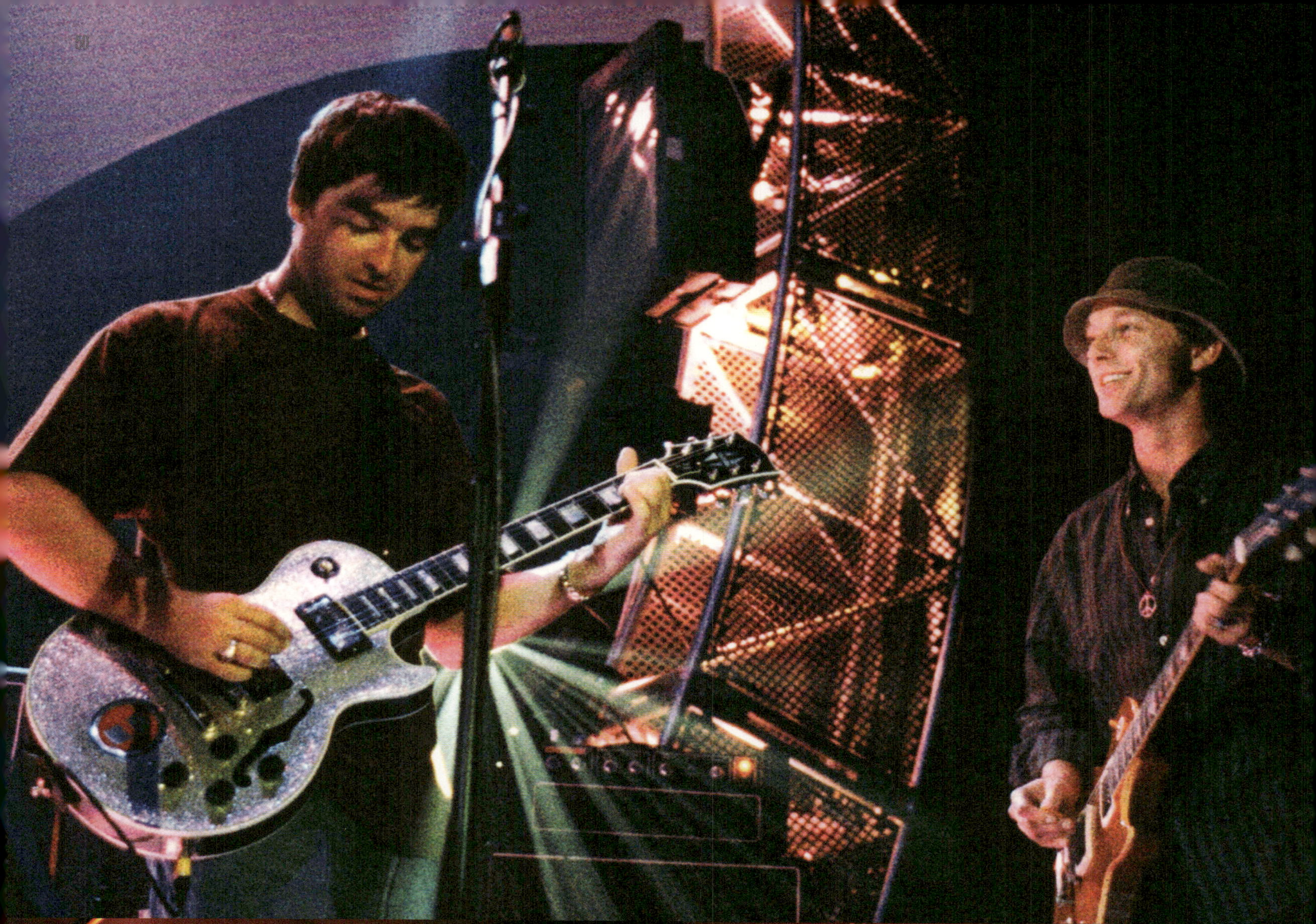

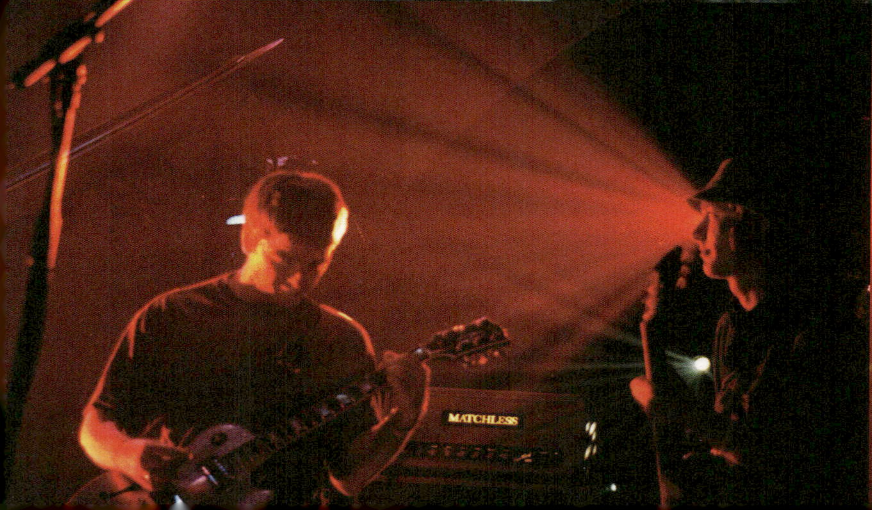
MATCHLESS

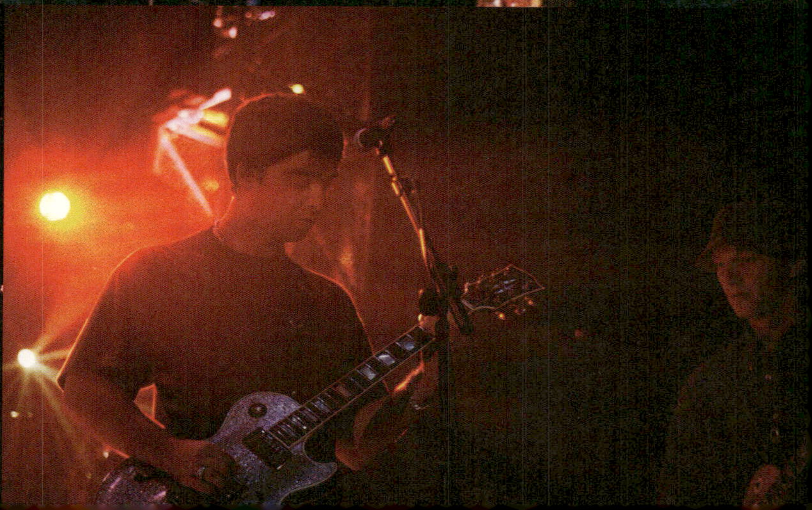

IF OASIS WERE THE BEATLES AND BLUR THE KINKS THEN OCEAN COLOUR SCENE WERE THE SMALL FACES

FLAMING CORK FESTIVAL, 1997.

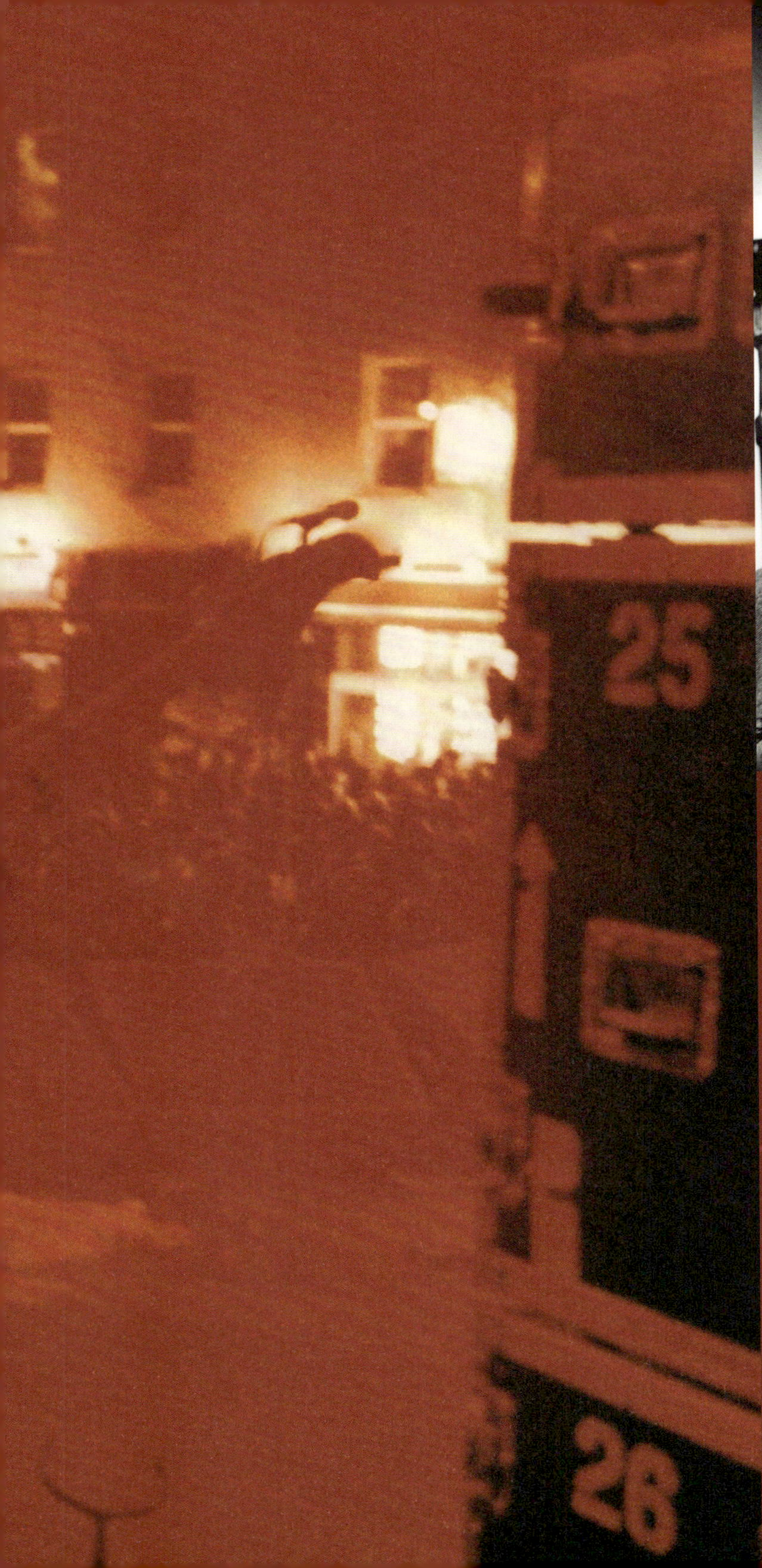
25
26

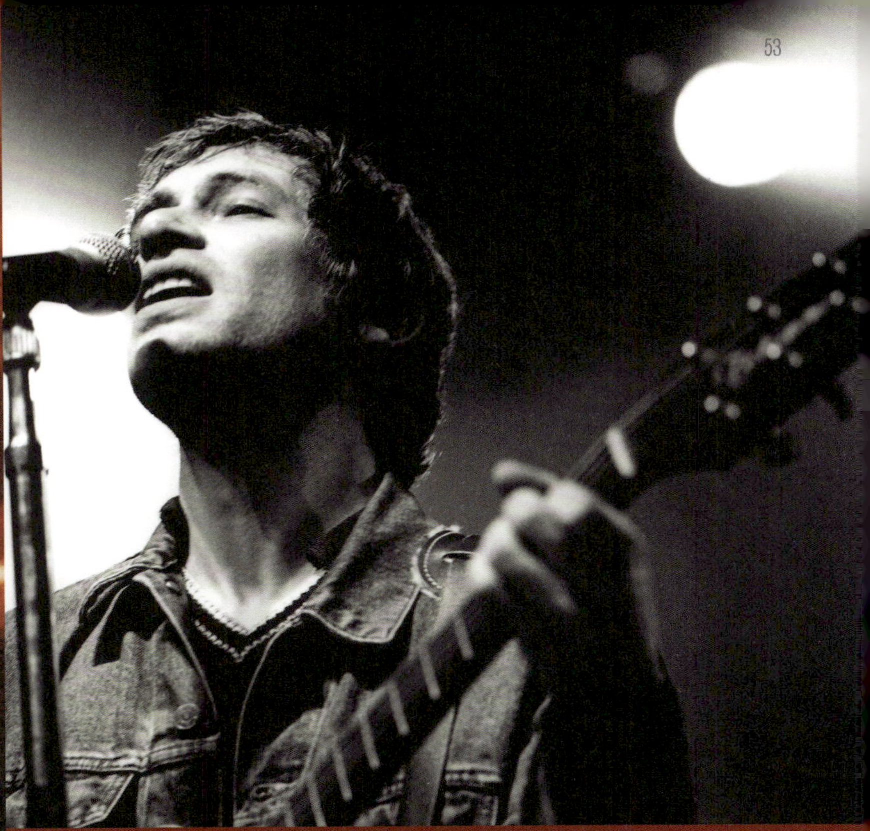

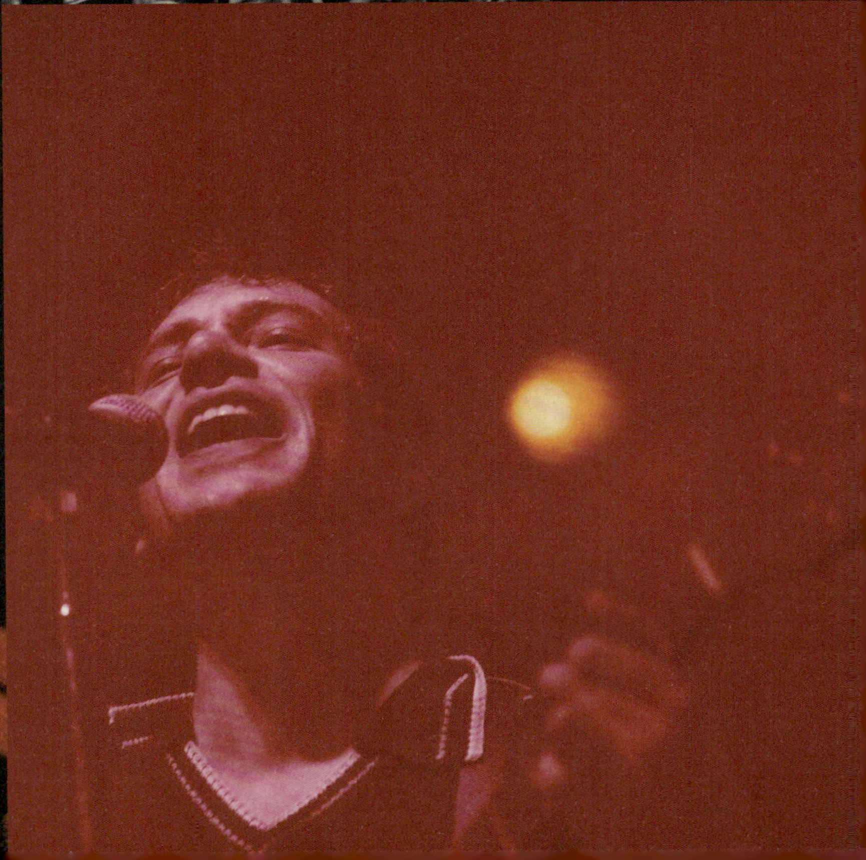

OCS HEADLINED AT GLASTONBURY IN 1997 WHICH WAS FANTASTIC. THEY WERE AT THEIR PEAK. WE ALL STAYED AT A HOTEL AND GOT BUSSED IN TO THE FESTIVAL (STEVE: FUCK THAT CAMPING LARK! WHAT NO TROUSER PRESS?) I GOT TO MEET RAY DAVIES AND PETE TOWNSHEND WHILE WE WERE HANGING AROUND. THERE WAS A REALLY GOOD ATMOSPHERE. I REMEMBER I WAS STANDING BY THE SIDE OF THE STAGE AS RADIOHEAD OR WHOEVER CAME OFF AND THEN IT WAS OCS TIME TO GO ON. NOW WE'RE ALL OF A SIMILAR AGE AND LOOK, SAME FISH HAIRCUTS, WE WORE EACH OTHER'S CLOTHES AND I WAS STANDING IN FRONT OF THE BAND FILMING THEM AS THEY WALKED TO THE STAGE. SO I'M WALKING BACKWARDS ONTO THE STAGE AND SUDDENLY ALL THE LIGHTS COME UP AND THE CROWD GO MENTAL AS THEY THINK I'M THE BAND. YOU COULD FEEL THE ELECTRICITY FROM THE CROWD, FOR JUST A SPLIT SECOND I GOT A GLIMPSE OF THE BUZZ THEY MUST GET FROM GOING OUT ON STAGE TO A HUNDRED THOUSAND FANS, IT WAS AMAZING. THE HAIRS ON THE BACK OF MY NECK STILL GO WHEN I THINK ABOUT IT. **TONY BRIGGS**

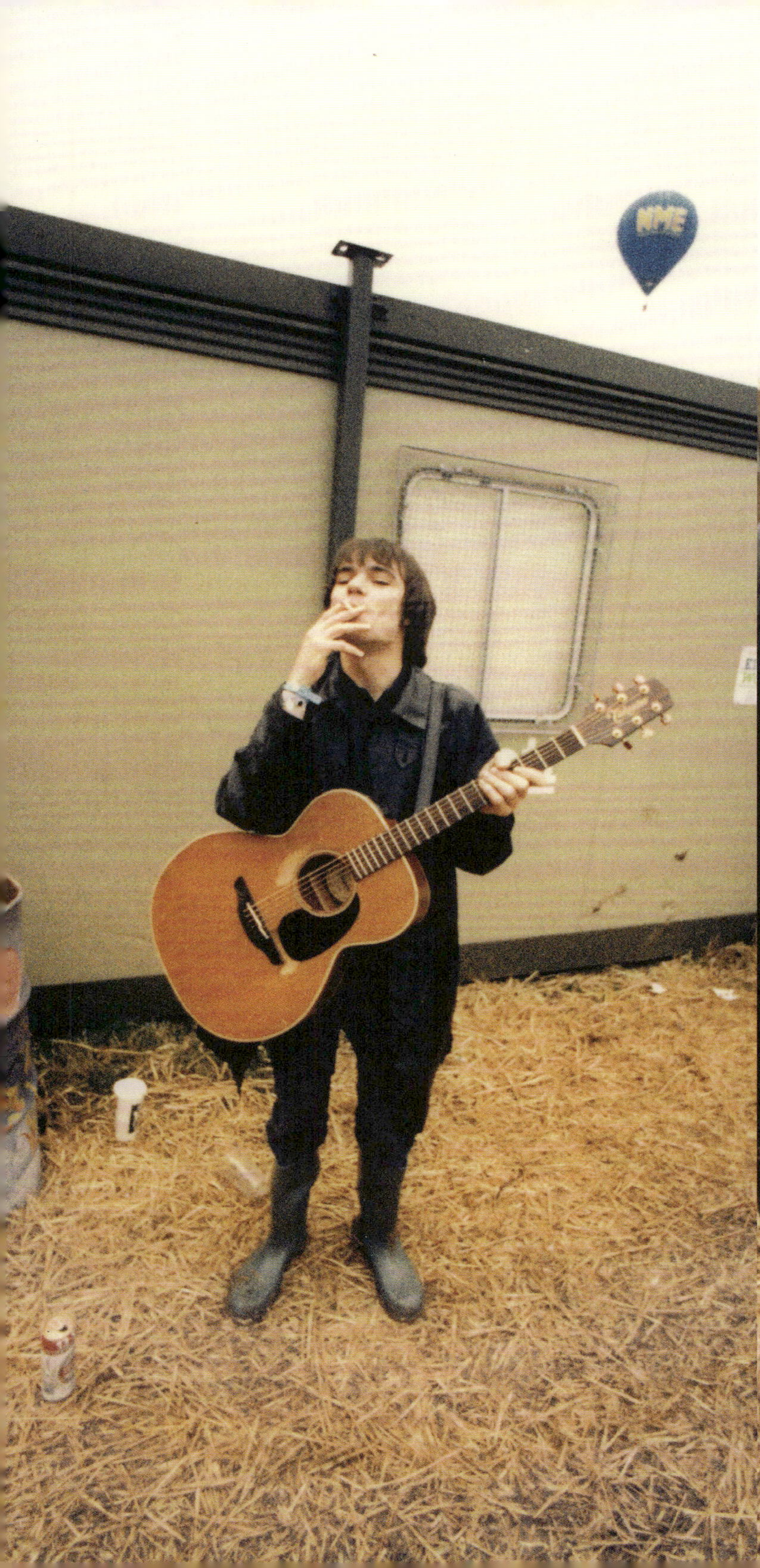
NME

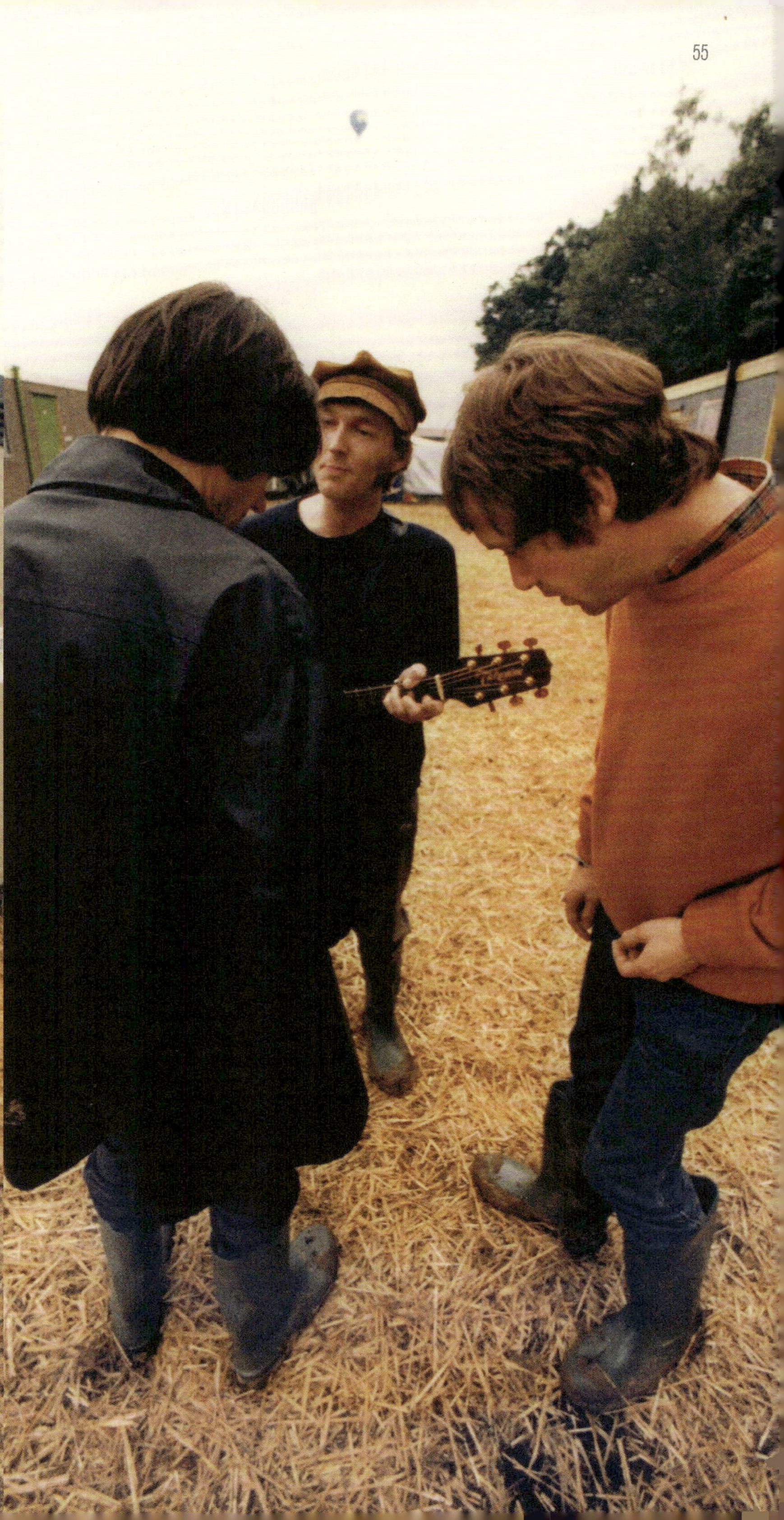

56

57

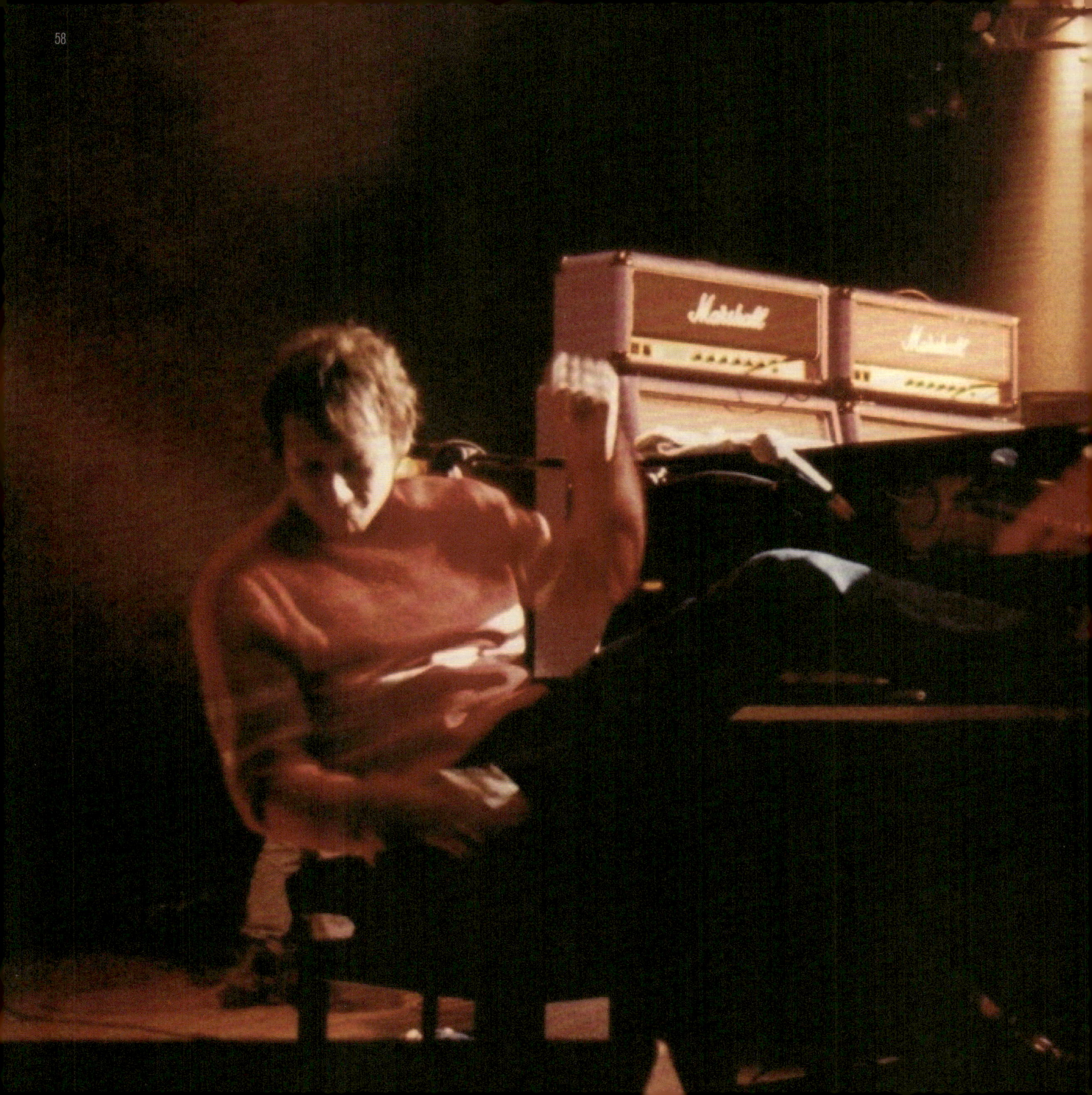
Marshall
Marshall

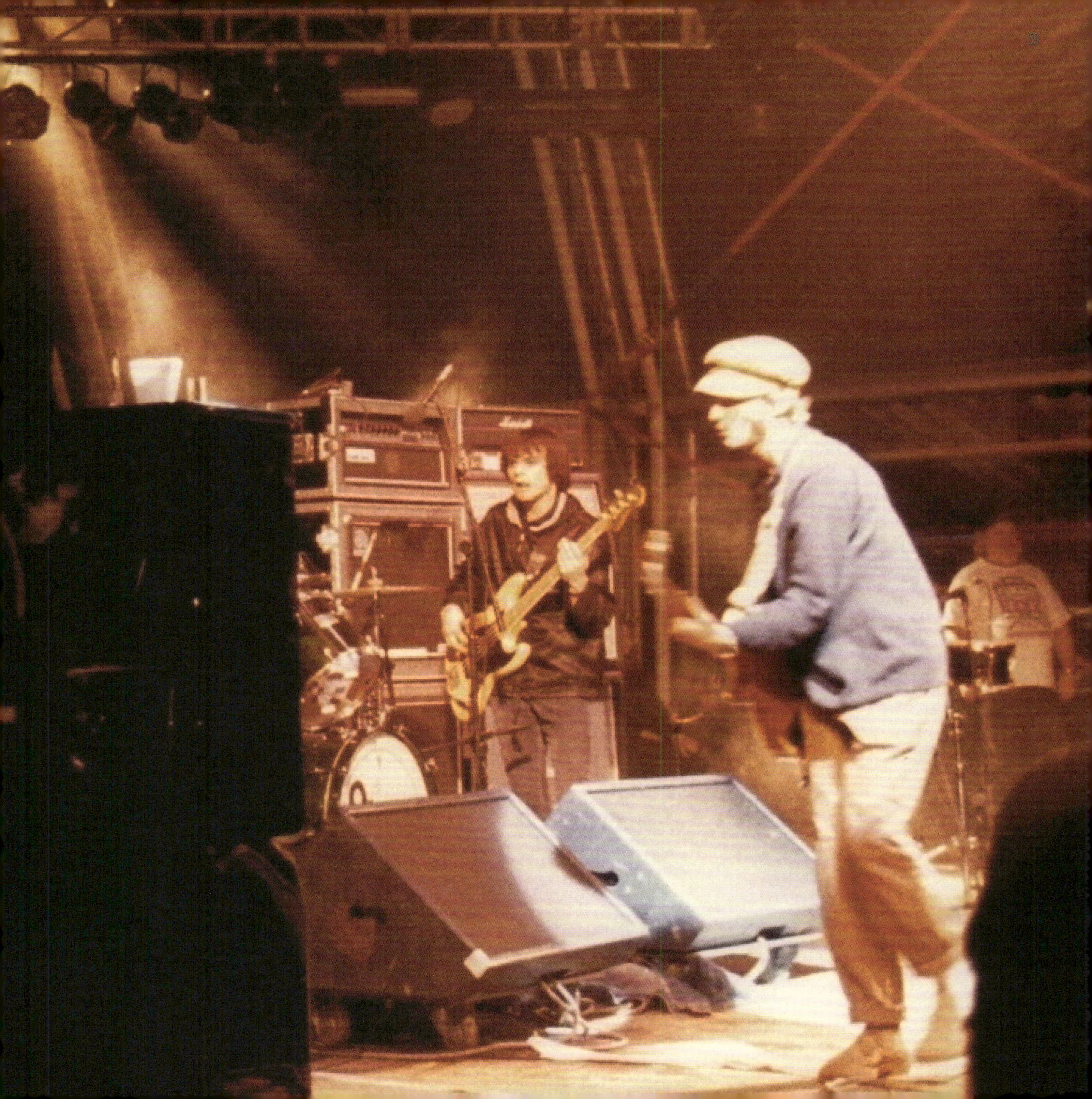

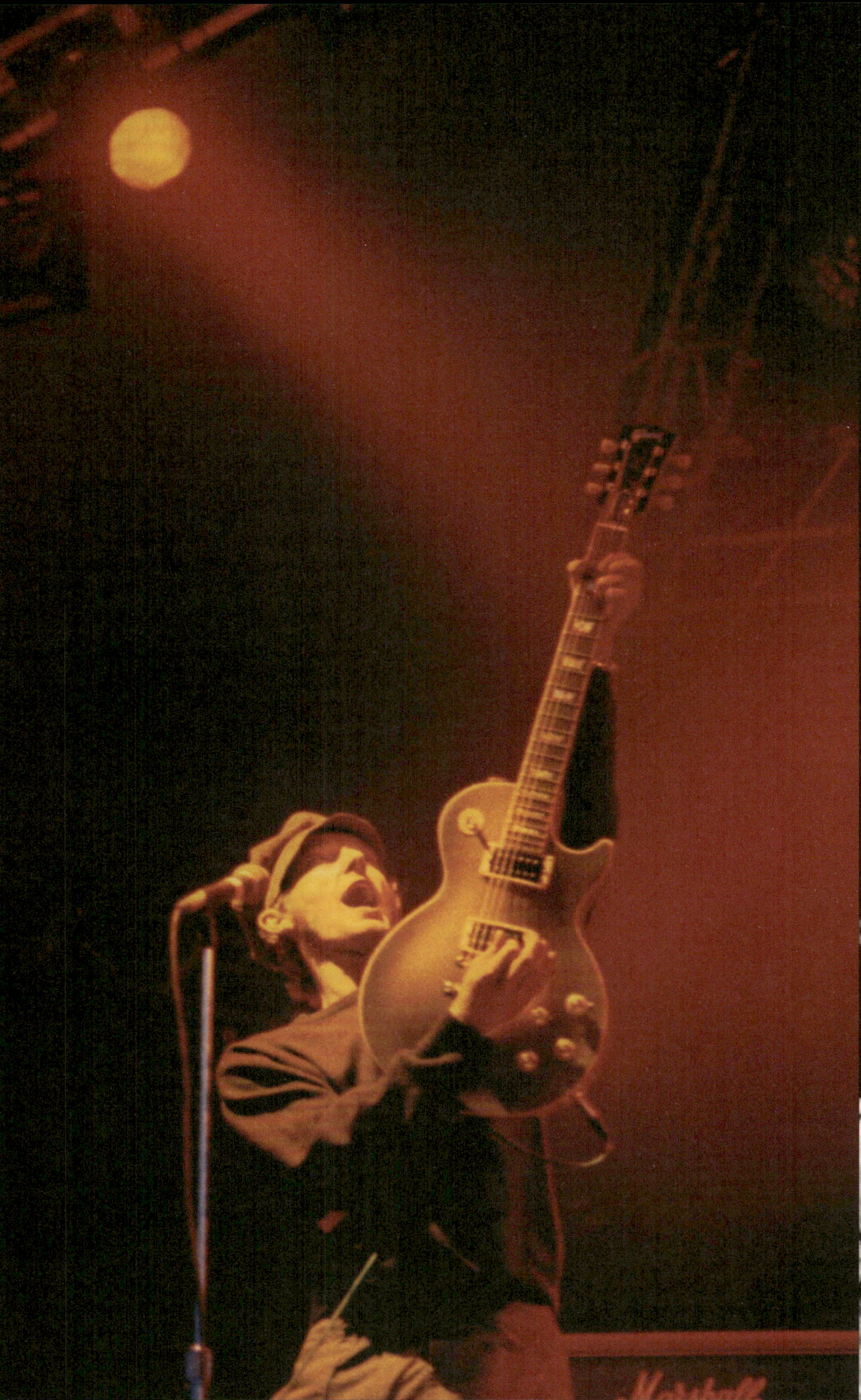
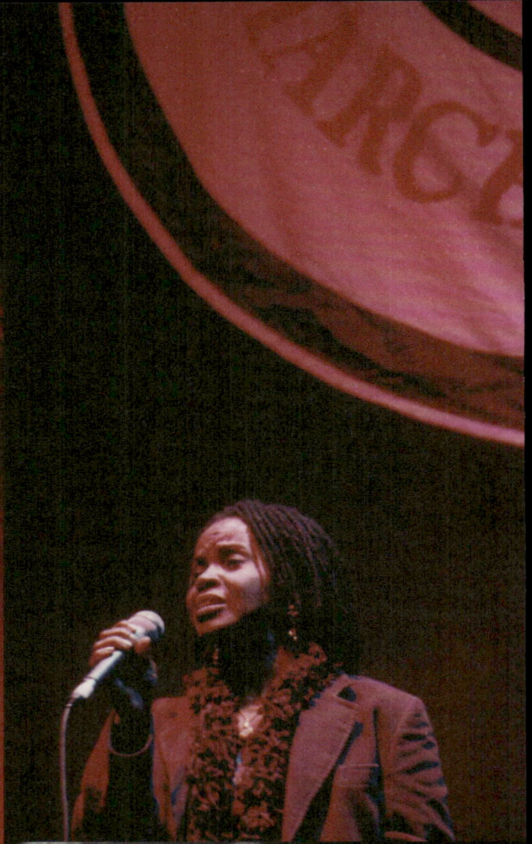
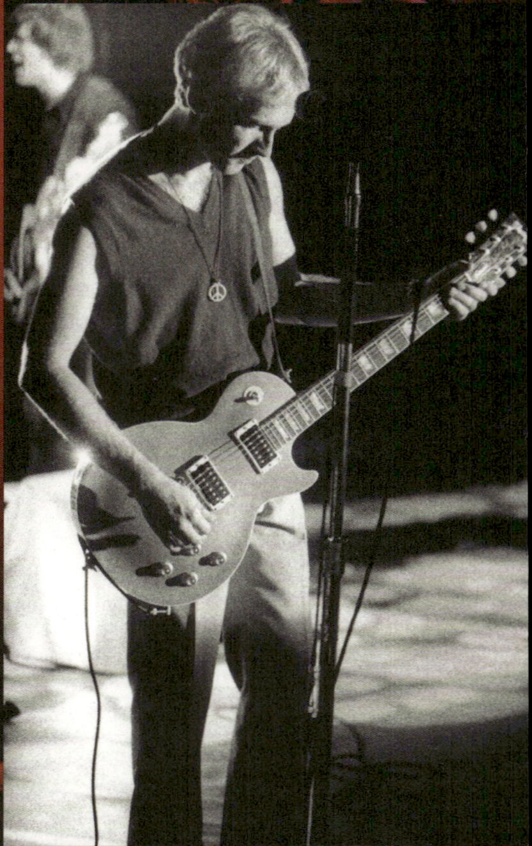

IT'S THE ONLY THING I'VE EVER REALLY KNOWN, I DON'T KNOW WHAT I'D DO OTHERWISE. **SIMON FOWLER**

NEXT I WENT TO SEE THE BAND AT READING HEXAGON. PAUL WELLER AND NOEL GALLAGHER WERE BOTH THERE. I REMEMBER WELLER PLAYED THAT'S ENTERTAINMENT FOR STEVE IN THE DRESSING ROOM. I GOT SOME GOOD PICTURES OF PAUL AND NOEL ON STAGE WITH OCS THAT NIGHT, THEY WERE ALL OVER THE MUSIC PRESS (THEY COULDN'T IGNORE THEM NOW). THIS WAS REALLY THE FIRST TIME I SAW THE BAND ON A PROPER STAGE AND THEY WERE AMAZING. DEFINITELY MAYBE WAS OUT BY THIS TIME AND OASIS WERE MASSIVE SO TO CATCH NOEL DURING THIS EARLY PERIOD WAS SPECIAL.
TONY BRIGGS

63

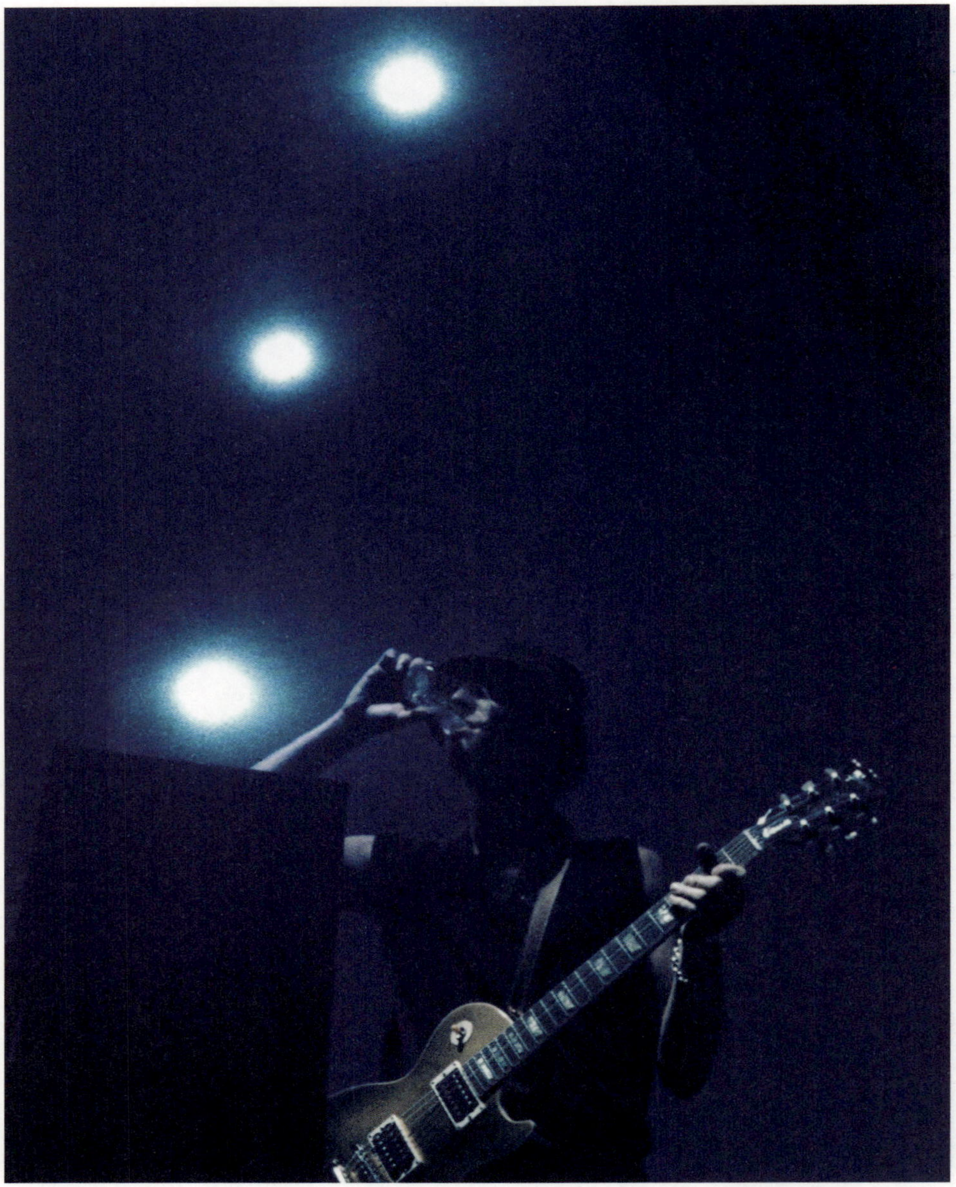

"THE MOST EXCITING BAND IN BRITAIN TODAY," CHRIS EVANS AGREED. ANCHOR TO TFI, FRIDAY NIGHT'S TELEVISION MUST - A READY STEADY GO FOR A NINETIES MOVEMENT DISCOVERING THEIR OWN GENERATION - THE RIVERBOAT SONG NOT ONLY BECAME THE OPENING THEME, BUT THE WALK ON MUSIC FOR EVERY GUEST TOO.'

66

WE WENT TO MADRID FOR A BIG SPANISH MUSIC FESTIVAL (FESTI MAD). YOU CAN SEE CHOPPER WEARING FLIP-FLOPS AND ONE OF MY SHIRTS AS HIS BAG GOT LOST ON THE FLIGHT (INTENTIONALLY MAYBE?). THIS IS WHERE HE AND I HAD THE IDEA FOR THE HUNDRED MILE HIGH CITY VIDEO USING THE WHITE PODIUMS, WELL WE NICKED THE IDEA OFF AN OLD WHO ALBUM COVER. **TONY BRIGGS**

68

FESTI MAD, MADRID. A RHYTHM SECTION SO STRONG YOU COULD LEAN AGAINST IT. **TONY BRIGGS**

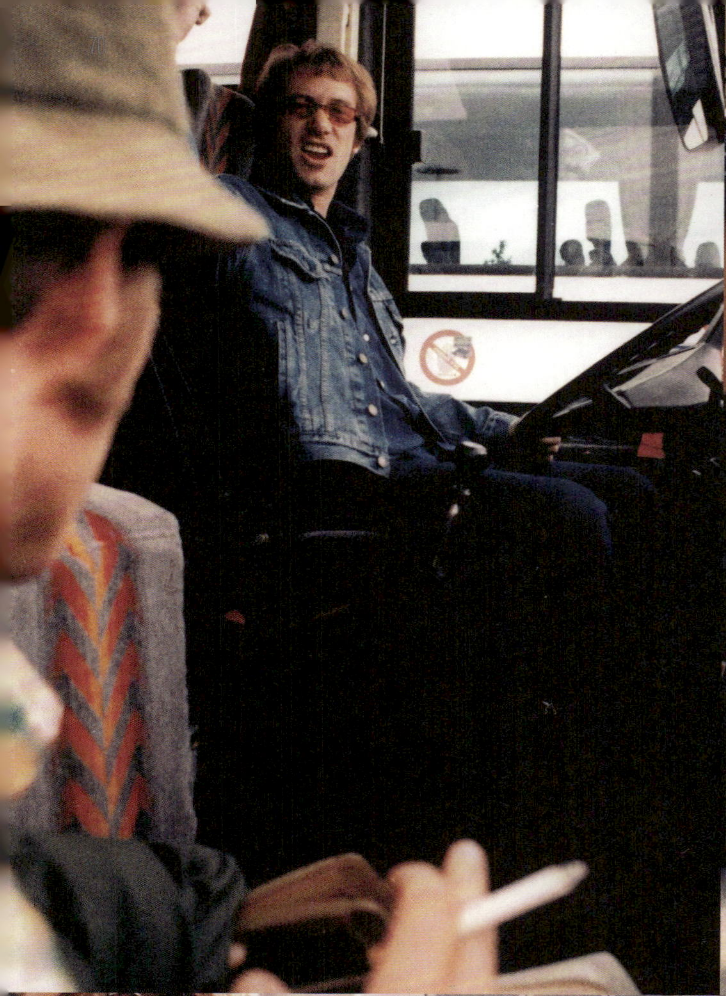

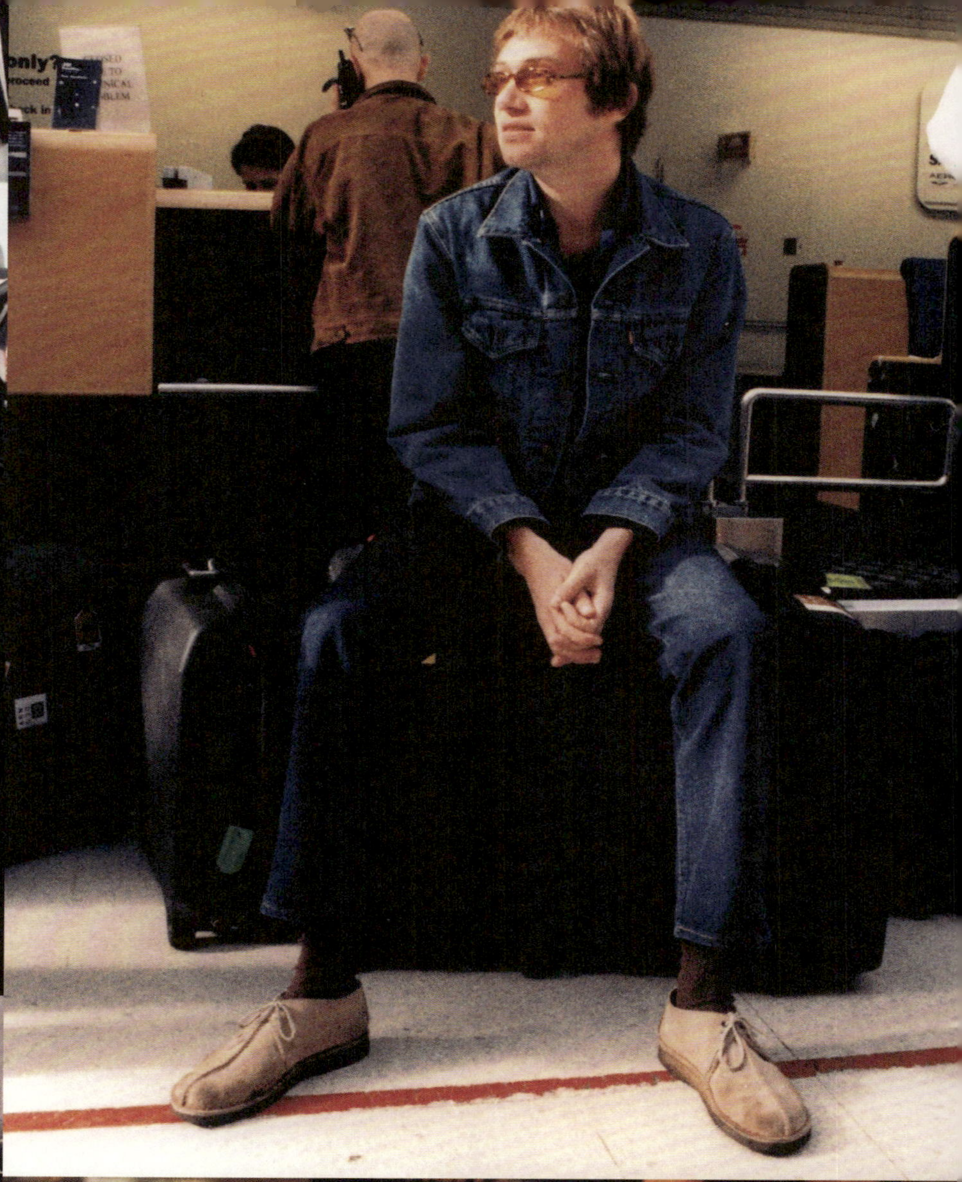
only?
proceed

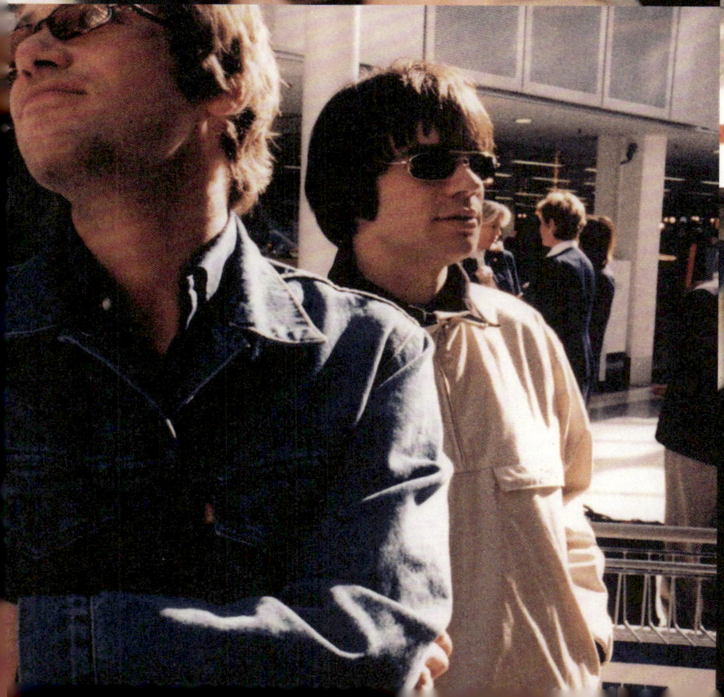

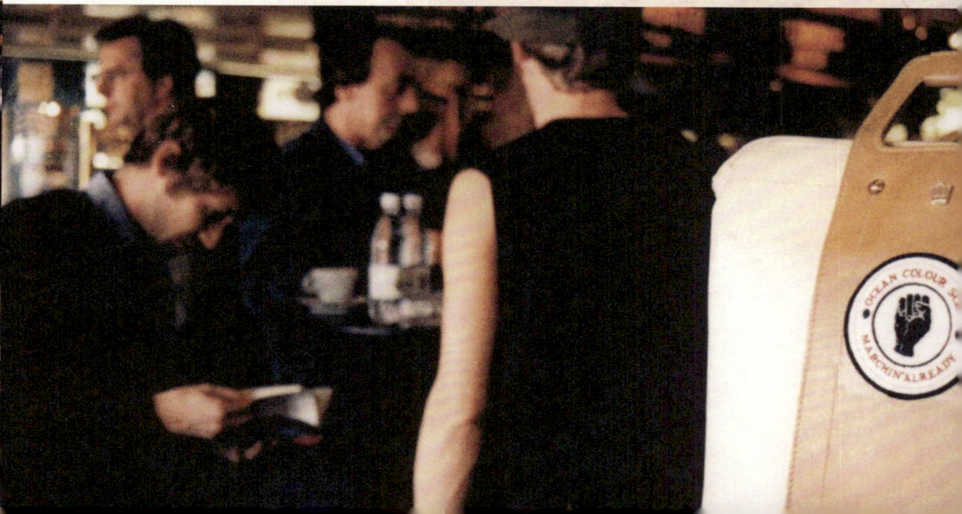
MARCHIN'ALREADY

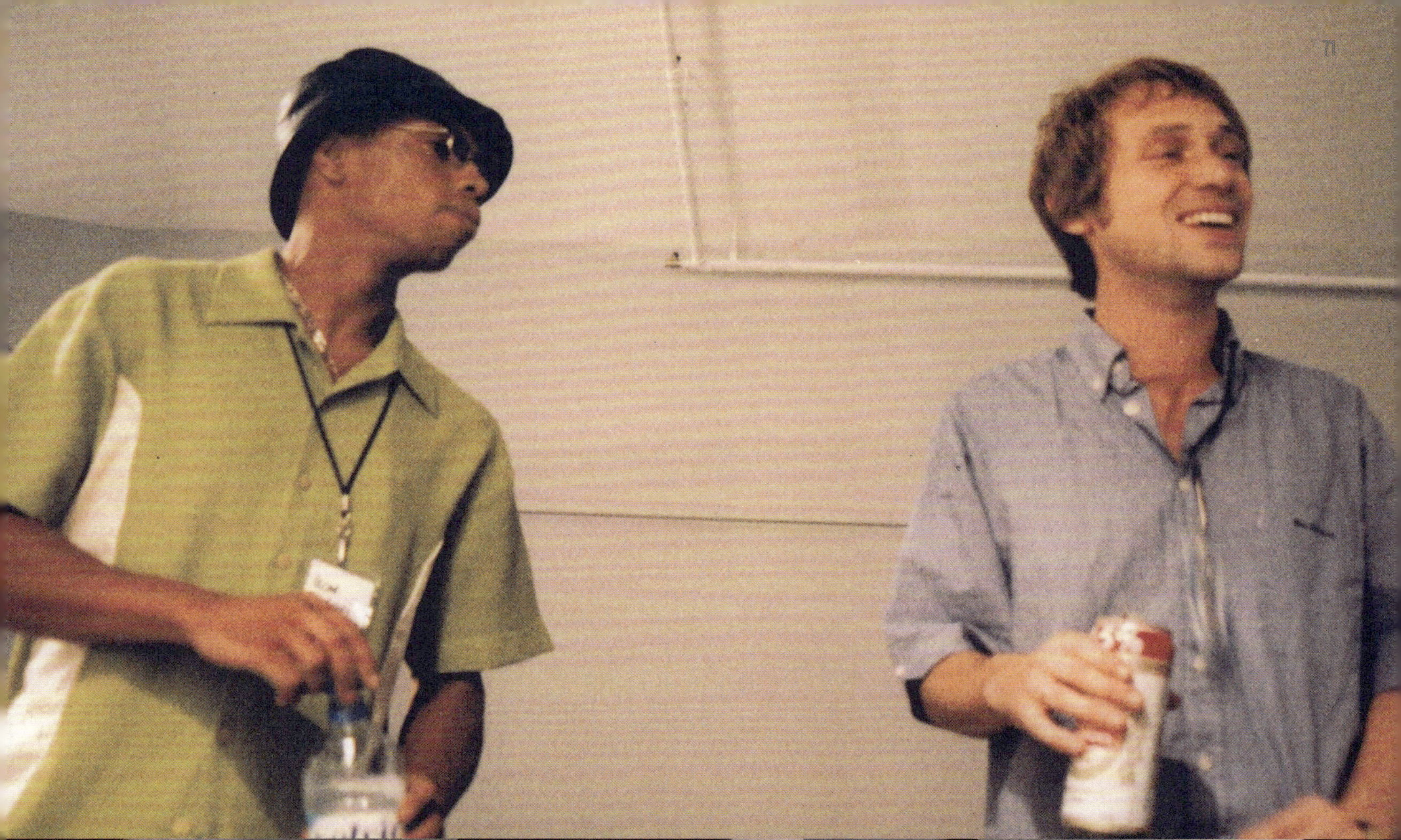

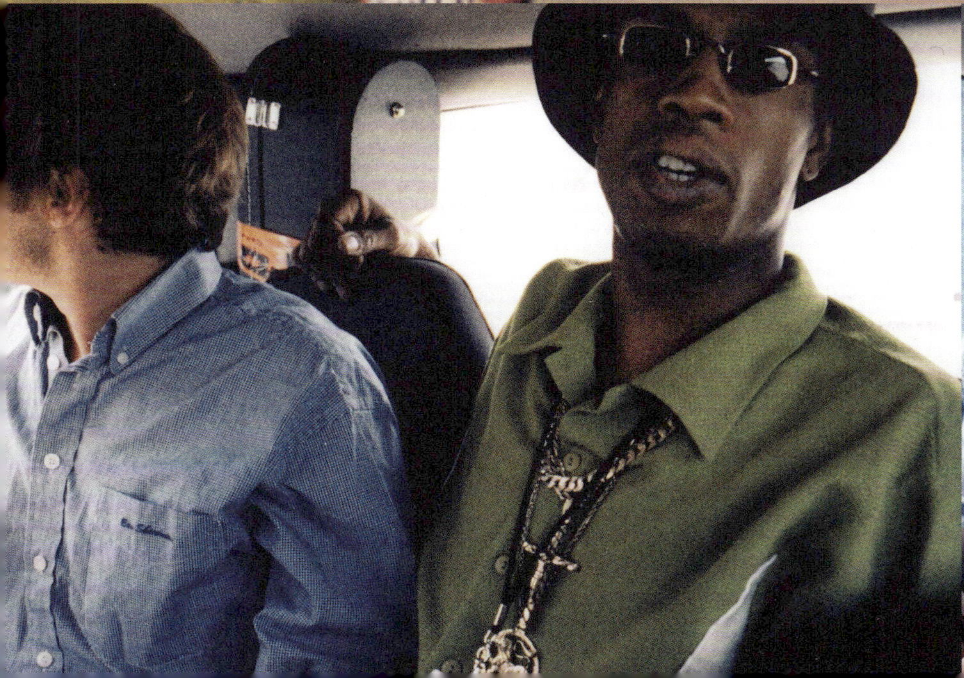

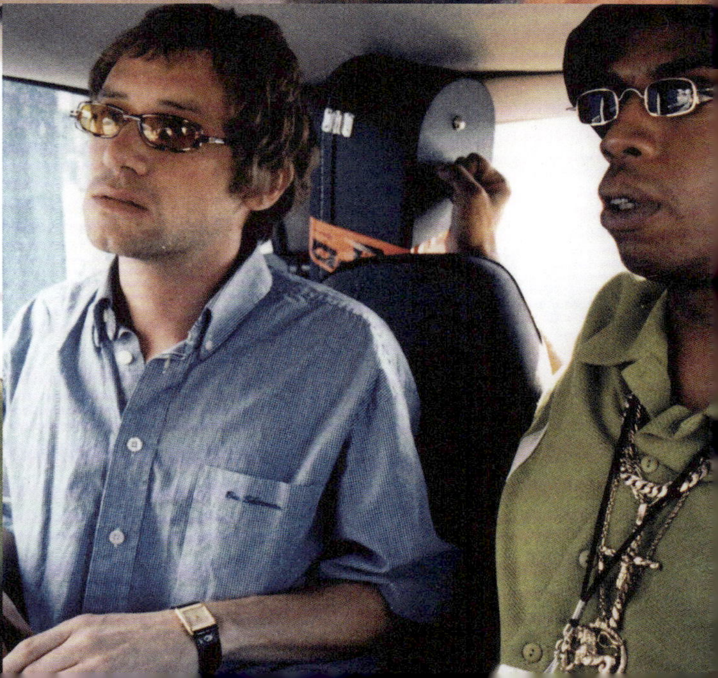

72

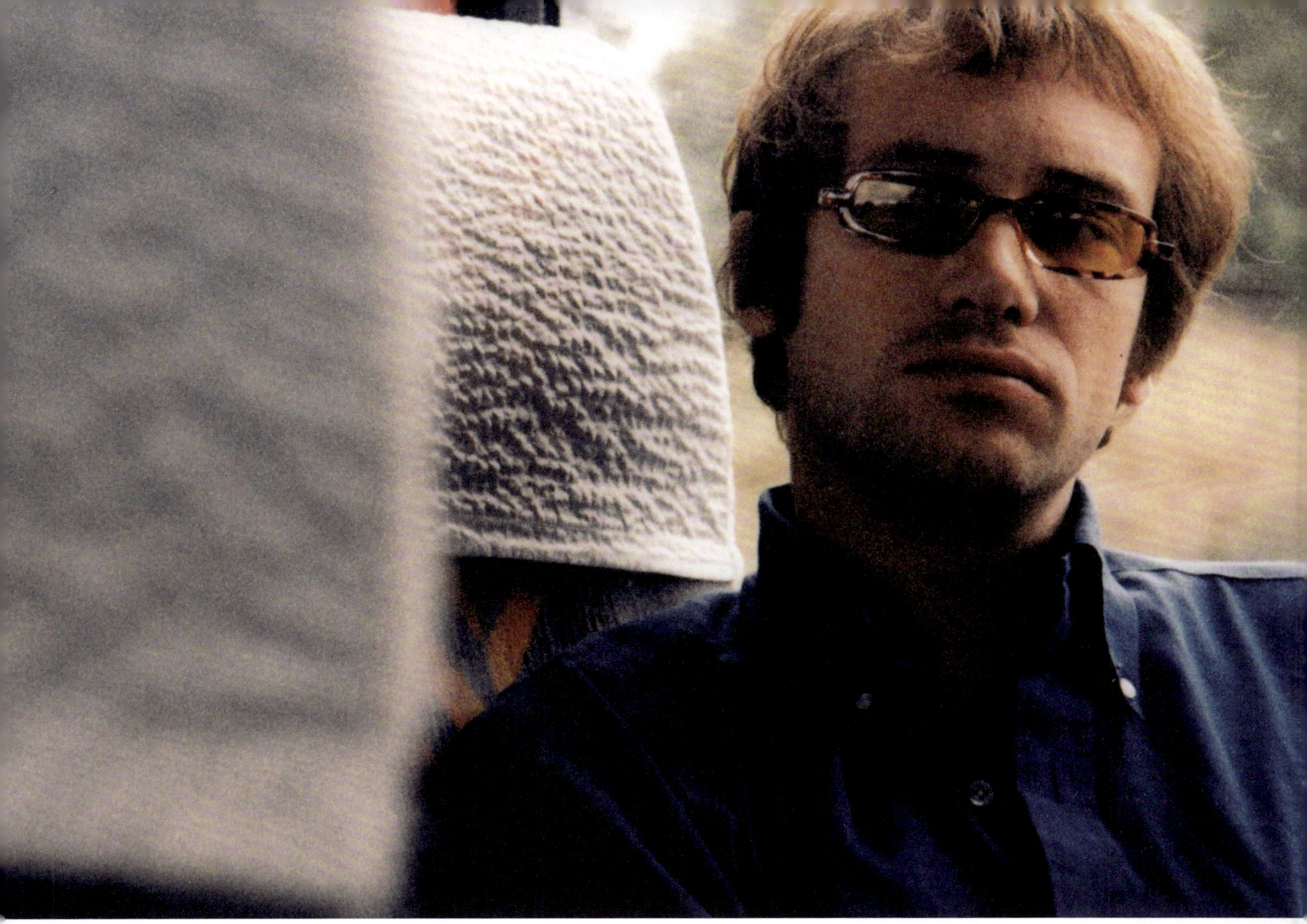

74

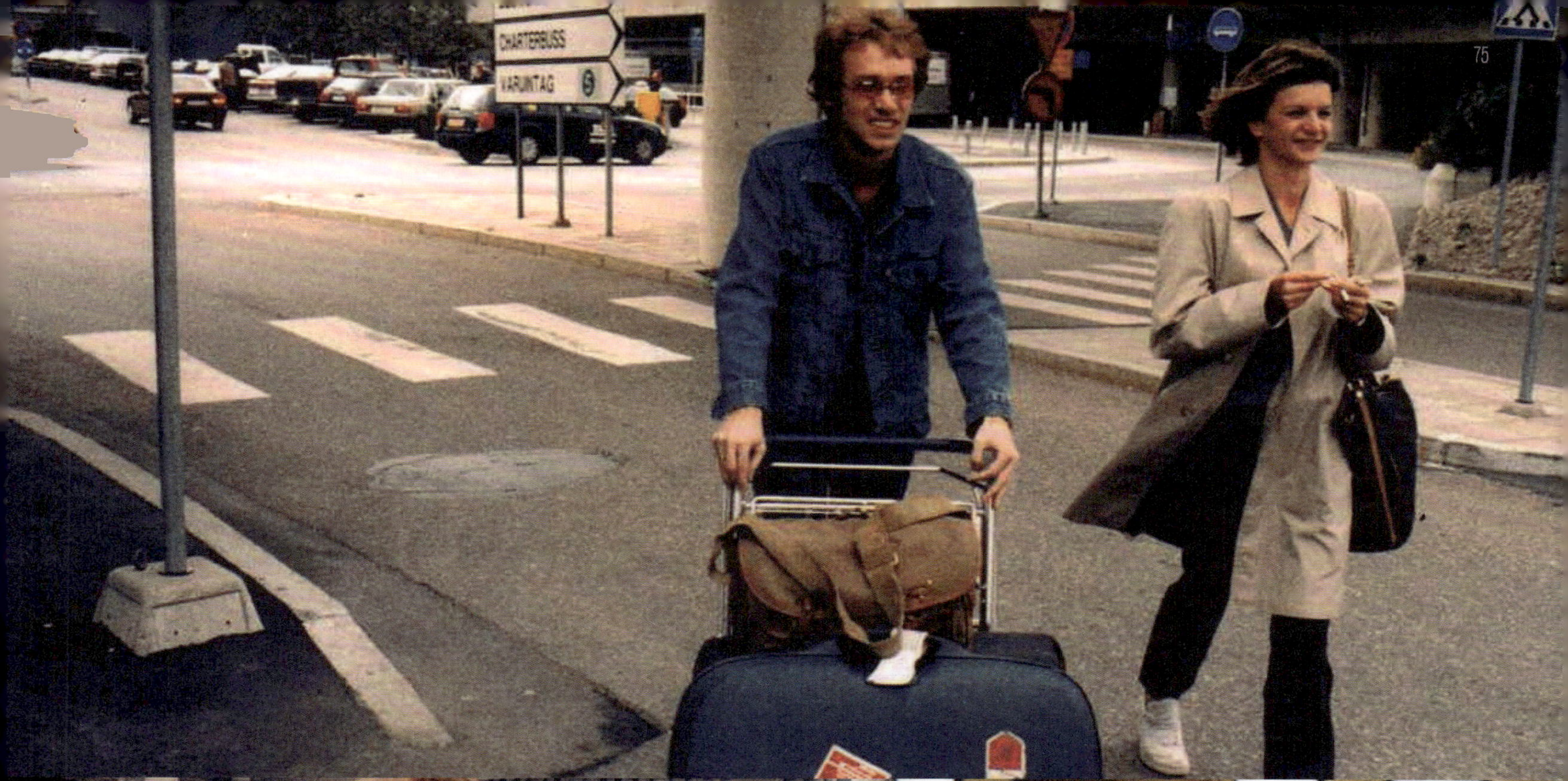
CHARTERBUSS

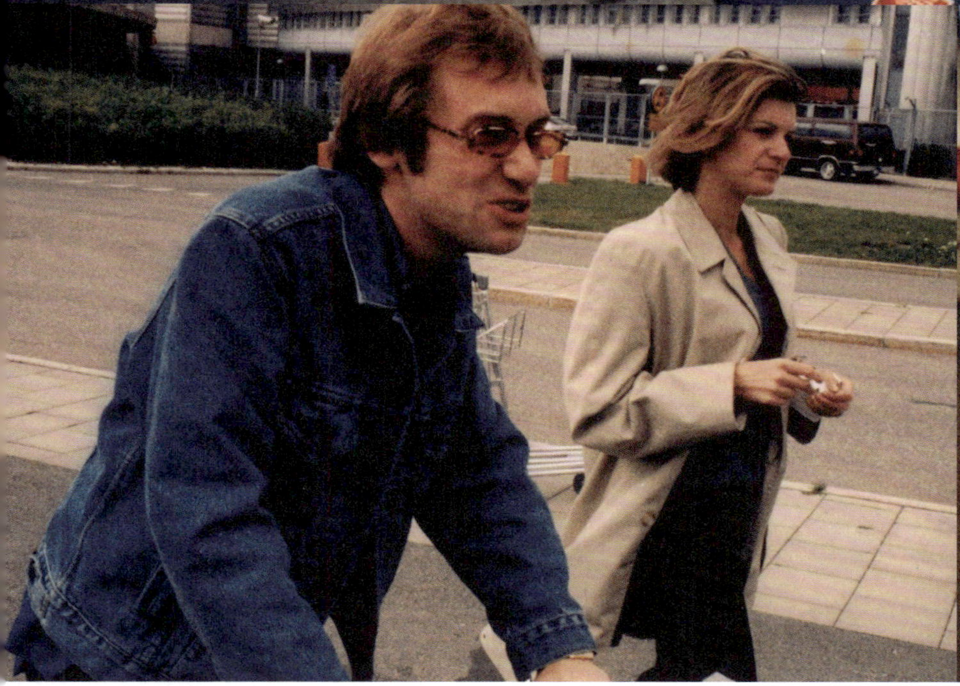

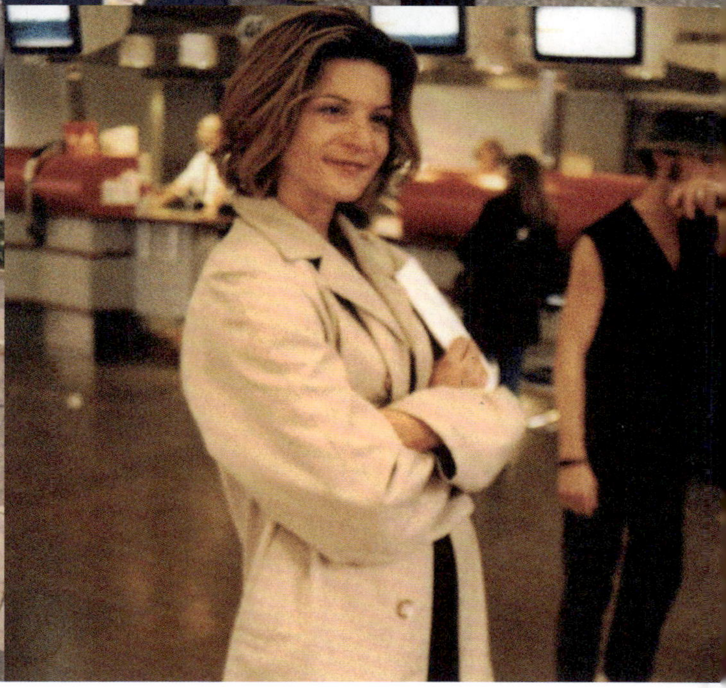

76

We first played in Scotland before many of you were in secondary school. We've always had a gentleman's laugh up here and being so far north it meant we were miles from London. At the time that was often the best place to be.

The love of music, dancing & drinking is an admirable part of the celtic outlook on life & that has made the Scots the top fans on these islands, along with the Irish.

Long live music, dancing and drinking and may your God go with you.

Your round.

Simon F.

78

THE LEGEND PP ARNOLD WITH STEVE. ALICE TOOK THIS PRESS PICTURE (AND THE 7" SLEEVE) FOR DIFFERENT DRUM, WHICH STEVE ALSO PRODUCED AND PLAYED ON. THE PROMO I MADE IS MY NOD TO READY STEADY GO! **TONY BRIGGS**

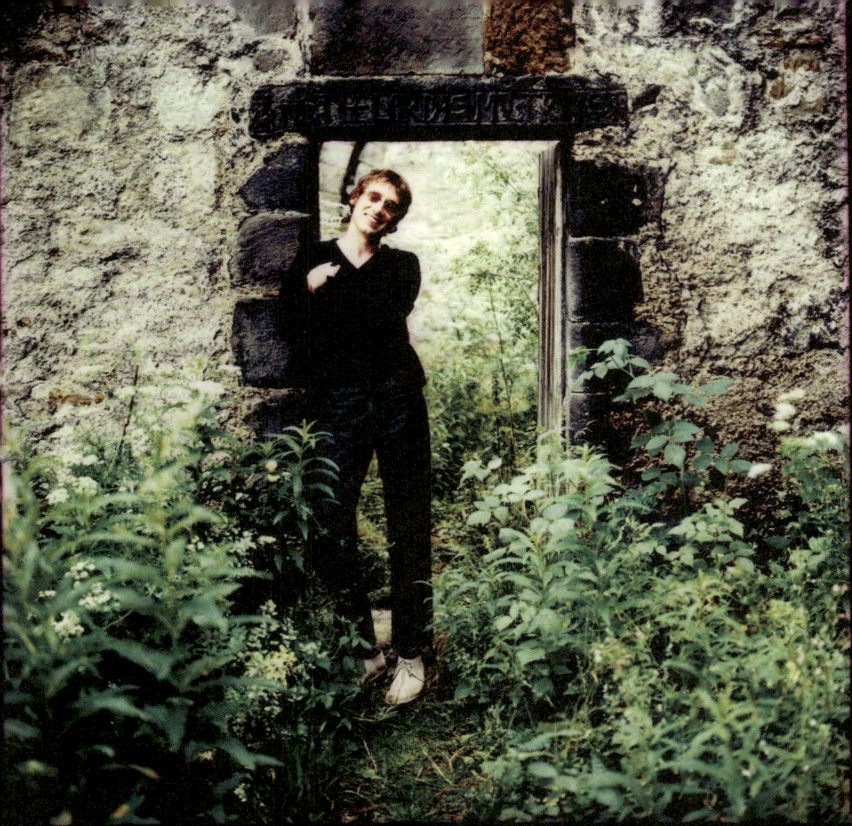

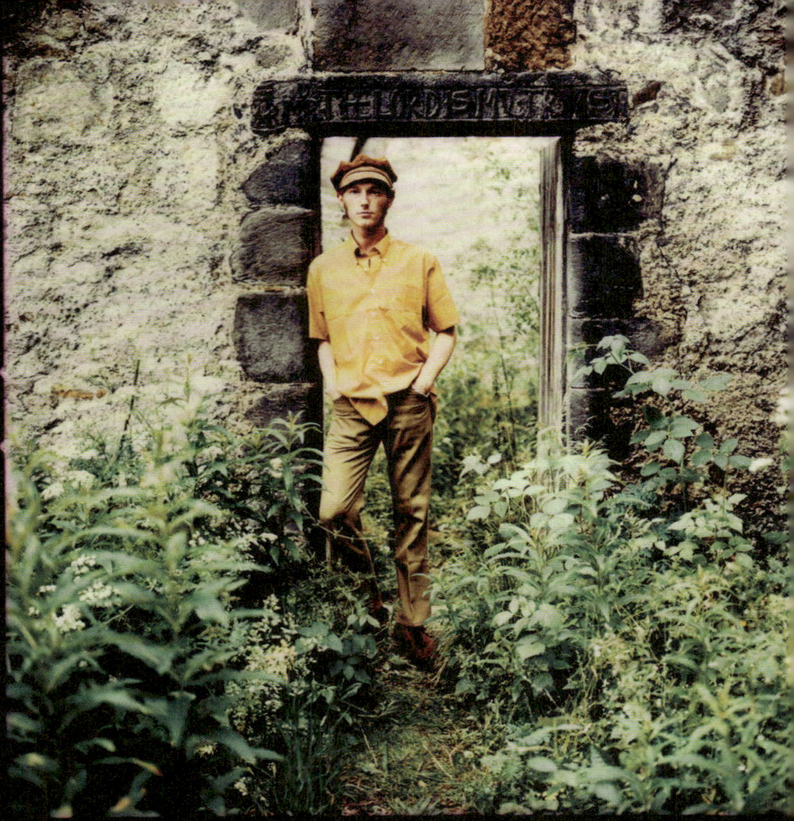

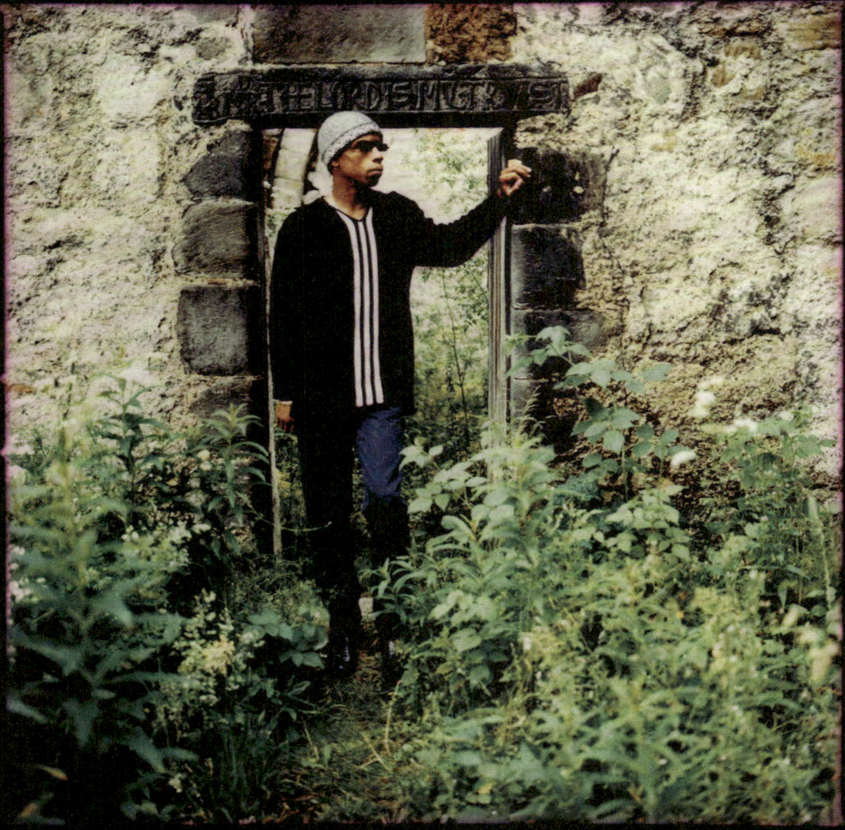

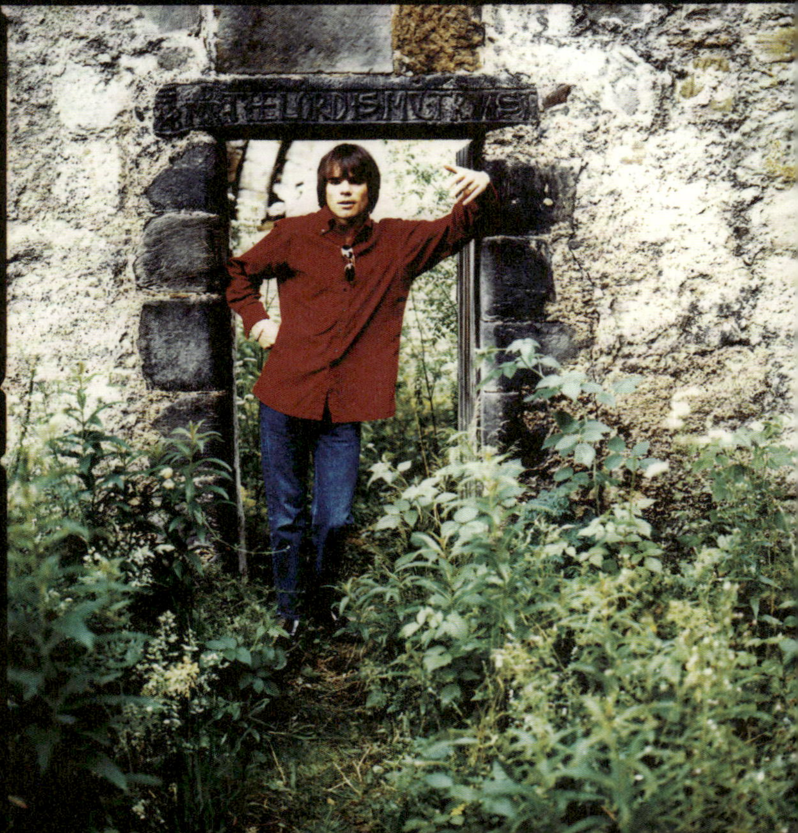

marchin' already Ocean Colour Scene

WE SHOT THE MARCHIN ALREADY SLEEVE IN SCOTLAND. WE HAD BEEN UP THERE FOR T IN THE PARK. THE GIG WAS ACTUALLY ON MY BIRTHDAY AND DAMON DEDICATED A TRACK TO ME IN FRONT OF ALL THOSE PEOPLE. I REMEMBER WHEN CHRIS ANNOUNCED THE BAND ONTO THE STAGE HE TOOK STEVE (THE DOG) ON WITH HIM IN HIS LITTLE BURBERRY COAT. WE PARTIED REALLY HARD THAT WEEKEND... PROPER RECORD COMPANY TYPE BULL SHIT, BRILLIANT! THE FOLLOWING MORNING IT WAS BY COMPLETE CHANCE THAT PETE (KELSEY) AND I FOUND THE LOCATION THAT WE SHOT THE MARCHIN' ALREADY STUFF IN. AN OLD RUINED PRIORY IN THE GROUNDS OF THE HOTEL. WITH MORE LUCK THAN JUDGEMENT IT ALL CAME TOGETHER REALLY WELL, THANKS TO PETE. **TONY BRIGGS**

WHEN MOTHER EARTH WERE STARTING UP I BROUGHT IN A 7" OF AN EARLY OCS TUNE SWAY TO SAMPLE FOR OUR FIRST LP (NEVER DID ASK PERMISSION, SORRY LADS!). THEN LATER DOWN THE LINE, I SAW THEM IN A FULL ON PERFORMANCE WHILE I WAS PLAYING GUITAR IN PAUL'S BAND. THEY WEREN'T TAKING THEIR SET LIGHTLY. THEY MEANT IT. THE CROWD KNEW IT, WE KNEW IT. WE HAD TO GO ON AFTER THEM ASWELL. THEY MADE YOU WANNA RISE TO THE SITUATION. UP YOUR GAME, Y'KNOW? TONY WAS THEIR DOCUMENTING THE MOMENT OF COURSE. HE SPOTTED THAT OLD DOORWAY RUIN FOR THE COVER OF MARCHIN' ALREADY WHEN WE WERE BACK AT THE HOTEL. ANYWAY, A NON-STOP GROUP... NOT SURE I EVER NOTICED AN 'OFF' SWITCH TO THEIR ENERGY COME TO THINK OF IT, QUITE A FORCEFUL FOUR PEICE IN FACT WITH TALL TUNES AND A SHARP LOOK WHICH I THINK IS SOMETHING THAT TONY HAS MANAGED TO CAPTURE IN THESE PAGES. **MATT DEIGHTON**

83

HUNDREAD

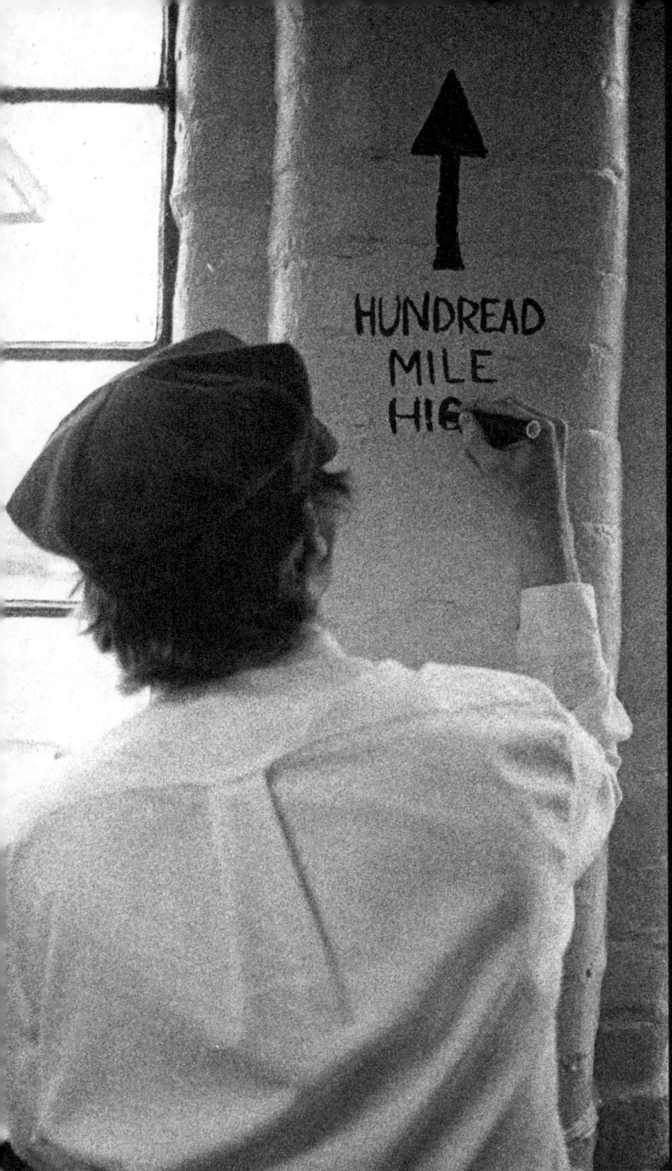
HUNDREAD
MILE
HIG

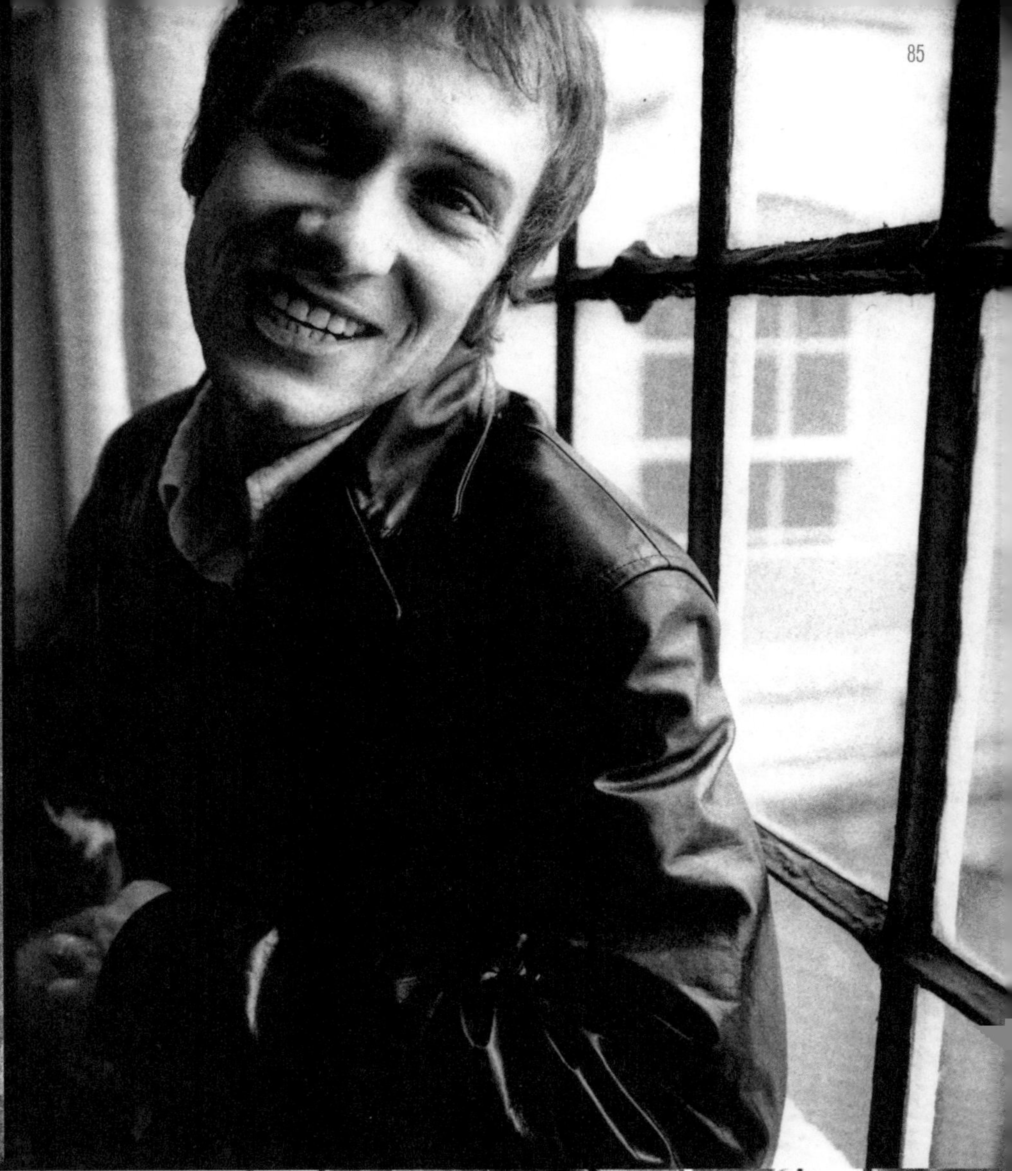

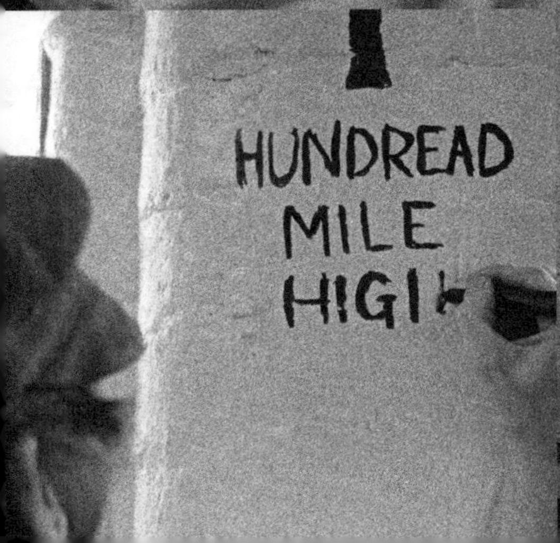
HUNDREAD
MILE
HIG

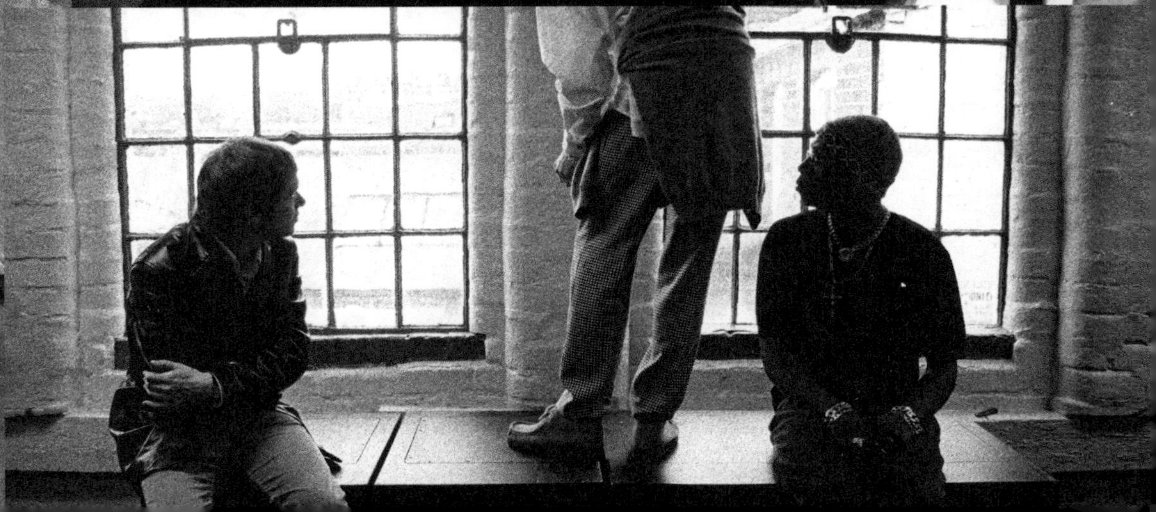

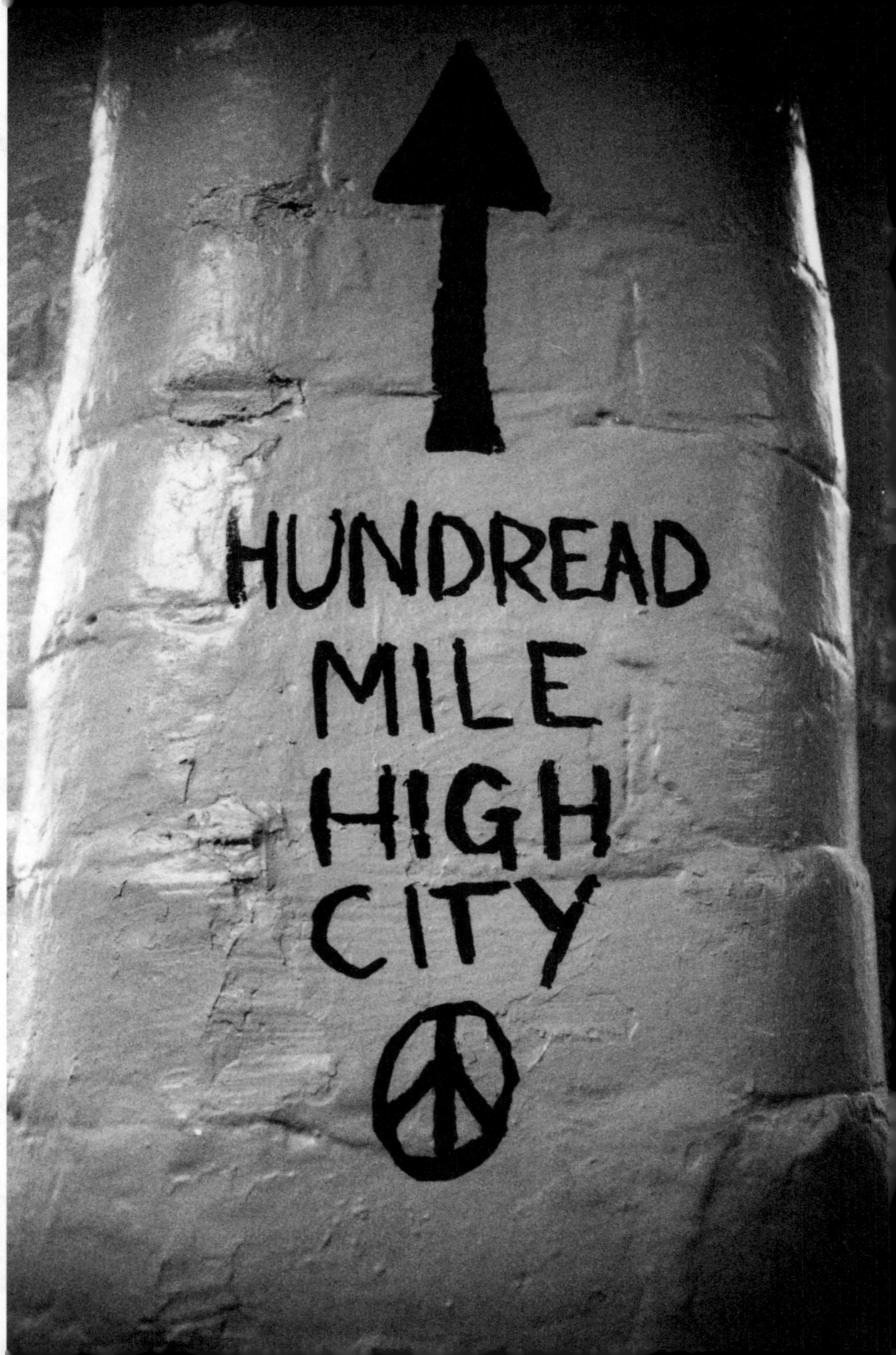
HUNDREAD
MILE
HIGH
CITY

HUNDREAD
MILE
HIGH
CITY

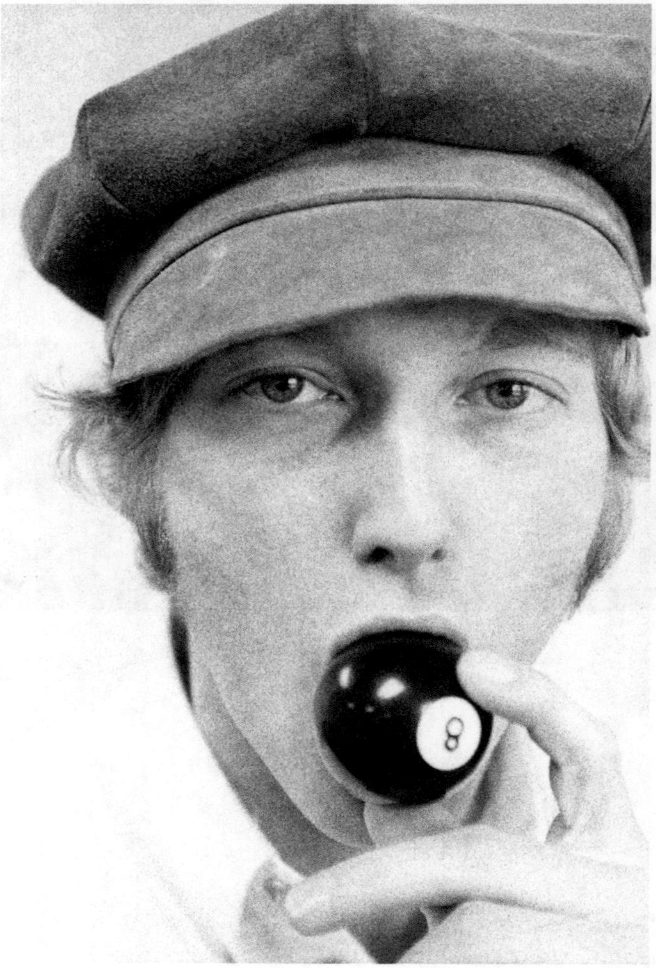
8

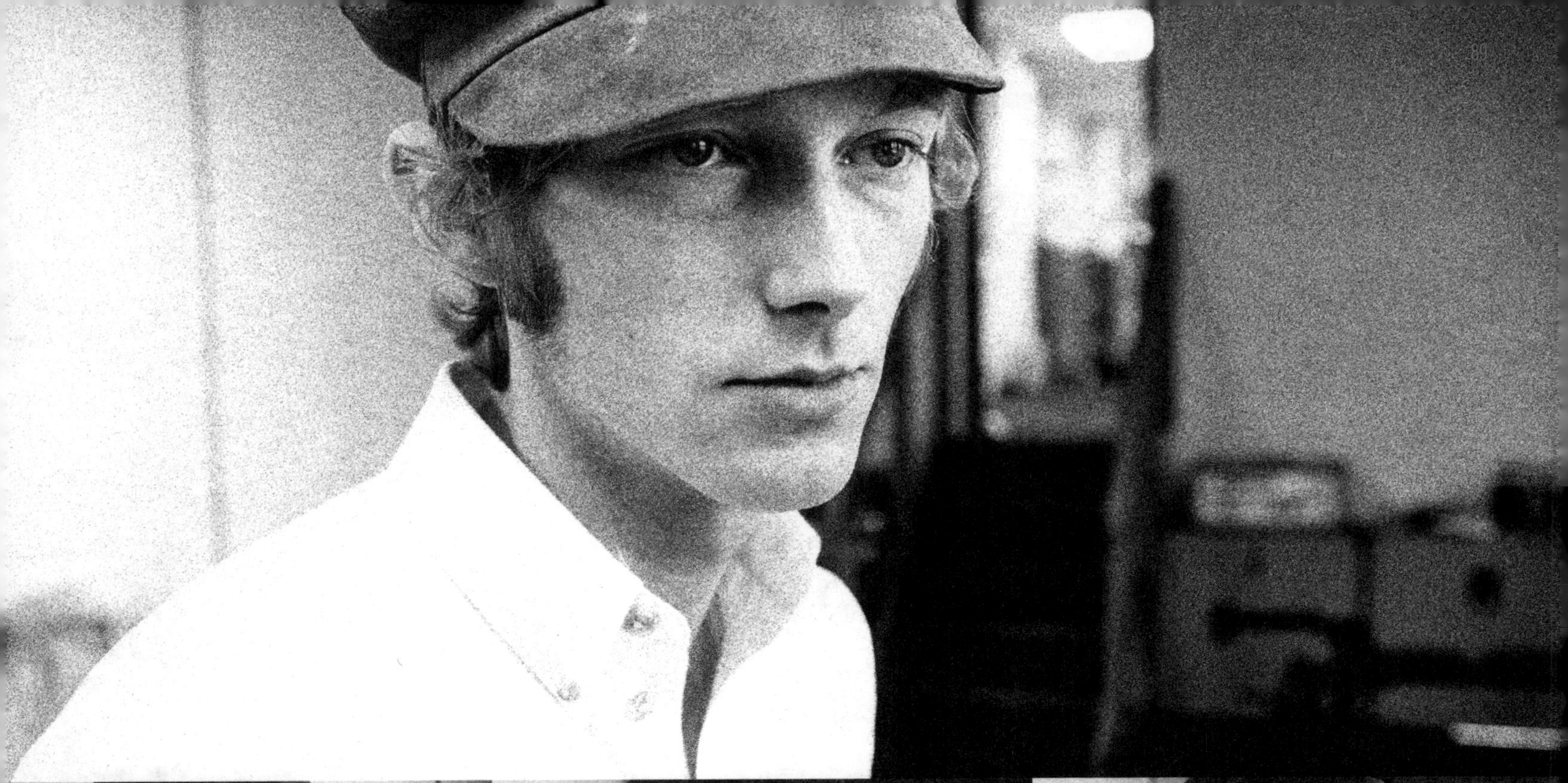

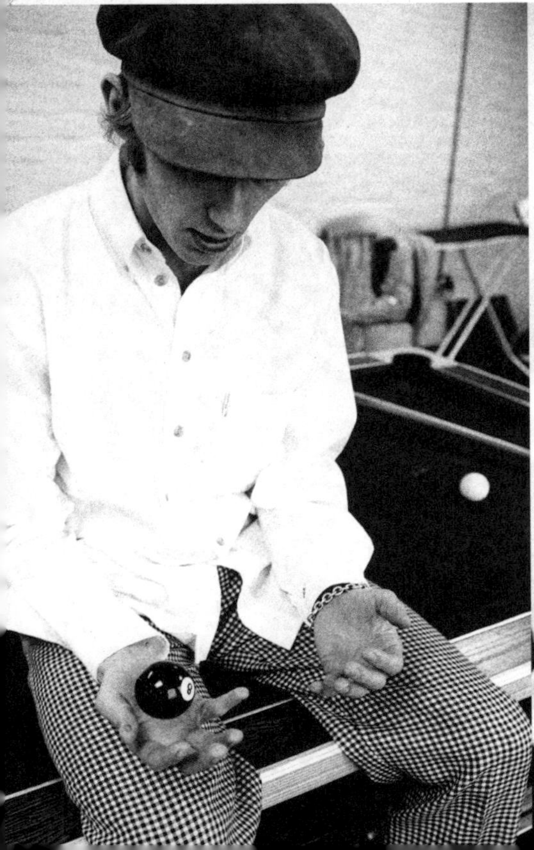

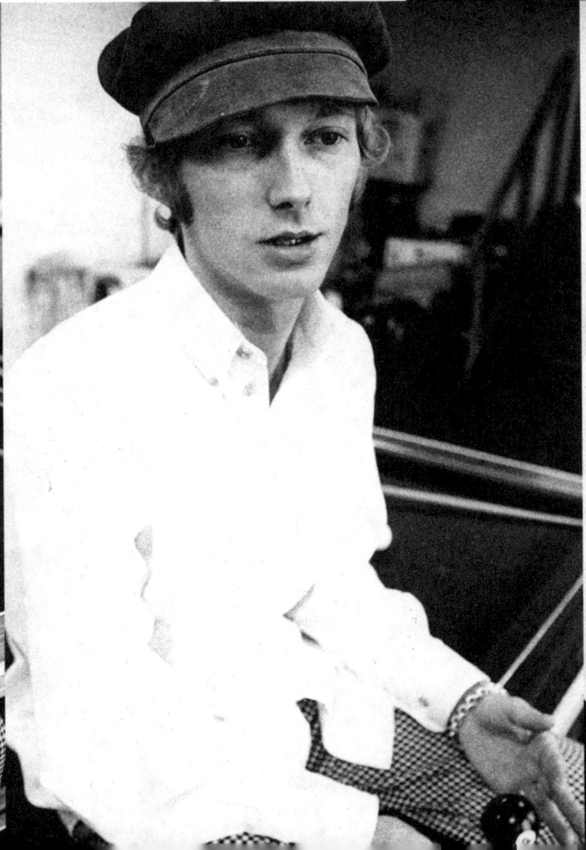

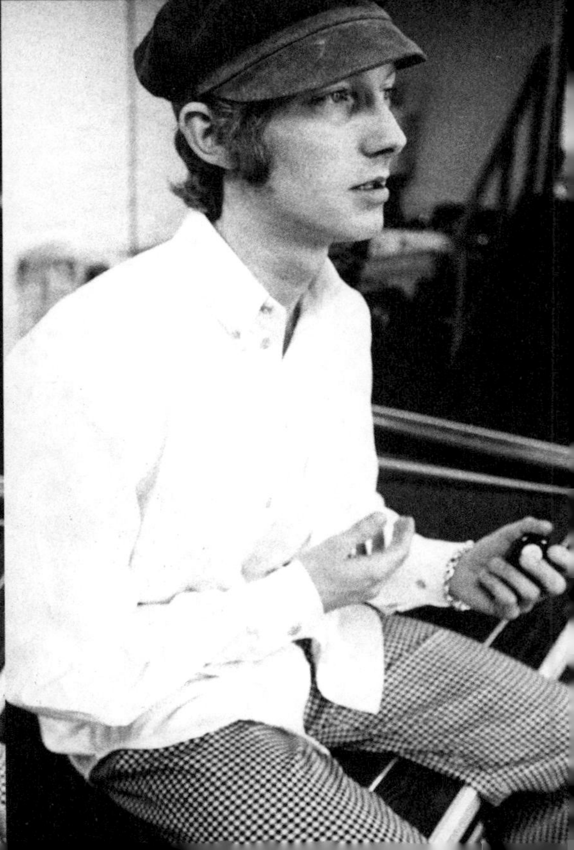

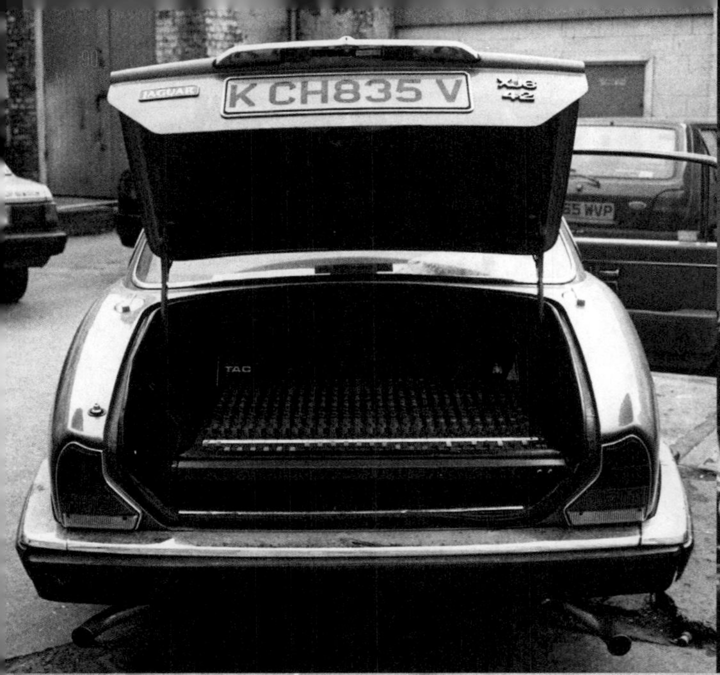
JAGUAR
K CH835 V
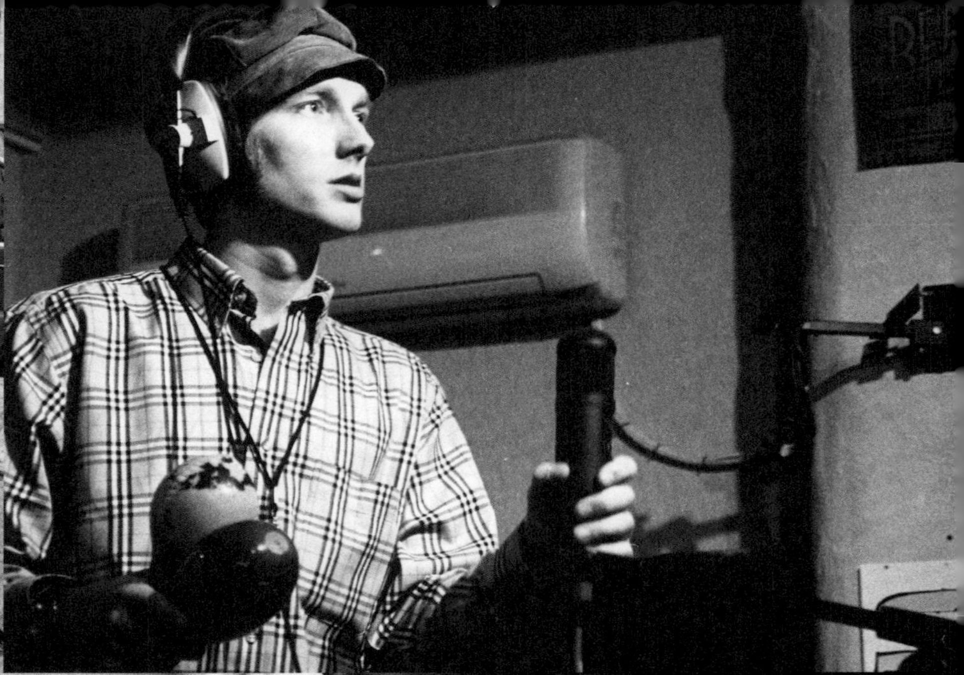
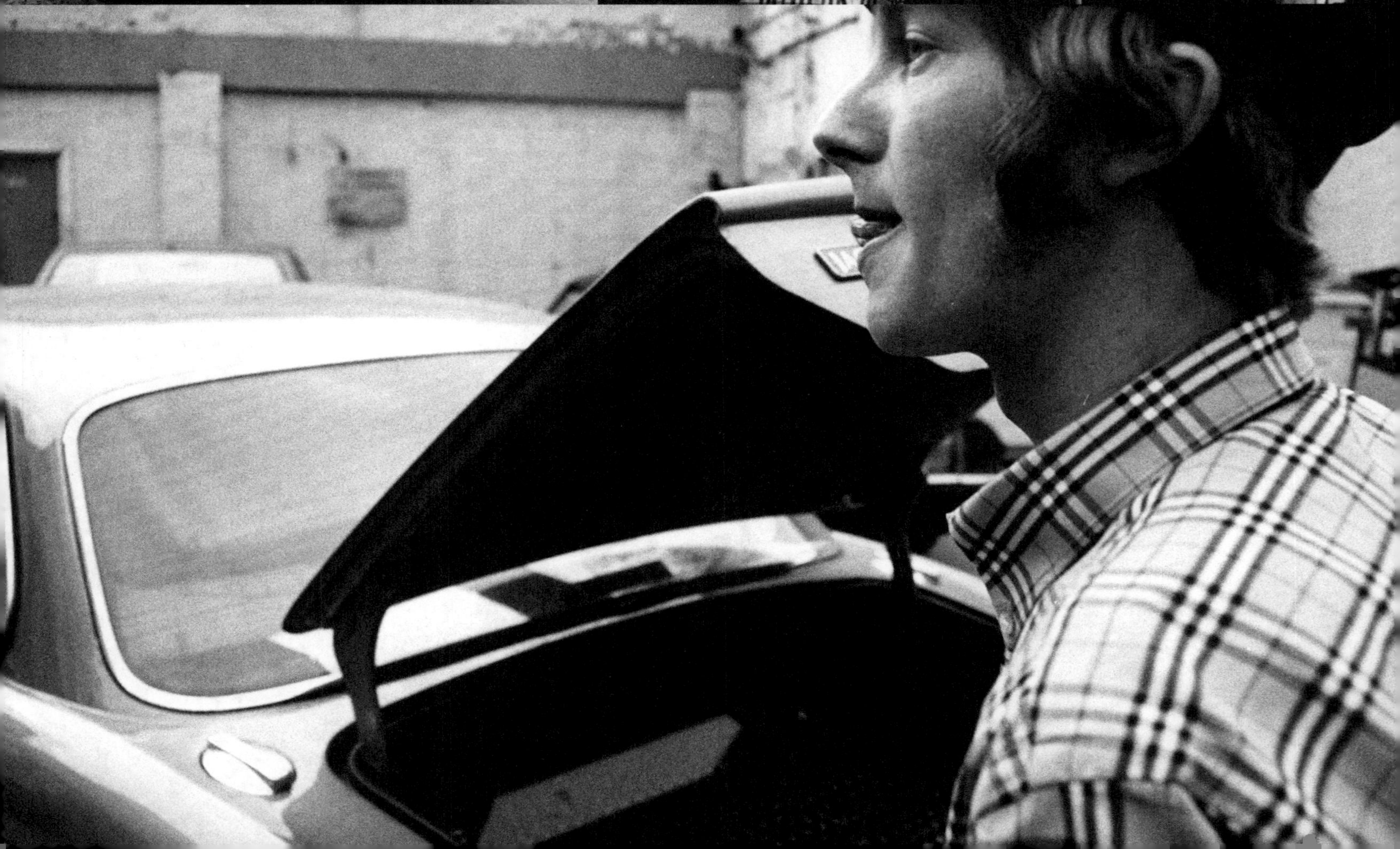

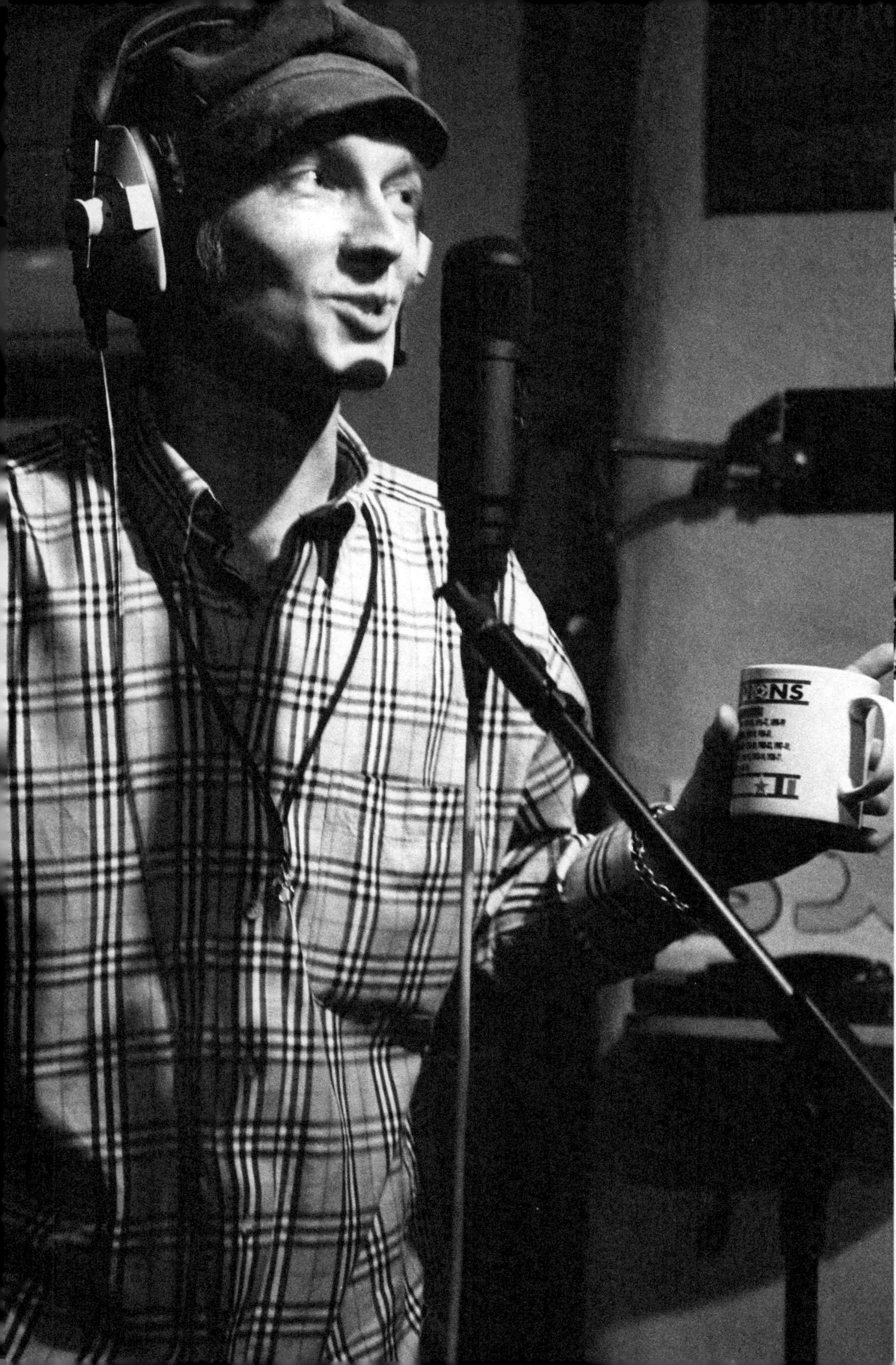

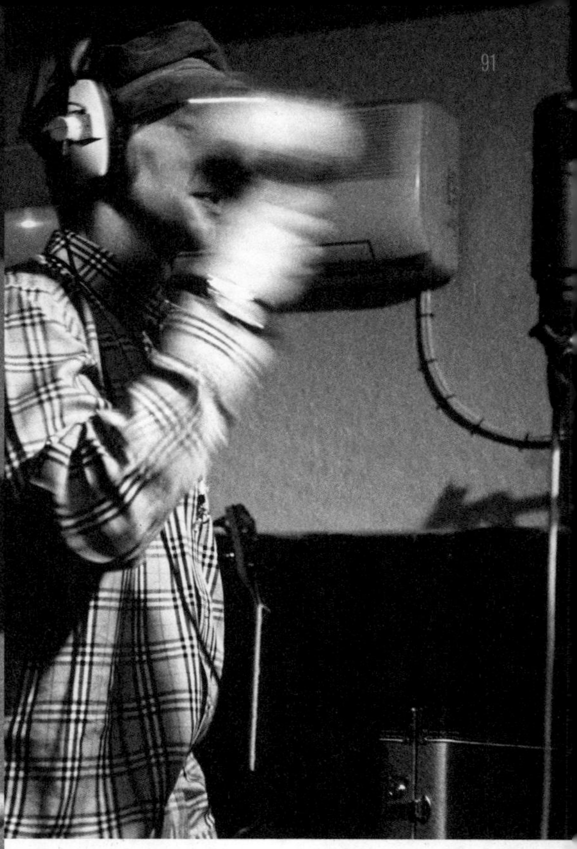

92

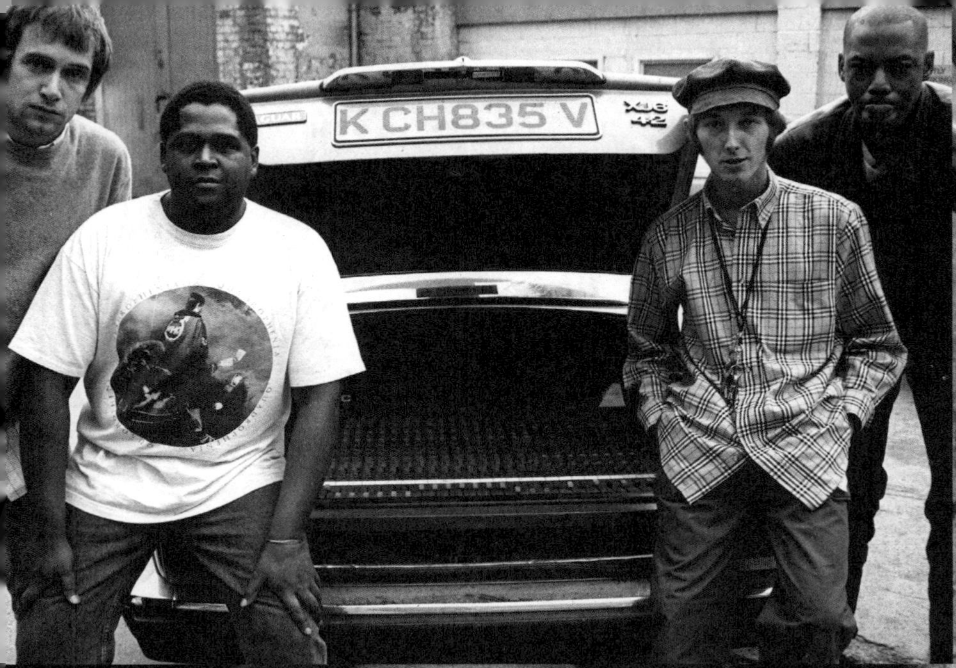
K CH835 V

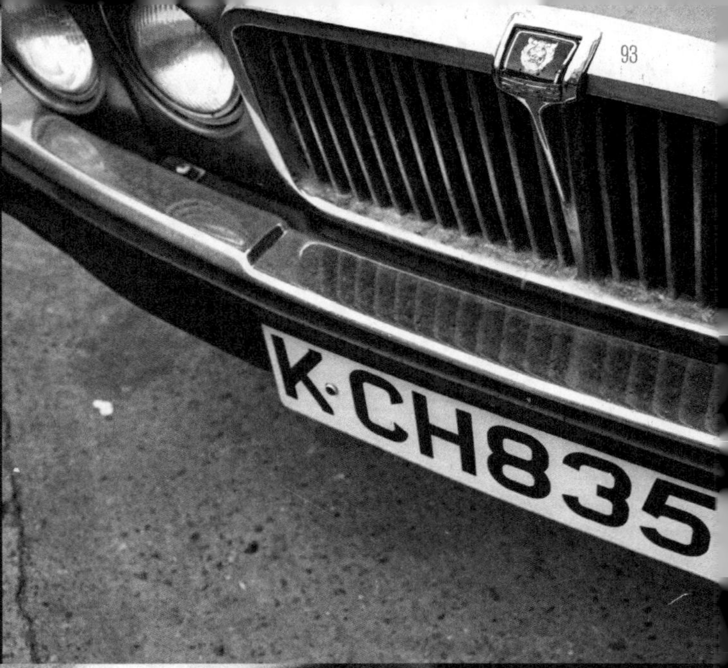
K·CH835

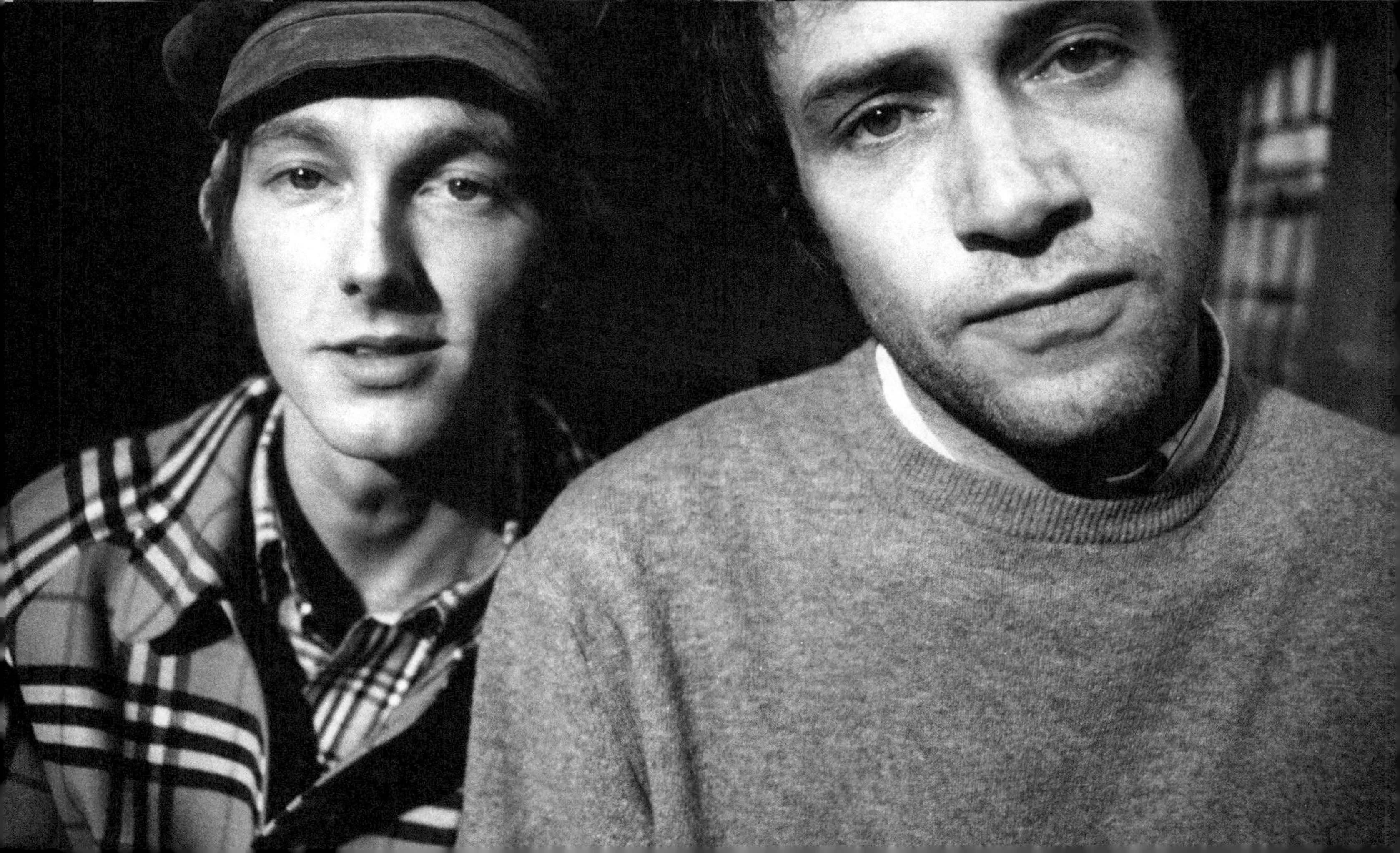

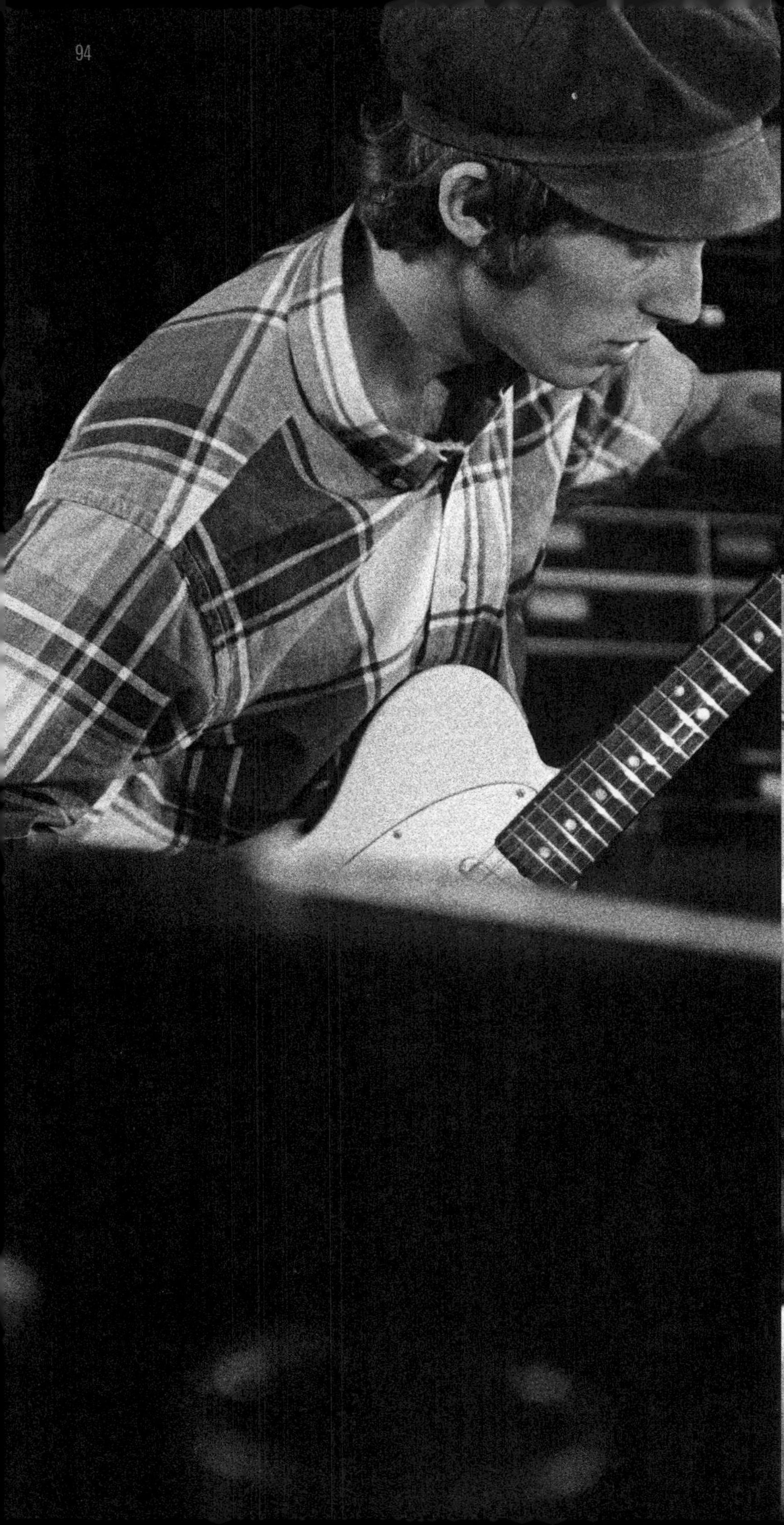

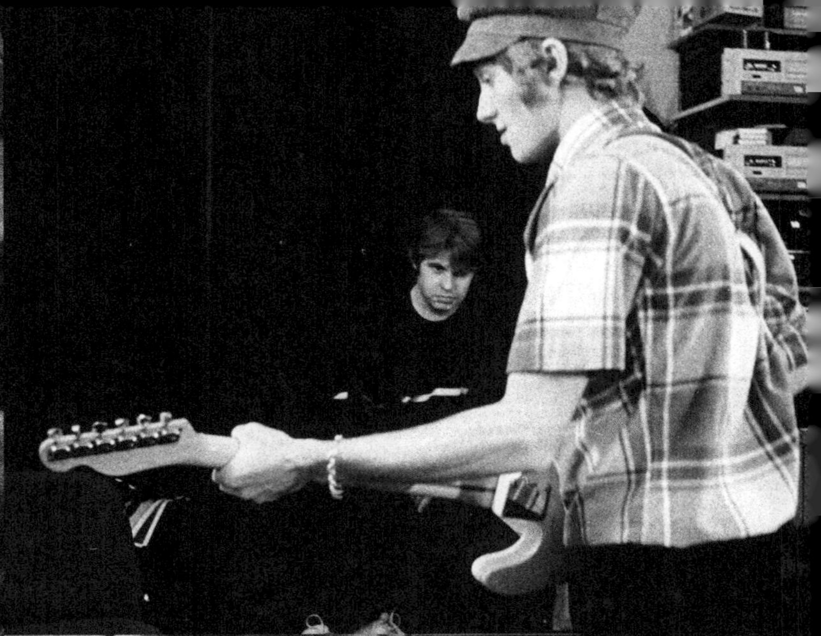

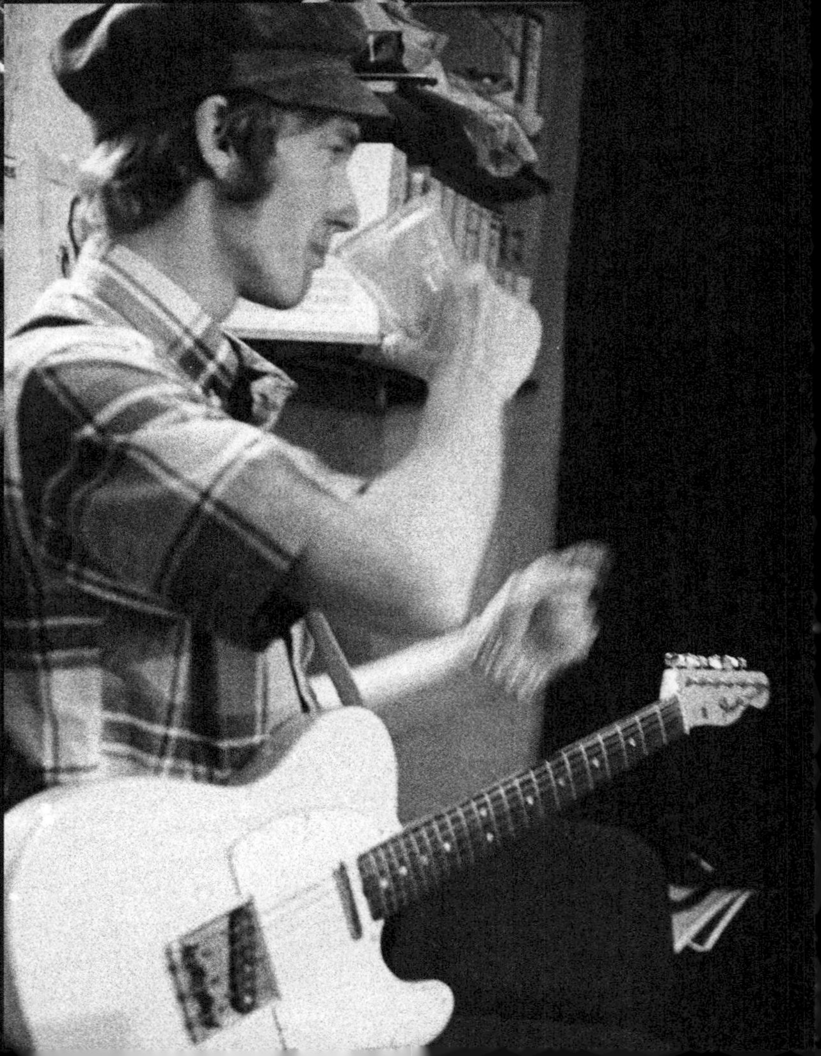

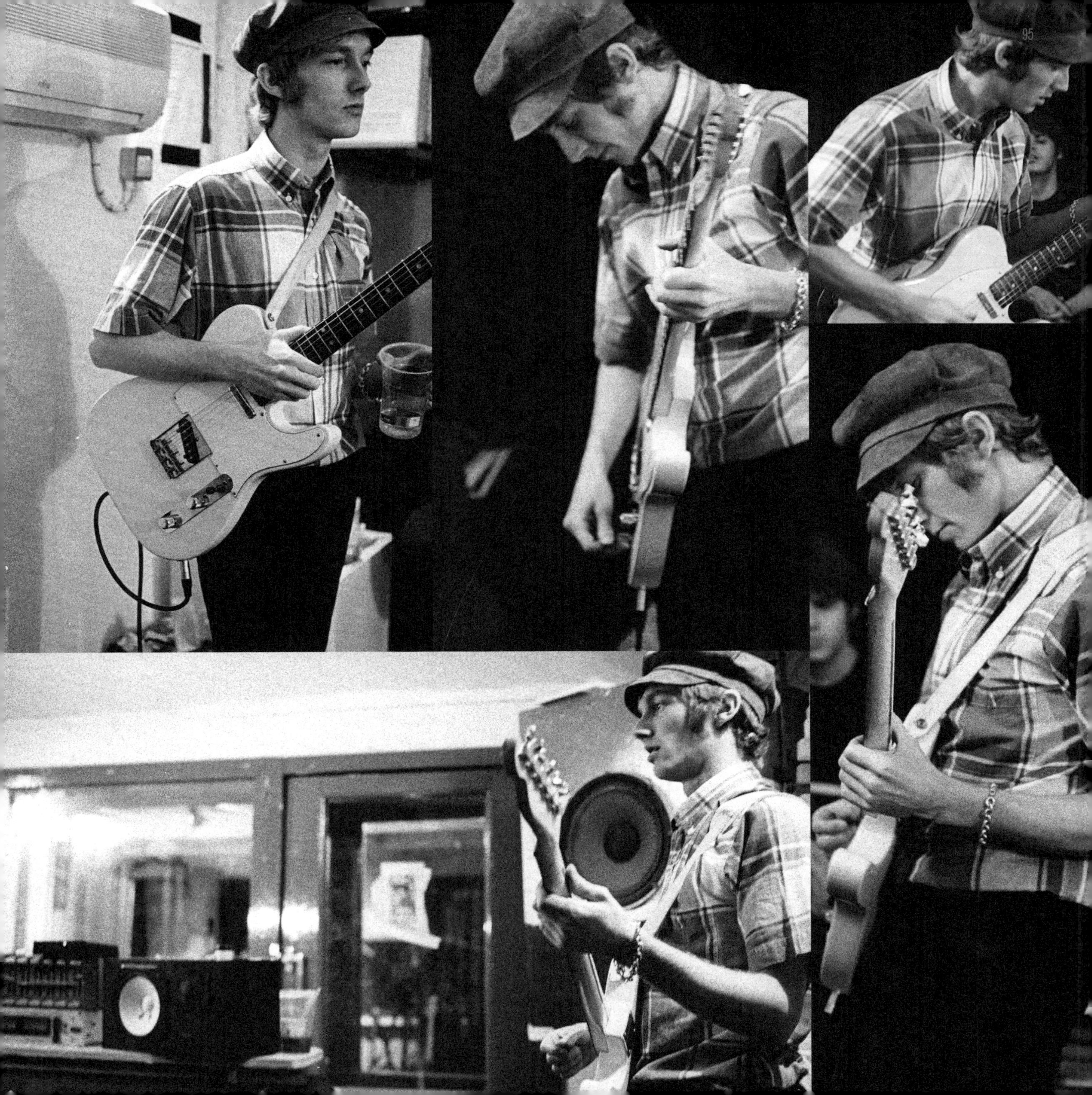

ALICE'S LEVIS (USED ON THE BACK OF THE TOUR PROGRAM)

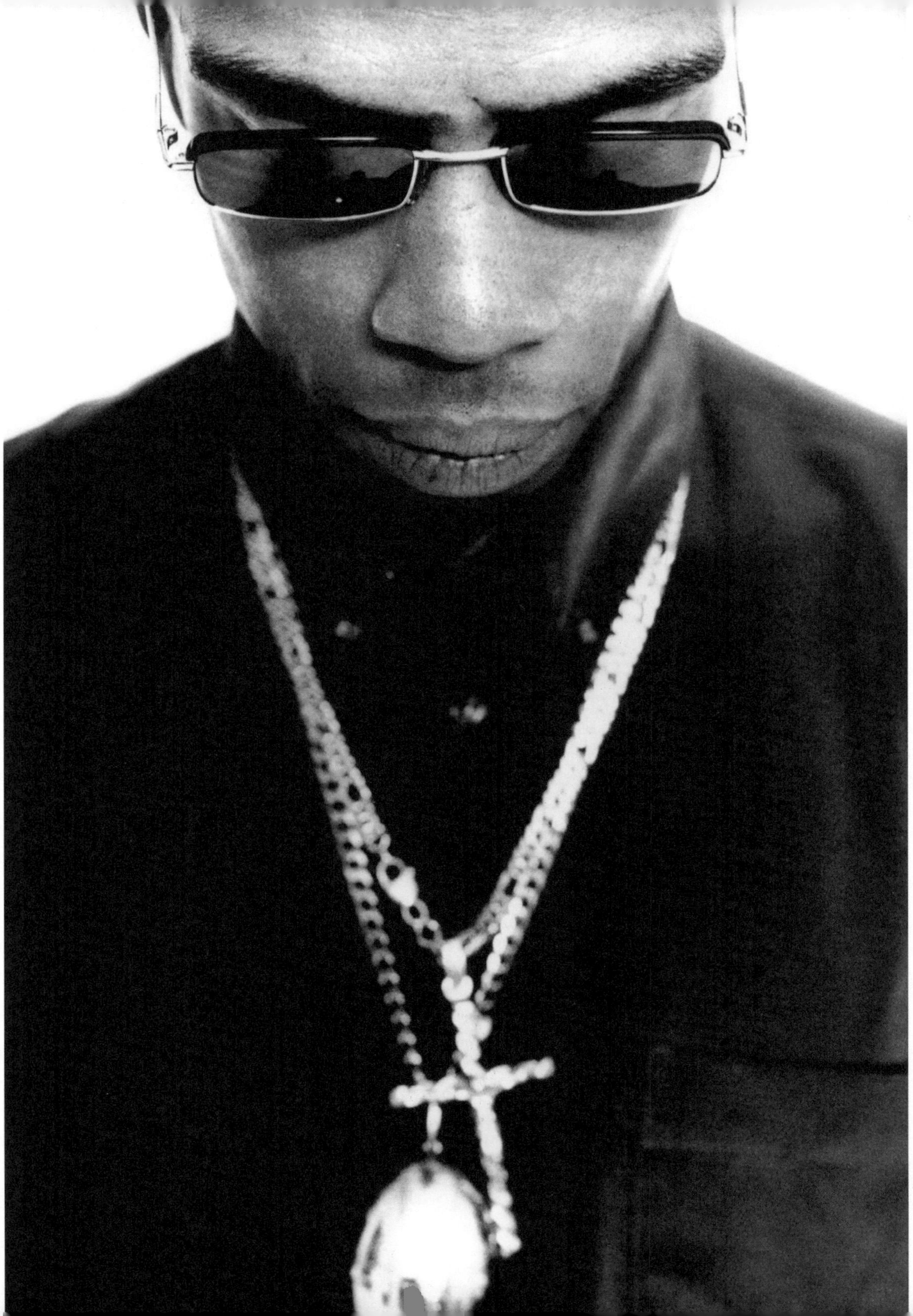

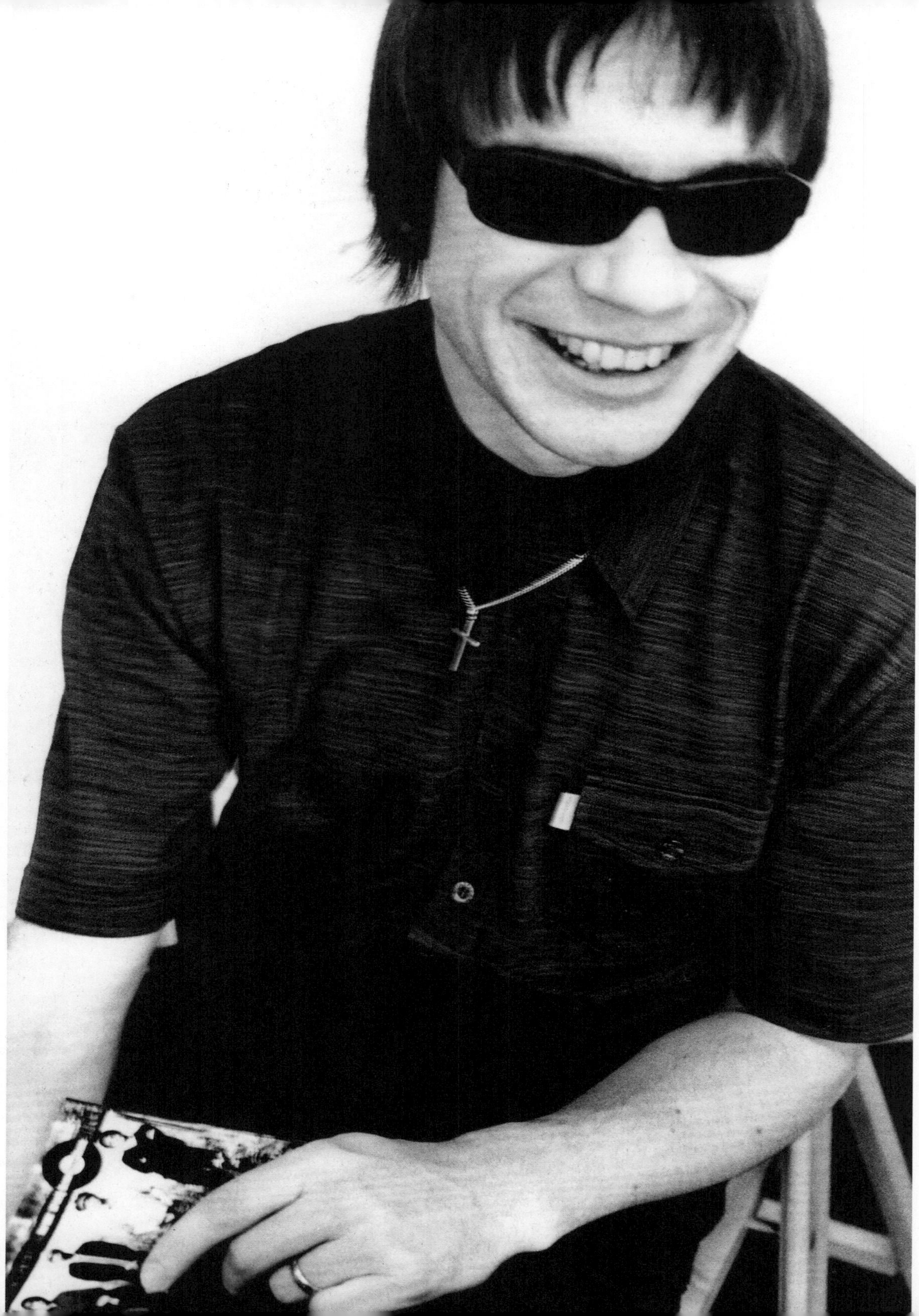

99

5AM ON A WINDY MORNING AND WE'RE SHOOTING STEVE'S PRIZED LAMBRETTA ON THE EDGE OF A CLIFFTOP. TONY KNEW THE IMPORTANCE OF CHECKING THE BRAKES FIRST. **GERRARD SAINT**

SOUL DRIVER

TONY BRIGGS

I'm from Sunderland, the Fulwell End, I've been a photographer for hire since I moved to London in 1988. I've always taken pictures and my influences have always been the 60's, the mod scene, David Bailey, The Who, Small Faces. I had Jam record covers pinned on my bedroom wall as a kid, so then for me, twenty years later to have worked with Paul Weller and to have my own photos on Ocean Colour Scene album covers was amazing.

I tried my hand playing in bands but I never had it so I knew shooting bands was the closest I could get. Despite my lack of musical ability I've had Steve White teaching me some drum licks and Weller and Cradock showing me guitar riffs and Damon running me through bass lines, what a jammy bastard.

Most of my pictures of this period are just self-portraits, they're how I see myself. They are all very mod influenced, all shot on film, all un-retouched. There are no special effects, no tricks, it's just story telling. I always try to shoot in technicolor, making things larger than life, but when shooting musicians black and white sometimes makes it more interesting, more intense. It adds that extra glamour. These ideas are not original but they say imitation is the greatest form of flattery.

One of my first proper music jobs was shooting Portishead's press shots for their Dummy album for Tony Crean at Go Discs. This was around the time when Paul Weller was starting his solo career and Go Discs had just signed him. Gerard Saint at Big Active had introduced me to Sean Bye and then Sean introduced me to the band. It was 1994 and Gez knew I was into the same sort of music, clothes, scooters, then once I met the boys we just clicked.

Sean and Gez invited me down to see the band showcase at some tiny venue in Piccadilly. I was sitting really close to the stage and they just blew me away. After that gig we arranged to do a photo shoot and I met them down at Holborn Studios and shot about a dozen rolls of film.

Sean Bye was the band's original record company product manager at MCA. Sean tragically died very young just months afterwards. I've dedicated this book to the memory of Sean. Then a lovely young up and coming fella called Matt Cook took over. A lot of the band's commercial success was orchestrated by Matt.

After Moseley Shoals, Gez left and Pete Kelsey took over, I can't remember why. Pete went on to do all the design for Marchin' Already.

Looking back through all the covers through Moseley Shoals and Marchin Already it does look like a decent body of work, you can tell they're all painted by the same brush, they have a look, a feel, a direction. It's nothing original that I can take credit for, all of it is heavily influenced by The Who, The Jam, The Small Faces; the mod scene in general. Steve's granddad's medals, the spirit of 66 Lambretta, the magic carpet, the bowling shoes and tins of talcum powder, the Black Power/ Northern Soul patch, it all tells that story.

Saturday Night, Sunday Morning was the Marchin' Already tour programme (1998) that Chris Cradock and Pete Kelsey and I put together. Matt Cook managed to get Levi's to put some money in to have me make a short film of the tour and we sold 50,000 tour programmes.

Matt was legendary at this sort of thing, The Mini Cooper/Italian Job connection was Matt's idea and Mini gave the band a brand new Mini Cooper each!

Simon is the best vocalist I've ever heard and I think he's a genuine artist and a beautiful song writer, but he took life quite seriously at times and was difficult to reach. Steve and Damon and I were close for a long while, we had similar taste in many things, we socialized and shopped together in London regularly. Matt used to get a lot of cool sponsorship for us; Ben Sherman, Levis, Merc, Fred Perry, and Clarks used to send us stuff. No wonder we all looked the bloody same.

I would like to think I had an effect on the band's success, their public image, but in reality they would have sold just as many records in brown paper bags. They've made some mistakes but they always just did what they did and carried on regardless. You got to respect them for that. If they hadn't cracked it they'd still be playing the same music in the pubs in Birmingham.

They have always been very defensive, Steve in particular but I think it's from their time of being fucked over by record companies and the music press (all before my time really). It took its toll but they just did what they did, they take their music and their image very personally. That's not a criticism, taking things personally. It's the personal things that matter. I know some bands have a leader, the writer who controls everything, takes the glory and all the money but OCS were always a democracy, there was always an even split four ways.

After photographing the band for several years I was running out of ideas and patience, the band were always difficult to keep interested and never EVER gave me much time so inevitably the pictures became repetitive. So I moved on (well, I got sacked, cheers Chris) but with no complaints. I'm just glad that I was there at the right time. I'd like to thank them all for taking me along for the ride, the few years I spent with them have been some of the interesting of my career.

Since the heady days of Moseley Shoals and Marchin Already I have kept in touch, Oscar has always asked after Alice and Steve (the dog) I told him the dog died years ago but he still always asks, he was always a genuinely nice bloke to work with. I've seen Steve many times at OCS and Weller gigs and have worked with him on two later albums, One For The Road and On The Ley Line when I think I produced some great photography reminiscent of the glory days. Not to mention a great little low budget 16mm video I made for 'I Told You So' shot in the Greenwich Tunnel with Dom Delaney.

Little known facts: one of the original Quadrophenia pictures by Ethan Russell was of Terry 'Chad' Kennett in the Greenwich tunnel in a target t-shirt. It is also said that the tunnel is built on a ley line.

I still see Damon as often as I can, I've done some great work with Trio Valore (Damon and Steve White), I'm a huge fan. To be honest, Damon seems the happiest of all of them. I've lost contact with Chris but I hope he's well, we had some great times. The last time I saw Simon Foxy Fowler was at the Garage in Islington a few years back. I was chatting to him for about 20 minutes after the gig before I realised he thought I was someone else. For fucks sake…

1989-

Ocean Colour Scene (Simon Fowler born - 25.05.65, Steve Cradock born - 22.08.69, Damon Minchella born - 01.06.69, Oscar Harrison born - 15.04.65) formed at a time when the United Kingdom was in the grip of promoters organising parties in fields and disused warehouses in and around the M25, in the Home Counties surrounding London. These raves were often attended by thousands of young, buzzing, bright eyed and bushy tailed ravers wearing Timberland boots, baggy tracky bottoms and baggy Champion sweatshirts.

The year also provided a platform to launch Madchester and a new era for the Manc's beloved Hacienda. Voodoo Ray and 808 State were massive hits on the scene and so were the Happy Mondays, who bridged both the rave culture and indie scene with songs that included Wrote For Luck (WFL) and Hallelujah. The Mondays were soon joined by their Manc pals, the Stone Roses, who thrilled the nation with Fools Gold and their debut album, and went on to set a new standard with their Spike Island gig the following year. The end of the 80's had a storming sense of vitality, rave had gate-crashed its way through the nation, sweeping aside all that had gone before. What it did was clear the deck of all the previous 'tribes' - the mods, skinheads, punks and so forth, and this was something that British youth culture would never recover from. Coming off the back of rave, the 90's also heralded something promising. The Stone Roses gave us a taster with their Spike Island gig but the momentum couldn't be sustained and, sadly, the excitement that had been so inspiring and motivating gradually waned. But being British it was only going to be a matter of time (about four years) before the next 'big' thing was to ignite. This, of course, was Oasis.

Before OCS formed all the members had acquired experience playing in different bands. Simon Fowler and Damon Minchella had been with the Fanatics, Steve Cradock with The Boys and Oscar Harrison had been drumming for reggae outfit Echo Base (and a stint with the Fanatics).

The Boys had been playing to the more serious, tailor-made, mod circuit and were a well-respected outfit. They had first formed in 1988 with Cradock starting out on bass. Chris Cradock (Steve's dad, an ex-police officer) got involved as the band's manager and they self-released an EP called Happy Days.

Their influences were firmly rooted in the rock, pop and soul of the 1960's. The influence of the 60's (and then the Stone Roses) was something that each band member recognised in each other. The foundations for OCS were laid following a chance meeting at a Stone Roses concert at the Irish centre in Birmingham (the same venue where The Boys once supported Steve Marriot). Then, once The Boys had collapsed and Harrison had left Echo Base, Cradock, Fowler, Minchella and Harrison formed Ocean Colour Scene.

Retaining support from Chris Cradock the family home's garage space was taken over to be used for rehearsals and, as the band cracked on with writing new material, the Madchester scene machine was taking off at a pace and somehow this would be linked to Ocean Colour Scenes destiny too.

OCS played their first gig at the Stoke Wheatsheaf. In the audience was the former manager of The Beat, John Mostyn, He saw their potential and quickly signed them to Phffft Records, who were based in Birmingham. A few months later in September (1990) their debut single Sway was released. Their debut television appearance on The Word (Channel Four) soon followed.

Being signed to an indie label suited the attitudes of OCS but it was a short lived affair. Phonogram got involved and Phffft manufactured a licensing deal with Fontana for an impressive £600,000. Not that the band benefited from it. What they did get, however, was a five album deal, which initially promised much but this was not to going to be quite such a simple evolution.

The band set out on their first major tour, Yesterday Today, to support their latest single of the same name. Other singles released on Fontana over the next two years included the re-release of Sway, Giving It All Away and Do Yourself a Favour. The band's debut album, simply titled Ocean Colour Scene, was released in May 1992. It was during this period that OCS first met Paul Weller and Brendan Lynch, who would both be integral to the development of the band when they resurfaced in the mid-90's with a new lease of life and a new bag of demos (which would become the Moseley Shoals album).

By 1993 Ocean Colour Scene had toured Japan and America and had begun working on new songs for their next album but they had also fallen out of favour with Fontana. An outcome of this was that the band managed to remove themselves from their contract with the label. This pleased the band and they believed it was the right thing to do. It also meant they were label-less and it would remain this way until Jon Walsh became involved, signed them up and the rest, as they say, is history and, for the purposes of this book, the band's Moseley Shoals and Marchin' Already history.

1992
OCEAN COLOUR SCENE

1. *Talk On*
2. *How About You*
3. *Giving It All Away*
4. *Justine*
5. *Do Yourself a Favour*
6. *Third Shade of Green*
7. *Sway*
8. *Penny Pinching Rainy Heaven Days*
9. *One of Those Days*
10. *Is She Coming Home*
11. *Blue Deep Ocean*
12. *Reprise.*

Eyebrows raised by some, cheeky grins from others. Whatever your reaction the Shamans Ebeneezer Goode was brilliant. It certainly gave most of us some much needed respite from the Abba revival and Whitney Houston's I Will Always Love You (which stayed in the top slot for over three months, spewing into 1993).

This year also seemed to be dominated by Simply Red's Stars and other forgettable albums from Erasure and INXS. But the Brit Award for Best Breakthrough Act went, rightly so, to Nirvana. Countless British teenage kids got turned on to grunge… for good or for bad!

Ocean Colour Scene's debut album came at a time when Madchester was all but a dirty word, the sense of the second summer of love 'rave on' days was well and truly over and mother Brit Pop hadn't even been shagged yet. It was a mixed up time with little direction, the rave casualties were piling up and many young people simply didn't quite know which way to sway.

ADAM COOPER

I first saw the Boys at a rally in 1989. They were playing with another local band called the Pictures. The crowd loved them and they sold their single Happy Days too, which they had brought with them. They handed out loads of free badges too. Their band logo was a replica of what Weller used on his guitar.

Up until seeing them I had only read about them in the Phoenix List and the CCI letters. They were proper moddy, all suited and booted, and I remember the bass playing dressed in his Cavern suit. Cradock looked good, but then he was part of the Colliboshers scene anyway.

The Boys had a good sound. I recall they played a lot of Jam covers but they had good songs of their own too. They had that poppy, mod revival sound. Then I saw them at the end in late '89. Their look had totally changed. They were wearing cycling shirts and shorts and everyone was like 'what the fuck are you doing?' They had totally blown out the whole mod look. I'm not sure whether they lasted the whole gig because people were booing them. They also upset Tony Class too because someone in the band pissed in a pint glass in front of Tony's missus and Tony told them that they wouldn't play for him again. I think The Boys broke up soon after that anyway. But then they were a bit of a whirlwind. They kind of appeared on the scene and then they were gone.

TIM DORNEY (FLOWERED UP)

Ocean Colour Scene did a tour with us in 1990. We did a second tour which was our first headlining tour. Ocean Colour Scene shared the support slot with another band called 530. We played Newcastle and places like the Tic Toc in Coventry. The first time that I met the band was at the Tic Toc. They were really good live and sounded really good too. In fact we ended up stealing their sound man 'coz he made them sound that good. What I do recall about them was that they were dead tight as a band. Plus they had Oscar on the drums and he was mustard. The band were really nice people but their crew were an absolute nightmare. They would never be happy with anyone else using their equipment. We had a few run-ins with them over monitors and stuff on that level. But the band themselves were all reasonable blokes and wouldn't go around throwing strops.

I know some people tried putting them in with the 'baggy' bands but they weren't baggy at all. They weren't as moddy or as 60's influenced back then either. I suppose they were a bit more Brit Popish. Or what would later become known as Brit Pop.

Around that time the crowds at gigs was still healthy. I remember one of the Tic Toc gigs. We were supposed to play in the back room of this grotty venue on a housing estate in Coventry but so many people turned out they had to upgrade us to the bigger room.

The thing is Ocean Colour Scene were good, crafting songwriters and knew how to put a good tune together. When they were in their mid-90's period I was more into dance music, house and techno, but I still liked the stuff I saw they were doing on shows like Chris Evans's. I met Chris (Cradock) a few times during the early days and then again when I was with Republica. We played a gig in Chicago and Ocean Colour Scene were our support. This was around 1996. I remember strolling into the sound-check and saying "Alright lads, still supporting us are you?".

CHRIS GRIFFITHS (THE REAL PEOPLE)

We first met OCS around '90/'91. Both of our bands had just released our first albums and we use to gig together. OCS would play Liverpool with us and we would play Birmingham with them. We also played a few festivals and hung out, these included Glastonbury and Hultsfred in Sweden. We became very close friends and stayed in touch. Later, when OCS toured the Moseley Shoals album, they invited the Real People on the tour, which really helped us as we had just released What's on the Outside.

Steve played piano for us on the tour on the track Rayners Lane and on one of the tours I remember Paul Weller got up and said, "If there were more people like OCS in the music business the music industry would be a much better place". Even now the Real People still get asked to tour with OCS. There's also some footage (on

YouTube) of us playing Day Tripper at the Royal Albert Hall with OCS and Noel Gallagher.

My brother Tony and I also sang backing vocals on Profit and Peace and the track I Am the News from the Northern Already album. OCS also covered a Real People song 'Start Of the Day' on the 'Flying Squad' album. Tony and I also co-wrote the Pleasure Seekers on Steve's solo album. We both hold OCS in high regards, as fantastic musicians and song writers.

TONY MCCARROL (OASIS)

I first became aware of Ocean Colour Scene around the end of 1994. Paul Weller had been attending shows towards the end of that year and I'm sure it was his belief in the band that brought them to our and many other people's attention.

Various tapes were bandied about the bus and it wasn't long before OCS were offered a support slot for an upcoming tour. We enjoyed many shows together and I soon realised that this lot, like ourselves, had worked hard to achieve what they had. In that I'm referring mainly to the unique sound they had developed.

The gigs were full of energy and I can only imagine seeing a line-up today containing the names Oasis and Ocean Colour Scene in a moderately sized building. Two of the biggest names of the nineties together under the same roof. Unbelievable, Amazing Times!!

The lads were absolutely fantastic musicians but, above all, the nicest bunch of blokes you could want to meet. You really wanted to see them go to the top and I'm proud to say that I was part of that journey. They were totally laid back and completely comfortable in what they were doing and in their style. Like ourselves, it was only a matter of time before the world took note. As it stands (07/08/13) I know I will be attending their show at the V Festival in a couple of weeks and am totally looking forward to it.

1996
MOSELEY SHOALS

1. The Riverboat Song
2. The Day We Caught the Train
3. The Circle
4. Lining Your Pockets
5. Fleeting Mind
6. 40 Past Midnight
7. One For the Road
8. It's My Shadow
9. Policeman and Pirates
10. The Downstream
11. You've Got It Bad
12. Get Away

The first number one record of 1996 was Jesus To A Child by George Michael, closely followed by Babylon Zoo's Spaceman (from the Levi advert). Take That disbanded - and a help line was set up for distressed fan and piss takers alike. Euro 96 fans chanted along to Three Lions by Baddiel & Skinner and the Lightning Seeds and Spice World was born with Wannabe in July. The Stone Roses Second Coming of the previous year had promised much but was over shadowed by Oasis's Definitely Maybe. Thankfully, what 1995 and Oasis had done was to get British youth interested in real, live bands again.

1995 was also the year that Ronnie Scott and Chas Chandler both died, and Jarvis Cocker interrupted Michael Jacksons performance at the Brit awards. This same year Oasis picked up Best Album for What's the Story, Best Video for Wonderwall and Best British Group (well they were from Manchester). 1996 simply belonged to Oasis but their pal, Paul Weller, picked up Best British Male Solo Artist. And in this year, Ocean Colour Scene joined Oasis at Knebworth on a sunny August afternoon… and so did a lot of other people.

This was also the year that gave us Brit Pop and some excellent bands, including Kula Shaker, Pulp and Supergrass, who were joined by the Chemical Brothers Setting Sun, Fire Starter - Prodigy, Underworld - Born Slippy and Oasis's What's the Story was the second biggest selling album of year (just piped by Alanis Morisette's Jagged Little Pill). OCS's outstanding Moseley shoals came in as the tenth best seller, selling over a million copies.

Moseley Shoals opens with a Cradock guitar lick that instantly pricks up the listener's ears and leaves them asking 'what is this all about?' A few more seconds and it's 'mmm, this is unusual - mmm I'm liking it!' The Riverboat Song. Before the song has finished it has left an impact that, for many, can only be compared to the first time the listener heard Wonderwall, Fools Gold or Wildwood.

There's something different, odd even, about the rhythm of the song. It's the way Harrison plays that jazzy style ride cymbal, slaps his snare and fills the gaps with tom tom rolls.

Fowler can sing - yes this guy can sing and he is backed by a hooky guitar riff and catchy bass line. Someone has found some maracas and it gives the song that Rolling Stones-esque feel. Two minutes into the song and the listener is humming along and taping along with the tambourine beat.

Cradock introduces a fine guitar solo and Paul Weller's organ part comes to the fore. The bands 60's influences are being clearly worn on their Paisley shirt sleeves. It's refreshing and most welcomed.

The song slips away, random maracas blend with guitar sounds and, before the song has seemingly ended, Fowler has introduced the Day We Caught the Train, his voice soon transformed into some strange, effected vocal. As the song progresses the listener is drawn into the lyrics. There is a story emerging and, once Jimmy and trains are mentioned, the listener cannot fail to evoke the image of Jimmy Cooper looking spaced out and rebellious with his eye liner on, sitting between two bowler hat wearing banker types on his return journey to Brighton, in an attempt to recapture better days.

The song itself is a journey through rum and coke and dirty jokes, with a further image of Groucho smoking a number ten. The listener is invited to sing along and join in by echoing feel no sorrow, something OCS audiences picked up on early on and became an integral part of the bands live experience.

The song ends but there's no time to relax because The Circle bursts in. Weller joins the band again, this time on guitar, the obvious relationship between Weller and the band evidently solid and strong.

By the time The Circle has arrived the listener is pleased that OCS have re-introduced themselves with such a brilliant album. Moseley Shoals is a spectacular home coming to where the band belong - playing and recording music. The third song on the album would become the fourth single release from the album.

Cradock and Weller's guitars sit comfortably beside each other. Harrison's relaxed drums have a Kenny 'Small Faces' Jones feel to them and Minchella provides a melodic bass line.

Three minutes in and the listener is fooled into thinking the song is about to end but it takes off again, pushed a bit further along by more guitars that sound like they could have been lifted from an early Faces album. The guitars sing to each other. The guitars have the final word before The Circle makes way for Lining Your Pockets. The band bonded, they drop the tempo down a notch. Fowler and a piano carry the song along. The song is roomy, beautiful and simple. Ronnie Lane could be supplying the bass part but it is just Minchella sharing his influences.

Fleeting Mind's bass line however, has an Entwistle like feel to it and the acoustic and lead guitar parts blend well together. This is the first song on the album that evidently hints of the bands late 60's folky psychedelic influences. There is a Love/Haight-Astbury feel but they have taken those influences and made them their own. It would work for them, often in the years to follow.

Next the 70's have arrived and they have been stewing and smouldering away, then the honky tonk feel of the piano on 40 Past Midnight reminds us that OCS can turn their hands to anything. Sure enough this is a band that has spent a lot of time discovering the sounds of the sixties and seventies. 40 Past Midnight could easily have shared a 1970's American stadium with the Faces, Stones or Humble Pie. This is rock music.

Weller is back for the next song, this time on piano and backing vocals. One For the Road has elements of a country rock song. Harrison employs the use of rim shots and Fowler implores the listener to get up and dance, smile, remember those we've known from other days and cried over, and then look towards each of our personal tomorrows. It's another beautiful song that could surely have been a contender for another single.

It's My Shadow is the song which experiments with percussion and sounds. The Lynch mob (Brendan and Max) are set to do their creative work. There are bongos, more maracas and rim shots. By the time this song has settled, the listener gets the impression that all of these songs are well-rehearsed and have been played time and time again by the band. There's a confidence in their own ability. Chris Cradock's belief in the band is affirmed.

Police and Pirates suggests more 1970's. Perhaps it's more British this time, perhaps more Bolan and Bowie in its structure. For sure it's a head nodder. It sounds like the band are having fun with this song. It puts a smile on the listeners face.

The following song, The Downstream, slows the album down again. The use of piano and minimal guitar is sublime and perfect for the song. This is the song that is slotted in the album, giving the listener the sense that the album is drawing to an end. It's the signal to have that last smoke and cup of tea of a long day.

But then it's all change again as You've Got it Bad shoots the tempo back up with a Harrison Motown style stomp. The beat is urgent, hasty. It has flare and ignites the song. This was always going to be a single. Cradock's guitars screech through a solo. There is an organ in there somewhere and rapid hi-hat beats. The Lynch mob are at it again, working creatively with the band. Then Harrison bursts back into the main part of the song. We're up again and Harrison leads the song out with phased, speedy, tom tom fills supported by Minchella's driving bass line.

There's a brief moment for the listener to catch their breath before Get Away signs off the album. It is total over seven minutes of brilliant musicianship, sounds, studio technique and imagination. Get Away employs wonderful harmonica, piano and acoustic guitar parts. Harrison plays his ride cymbal gently. This song is all about dynamics and, unexpectedly, Harrison increases the tempo and starts to fly.

Each band member is flying. The Ocean Colour Scene machine is flying. There are a multitude of sounds swirling around on this song. The listener cannot resist getting sucked into them. It's a fitting end to a mouth-watering collection of songs. Moseley Shoals, recorded at Moseley Shoals studios, the bands home from home.

DAMON MINCHELLA
FIRE & SKILL

I wasn't even supposed to be playing on it originally, Noel (Gallagher) was going to do it, but he couldn't work it out. And, so I said I'll do it because I had already been playing it in Paul Weller's band. I think the initial idea arose after a drunken meeting with Liam and Steve. So it was recorded and, what was even more shocking, was that it even went into the charts. I remember some miming going on, on TOTP, that included Allan White too and even Noel (who wasn't even on the record).

Around that time we were spending a lot of time with Oasis and Paul. I remember when Morning Glory came out, it was about two weeks before actually, and we were just about to go on tour with Paul Weller. Noel came to see us and gave us all cassette copies of the album. It even included the song that was a rip off of the Stevie Wonder song, which they had to scrap. Unfortunately, I taped over it when I should have kept it.

OASIS Our relationship with Oasis started after they asked us to support them around the time Live Forever came out. Noel had already heard some of our demos and had seen us playing with Paul. We went on to play loads of gigs with them and, in the early days, the exposure helped. But even by this time we were already getting radio play on Radio One and also Chris Evans was playing us.

There were many good gigs with Oasis and the one where they supported us at the Electric Ballroom was amazing. In fact that night we pulled a fast-one on purpose. There was a band called the Real People, who really helped Noel out in the early days, and they never really got the credit for it. The Real People were starting to get somewhere but it never really happened for them. Noel pulled a lot of their ideas and used them for Oasis's first album. Anyway, we didn't tell Noel that the Real People were also going to be supporting us at the Electric Ballroom, so on the night he had to meet them again and shake their hands.

It was a great gig and it was the first time Liam had sung Wonderwall live too. Chris Evans and Radio One were there that night and they recorded it, and by the following morning it was being played, along with Riverboat and Day Tripper, on the Chris Evans show.

That night there was a guy called Dave Bates (who had first signed us) who was also around when we did the first album. That album was a complete disaster, a complete car crash for EMI Records and for us. But Dave had the balls to come to the gig because he knew he was going to get it in the neck but I just shook his hand and said 'fair play to you man'. He said he was pleased that things had worked out for us and that was fine.

STUDIO Most of what we did in the studio happened really quickly. I mean 40 Past Midnight we did all in one day. The song had never been played before. There was a little piano riff that I think Oscar had. Then Steve played drums on it, Simon free-styled some vocals over it and I played bass whilst trying to engineer it at the same time. We just spent the whole day knocking it backwards and forwards until it was finished and we had a brand new song which came from absolutely nowhere.

Then there is a song like Get Away, which we had been pissing about with for ages. We had been doing various takes of it and we just edited various bits of the takes together.

Getting Brendan was great for us. Even before Brendan got involved we had recorded most of Moseley Shoals but what we couldn't do was mix it. Steve and I were hands on with the engineering and we could make it sound great but we couldn't mix it. We just didn't have that expertise that someone like Brendan had. So Brendan got involved, listened to what we had and said 'do you want me to do it?', to which we said 'yes, but we can't pay you'. But he agreed and then MCA got involved and they got Max Hayes in to help Brendan out.

There was something about us having our own studio that really helped. We owe a lot to Andy McDonald from Go Discs. We had met Andy during our time playing with Paul. He had heard some of our demos and loved them but he didn't have any room for us on his roster at the time. Instead he gave us ten grand and some recording equipment. So with that ten grand we rented out the studio that had been used by Dexy's Midnight Runners.

It was during those six months when we rented the studio that we recorded loads of demos and Jonny Walsh was coming down and telling us how much he loved what we were doing. I remember he turned up one day, just as we had recorded a whole new song that he had never heard before. That song was Fleeting Mind and he loved it.

GLASTONBURY Before Glastonbury we had already done Knebworth and headlined T in the Park, so we were used to playing the big stuff. But when it was put to our agent about who wants to headline at Glastonbury, neither us nor Radiohead wanted to headline. But eventually they said they would do it and I think they absolutely blew us off stage. I thought they were incredible that night and there was a bit when they were halfway through Paranoid Android, where he sings about the rain falling, and in that moment it started raining. In that moment Radiohead were electric. So yeah, that night we were good but they were amazing.

Going to Scotland was always really good for us. I think our connection began around the time of Riverboat, when we had a really small tour organised around the obvious Scottish venues but we also included some smaller ones in places like Perth, where people wouldn't normally play. So when Riverboat came out and went into the top twenty we had these Scottish promoters contacting us, asking if we were going to ditch them. But we said we were still going to do it and we did, and I think because of that the Scottish promoters loved us after that and so did the fans. And we did those small venues that were only meant to hold a couple of hundred people and, all of a sudden, there would be five hundred crammed in. There is something about Scottish audiences. If you are great they will love you for it but if you are shit, they'll kill you.

We always enjoyed playing Scotland after that. We enjoyed that connection and we had Oscar waving flags on stage at Stirling Castle and we loved it. To this day I think we are still the only band to sell out five nights at the Barrowlands. There was another thing about playing Scotland. When I used to go on stage the first thing I would do was go to the back of the stage because at the start was when all the pints of piss would come flying over, which was their way of showing us that they loved us. I remember Simon used to get covered in piss and all sorts of stuff.

Being in OCS during the Moseley Shoals and Marchin' Already albums was weird. We went from being nothing to being massive. We went straight into doing twenty all-sold-out arenas. In 1996 we were the seventh biggest selling (record sales) band in Europe. It was amazing but it was our day to day life. We were inside it all, still living our lives and still having to deal with everyday stuff like 'where's my wallet', 'where's my passport' and 'I've got to phone my mum and my dad'. Then we would go on stage and that would be incredible, then we would come off stage and everyone is having a party and that's incredible too and everything is fantastic. And this becomes a cycle of what happens every day. There's also time in the studio and what comes with that is pressure from the record company. It becomes a massive thing, which some people can handle and some people cannot. It started off as a little adventure between four blokes going 'cor, how can we be playing on TOTP' and 'how can there be eleven people turning up to us in Inverness', then suddenly the managers got an assistant and they've got an office, and our mates are no longer selling tee-shirts it's a merchandise company and over there is a rep from this company and another rep from that company. In amongst all this we are thinking that we are still us but everything around us has grown to be this huge thing - and no one asked us. I mean no one asked us if we needed this extra person to do this. Suddenly we were being told 'no you don't need to do this or that, we'll make that phone call for you or we'll sort out your car insurance'. We went along with it but it sometimes felt like being a baby. There were also times when we would get off tour and have to say to the tour manager 'what do we need to do today? I don't know what to do today - where's the itinerary?'.

MARCHIN' ALREADY The process for making this album was different. With Moseley Shoals we just made a record that we wanted to make. When we put out Riverboat we thought it was going be an underground thing. We really didn't think it was commercial. We kinda put it out just to keep some of the pressure off us. We were thinking that the songs like The Circle and Day We Caught the Train would be the ones that would, perhaps, make it into the top forty. But Riverboat came out and went ballistic. And we went from playing to five hundred people to five thousand. Re-negotiations opened up to get more money and then everyone's buying new cars and a new house. Instead of being in the studio from eleven in the morning to eleven in the evening I would be turning up maybe around half past eleven, Steve would be turning up at twelve, Simon would roll in at about two and then Oscar at about four. Then at about eight someone would say that they had to go because they had theatre tickets, or are going to look at a new car, or have a new girlfriend coming over and it created a different situation to what had been there before.

Plus whereas when we were doing Moseley Shoals we had loads of songs to choose from, when it came to Marchin' Already there were moments when we sort of said 'yep, that will do' and that was that. I think we presumed that because everyone's loving what we were doing, everything that we were doing must be good. It's an easy thing for bands to slip into. But it's not always the case. That's why Marchin' Already is good but it's not as good as Moseley Shoals. Plus there were different pressures coming from the record company, who were saying things like 'we need the record three months earlier'. With Moseley Shoals we hadn't had any of that. Marchin' Already was written under those sort of pressures.

By the same token we couldn't have made a Moseley Shoals volume two. Yes, Marchin' Already has some great highlights in it but I can see where the four-way unity was slipping a bit. And I think that the song writing suffered a little bit too. The mind-set in the past, when we would work on an idea until it was finished, just wasn't always available because we would have to put it down and go and do something else over there - shows in Scandinavia or something. This meant that the spark we had been working on was harder to get back when we returned to the studio. I think the mark of really great artists is when they can keep that side going, along with the business side of things. The more successful a band gets, the more commitments come with it. I think, as a band, we balanced that really well for a while and we still produced a good record in Marchin' Already, but it's not the record it should have been.

I think there were times when Steve and I were, perhaps, a bit too intense for Simon and Oscar because we were really getting into our music and it seemed different for them. But this is just me looking back now. At the time it was just all great.

TOURS For us, going to Spain was always amazing. We went to Spain a lot because we had a really passionate guy at the record label called Jose. He did everything to help us break in. We would headline at festivals and play in town squares. We would play to two thousand people in towns we had never heard of.

Germany was also really good to us. We did Germany in the old school way. At the first tour we would play to 100 people, then the next it was 200 and then it just kept building and building. Japan was just great. Japan is great for any band. They get into every detail of every single thing that you're doing. We had a great time in America even though, at that time, we didn't fit in because they were all into grunge. In the early days we went on tour with the House of Love and Catherine Wheel. The second time we went wasn't quite the same and we only did a few weeks. The usual thing, East coast to West coast. But it didn't really work and, if you don't get on the David Letterman show, it's just never going to happen. Nowadays it's very different because of YouTube and Twitter. But we still had some great times and played some great shows. Some daft ones too, where we would play to fifteen people in St Louis then to three thousand in New York.

BRIT POP At the time we felt like we were a massive part of the Brit Pop thing. Of course the name was stupid. We were lumped into it because we were lumped into the Oasis camp. There was all this fake division between Oasis and Blur. Next it became Brit Rock because we weren't pop, so Weller, Oasis and us became Brit Rock and then you had Time Out doing the dad rock thing. It was supposed to have been an insult but it wasn't because I was thinking 'well my dad had the White album and that was one of the first records I had ever heard, so I'm quite happy with that'

DJING I loved djing. The thing is that it's always boring before a gig. It's mostly just sitting in a dressing room and not really being able to drink. So I started djing and would love playing hip hop to our audience, especially because they would expect it to be just pure northern soul. Djing also used to help me get up for the gig.

Before the band went on stage we had several tunes that would get played. Green Onions was one of them. In the earlier days we had a Buffalo Springfield song. We used it because we liked it but also because back then we used to start the sets with You Got it Bad, which starts in F and Green Onions was in F Minor. This meant that as we were tuning we could play over it, then Green Onions could be faded out and we could start.

JON WALSH

It was fuckin' brilliant. It was fantastic. One of the most brilliant experiences of my life. OCS were a passion of mine and I totally believed in them. It was about who they were and what they represented… as well as the fact that their music was great. We were all a part of this amazing scene. There was Paul (Weller), Oasis, Ocean Colour Scene and I spent three years with them. We were always interacting and going to gigs. It was brilliant and full of great moments. I remember my mum came to one of the gigs at Hammersmith. We did four nights. My mum worked with this woman whose daughters were massive OCS and Oasis fans and she had arranged for them to come to the gig with her. They were standing in the VIP bar area, which was packed, and Liam and Noel were there. Noel spots my mum and walks straight up to her in front of all these people and goes 'alright Pam how's it going?'. It blew everyone, and the two daughters, away. It was a classic moment.

Ocean Colour Scene went stratospheric in the year that they did Knebworth. I remember that Oasis had needed to cancel some gigs in Edinburgh and Newcastle and OCS ended up supporting them at Whitley Bay ice rink. The whole day was just mental. We had got in there early and it was cold. They had put wooden boards all over the ice. Oasis were sound checking and Steve was playing Champagne Supernova along with them. Well, with Noel because Liam was nowhere to be seen. There was a dressing room and it had a long shelf going around the outside. I wandered in there and Steve and Simon were in there and Liam was sitting on this shelf. At first he totally blanked me and then he says 'D'ya fuckin' like our band?' and I replied 'yeah, yeah of course' but Liam just kept saying 'D'ya fuckin' like our band. Look it's my fuckin' band and if I wanna split them up then I'll fuckin' split the band up'. I was just nodding, 'cos he was just proper on one. Anyway, I go back to the hotel with some people from MCA, then we went back to the venue and by now it's rammed. We headed to catering to see if we could get a beer and Liam was there and still proper on one. It was mental. I remember seeing Noel and his face was ashen. He had the look of a bloke who just needed ten minutes on his own. But Oasis went on stage and they just blew the roof off that place. They totally fuckin' smashed it. It's up there in my top three most incredible gigs I've ever seen. They were out of this world. I was sitting on the side of the stage with Simon and Oscar and someone threw a shoe at Liam, who caught it and he just turns and looks at us with a certain look. It was an incredible moment. The whole gig was. When they played I Am the Walrus was one of the weakest songs in the set. Then Noel strummed the first few chords of Wonderwall and the whole audience sang the rest of the song. It was part of the feel of what was going on at the time and OCS were part of it.

I started working in A&R in 1990. I worked for a guy called Dave Bates. At the time OCS were a huge buzz. They had signed a deal with a label called Phffft Records but some of the majors wanted to sign them. This was all around the time of the Stone Roses. But Phffft said if you want the band you have to sign a label deal too. So if a major wanted to buy the band they had to buy the label to get the band. Dave Bates got involved to do the deal. He was a bit of a loon but also a bit of mentor to me. Just ask anyone else who worked in that department… Gilles Peterson or Norman Jay. Anyway a deal was done and it was for around the £800,000 mark. But the band were caught in the middle of it all and they got screwed. It was a disaster for the band. At the time their careers were basically fucked and the name OCS became synonymous with 'how not to do it'. There had been a huge deal at stake and it had just gone nowhere. Fucked! They were written off by the industry. I think it was one of the reasons why, later on, some of the press hated OCS so much.

I went on to sign them in 1995. I told Steve that the reason I signed them was because 'you are' and not because 'you wanna be'. Steve Cradock did not just get out of bed one morning and say I want to be a musician… he is one. It was the same with Fox, Oscar and Damon. It's what they were meant to be and do. OCS were the real deal.

For five years after that original deal they went off and worked in a little studio that became Moseley Shoals and wrote songs. Chris (Cradock) was managing them. He had been declared bankrupt and was living in the garage but they were going to do it.

Through some contact I had I was given a cassette of OCS. On it was all the tracks that would turn up on Moseley Shoals. It had all been done whilst Steve was playing in Paul's (Weller) band and they had a plethora of material. They had tons of songs that they had been working on for five years. It was key to their success.

At the time they had also signed a small publishing deal with Island Records. They believed enough in them to give them a small publishing deal but not enough to sign the band and release their records.

I got involved because I just knew it was their time. It was right for them. I told my MD, Nick Phillips, about OCS and I got in touch with Chris (Cradock). Fair play to Nick because he sanctioned the deal. I wanted to give the band something like 130 grand.

I arranged to go to see the band at their studios. Then a scout I knew mentioned to me that Paul Weller was doing a secret gig at the Blue Note in Hoxton. A few minutes after that conversation Chris rung me and said 'are you coming down to Birmingham today?'. I said 'well yes I was but I've heard Steve is going to be in London with Paul'. Chris replied 'well if he is he'll have to be going some because he (Paul) is here doing some backing vocals with us.' Two hours later I was in their studio. All their equipment was set up. They had their sixteen track, a little piano on the right hand side as you went in and on the wall were the words Birds Can't Drive. The place really felt of their vibe. They pretty much lived in there. And yes Paul was there. But the moment I walked into that studio I just knew it was going to happen. This was going to be OCS's time. I just knew they were for real!

I remember that I was meant to be back in London the following day because I had a mortgage interview arranged but I ended up staying in some shitty B&B in Moseley, where Paul was also staying.

They played me song after song and I was thinking 'this could be a single and that could be a single'. It was happening. For some reason I said to Steve 'have you ever thought about changing your name?' and he replied 'Jon it's the only thing they never took away from us.' In that moment I got it and never questioned anything about the band again!

Once I got back to London I made Nick a cassette of three or four tracks but I didn't put the band's name on the tape. I told Nick to listen to it over the weekend and I didn't give him any other details. Come Monday morning Nick was all 'I wanna do this deal', so we did the deal and went to celebrate down the Crown and Sceptre pub.

I tell you what though, Steve Cradock can be a handful. I mean him and Paul must have come out of the same test-tube. They are two of the most intense guys I have ever met. I have huge respect for both of them but they can be loons too. I remember soon after doing the deal we went to Brighton and stayed at one of the hotels just along from the Brighton Centre. We came out of the hotel and got on the tour bus, which only had to drive forty yards to the venue. This was what it was like with them.

It was October '95 and I recall sitting in Steve's Mini outside the studio and told me that he wanted the album out before Christmas. I had to tell him that we couldn't put the album out before Christmas because it would die. So instead we did 500 seven inches of You Got It Bad, which are now probably some of the rarest OCS records. But none of the radio stations would play it except for Gary Crowley. We did have our own in-house pluggers, one of which was Sally Edwards, who worked for MCA and, of course, married Steve and became Sally Cradock. That was how Sally met Steve.

Back then everything was done in-house - the promo work, the press. This helped to make the whole thing even more special. It felt like everyone was a part of it. My office was on the top floor, so the great thing was I only had to go down one floor to see the press people. We knew it was getting successful when we started having meetings that went from four people in the room to everyone in the office. Everyone in the building had some stake in the band. It was special and everyone believed in it and everyone enjoyed it. The company policy was to go out and 'ave it' and 'smash it' and we did. We had earned it. We were turning over millions of records.

Around December time we decided that the Riverboat Song was going to be the first single and the album would follow. The company policy was sort of two singles and an album. At this time Chris Evans still hadn't gotten hold of the record but it did get some genuinely good reactions from radio.

It was all getting ready to 'go' and it got to a point where I said to the band "please don't play me any more records… they are all good and could all be singles". We did agree to put incredible B-sides on though, and that went on to inspire the B-sides, Seasides and Free Rides album. I Wanna Stay Alive and Huckleberry Grove are two of my favourite tracks.

It was all coming together nicely and I remember Oscar was like a kid and, because he was the drummer and spent a lot of time sitting around, we used to hang out. I used to send him on little missions. One time I told him that I had a special treat for him and told him to jump in the motor. I took him to see Aston Villa and got him VIP seats. He loved it and then, after the game, I took him to see the Motor Show.

But Oscar was an enigma. He wouldn't often get involved with things. He was above it all, like some kind of Zen figure… the man… very cool. One day he says "Jon I wanna have a word with you. I want you to listen to this track and I think you should put it on the album". It just wasn't the sort of thing he did and he never did it again. That song was Brilliant Mind.

By this time the word was really getting around and it was a real buzz. Then, just before Moseley Shoals came out, I said the aim is to get it into the top 75. That was the target and anything more than that was a result. Our marketing team thought it may make the top 25. It ended up going into the top 10.

Then Chris Evans and the whole Riverboat thing kicked in and so much started to happen in a very short space of time. I remember one particular night (I also got nicked for driving my car down a one way street because I was racing to get to the band at TFI) when the band did TFI Friday. Paul (Weller) was there and I butted into a conversation he was having. He just cut me down dead. I was so embarrassed. I saw him later on and he was back to being 'alright Walshy' and so on.

The night that Chris Evans got on board was the night that he came to see the band at the Electric Ballroom. Steve hated the support band and he held me to make me watch them. They were a band that I had nearly signed. That same night was the night that Liam and Noel joined OCS on stage. It was an amazing night. I think it was the first night that Liam and Noel played Wonderwall. The following day Chris Evans played live recordings from the gig of Wonderwall, Riverboat and Day Tripper on his breakfast show and he was raving about them. From that point on Chris Evans was on board. He was key to helping to break OCS.

After a few weeks I remember being told that Moseley Shoals was at number seven and it was a real moment for me. It was a big record then and it's still a big record. I then wanted to do four singles off the album but the band didn't want to. They wanted to stick with three. I flew up to Scotland specifically to have a conversation with them about the fourth single. I explained to them that there were six singles on the album and it was the right thing for them to do four. Eventually they put their trust in me and came back saying 'okay, you're right'.

I said the follow up to Riverboat should be The Day We Caught the Train but Steve phoned me and said he didn't want that song to be the next single. He said he wanted You Got It Bad to be the next single. I said, "What? You want to put out the track that we did six months ago that none of the radio stations would touch. You want to bounce the album off of that?". He said, "Yeah that's exactly what I want to do. It's the right move". So that's what we did. The single did well and the album was doing really well. It didn't go out of the top ten for over six months. It was selling forty thousand a week. Next came the arenas and the festivals and it was all kicking off. The Brit Pop thing was also happening but we never felt like we were a part of that.

GERARD SAINT

I was really good friends with Jon (Walsh) when he was with MCA. We worked on a project with a US artist. We also had a mutual friend who we worked with whose name was Sean Bye. Jon told us about this 'fuckin' amazing band' and he wanted us to go and listen to some tracks. He played us something like four tracks. The Riverboat Song was one of them. I really liked the songs and it wasn't the band that I had remembered from a few years earlier. I had just lumped them in with all those other northern bands at the time but the songs that Jon played us were razor sharp and they felt really different.

So it was Jon who introduced me to OCS and then I went to see them at the Blue Note Club. We went to check them out and it was really sweaty, it was in the summer and it was really hot. It was a fantastic night and anything that MCA did back in those days was pretty 'rock and roll'. OCS were a fantastic live band and what they were doing had a really good vibe about it.

It was after this that we started to think about how we saw the band looking on their record sleeves. We played around with a few ideas and were keeping it all very graphic, very clean and not totally mod influenced. But we did do the band OCS logo based on that kind of mod target thing. It was one of the first things we did and it just felt right and it worked.

Then we got involved with Tony (Briggs) for the photo shoots and everything started to happen really quickly. We didn't have a lot of time to prepare the project for the Riverboat Song. We did shoots that involved them just mucking around, playing cards and things like that. Plus Tony's dog, Steve, was also getting in the shots. Steve (the dog) is a legend in his own right.

I would say that Steve Cradock was the most involved with all of the art projects, more so than the others anyway. We would prepare things as much as we could and how we thought they should be, then we would run it by Steve and most of the time he was alright with it. There were times when he had things he wanted to throw into the mix. The take on the Byrds Fifth Dimension thing with the 'carpet' was Steve's idea. He was really into that band and so we thought it would be a nice homage to the Byrds. I always thought it was a good thing that the band got involved. I mean the story comes from the band.

What we did for Moseley Shoals we sort of made up on the hop. We knew we wanted to do a location shoot with the band and Tony suggested some park in Leamington Spa. I think Tony had seen this incredible bandstand but we didn't end up using it. Instead we found the building that appears on the album sleeve and we shot the band in front of it. Steve was always keen on certain details. His hand had to be in his pocket in a certain way.

What I do remember about that photo shoot was that their attention span was pretty much non-existent. All they wanted to do was make records. For them the photo shoots were just something that they had to do and were a bit of a pain in the arse. On the day of the shoot it was snowing and Tony and I had to rescue some kid who had fallen in the lake. Oscar was like 'have we finished yet 'coz I need to get some chips?' and then he just 'fucked off'. I think Tony had only shot one roll of film. From this point on we tried to develop things around the vibe of the band. Tony got really involved with the band and got to know them on a really personal level.

I remember the day we shot for the Day We Caught the Train. There was Steve's Lambretta and I recall the brakes weren't working very well and we had to stop it taking a tumble off the cliff. That scooter was Steve's pride and joy.

For that shoot we had to get up really early (and we had a late night) because we wanted to catch the sun coming up. We wanted to try and emulate that Who Quarophenia thing, as if someone had gone off the cliff and just left the bike. We also took loads of shots of the beaches around that area. Again, using one of the beach shots was meant to echo one of the beach shots from the Who's Quadrophenia album. That shoot was one of the times when the band weren't with us but working together with OCS there was always loads of little reference points.

The thing about OCS was that they were very tight. It was hard to infiltrate their world sometimes because of their 'gang' thing. They didn't let people in who they couldn't trust. And the people they did let in, they would place at different levels. Steve was always the more vocal and more opinionated. I don't know how much of that had to do with the fact that Chris was managing the band. I mean Steve was having to live with the band thing 24/7. The first time I met Chris he picked me up from the station and took me to the Custard Factory. When we arrived the band were there, Steve's mum was there and it felt like you were being invited into a world that was a tight world, to do with the band. They definitely had their own code.

Steve had a hell of a lot of respect. I mean for things to do with music there were always respectful points of reference. Sometimes it was hard to understand why these things meant so much to him. Steve was always incredibly focussed on the detail of things. Maybe he got some of this from working with Weller, whom he was working with at the time. There had been the old OCS band and then they had come back as this sharp band.

We didn't do the Marchin' Already album but we did the B-sides album with the tax disc. We didn't want another album that we would just stick a picture of the band on. We tried to do something that reflected the wider idea of the band with out-takes and stuff. My brother is an avid collector of vintage tax discs and he had some 60's ones that I used as a base for the design. On one of the promo's that went out it was designed so that you could actually remove the disc. It was a great package and sort of related to the idea of travel... seasides!

PAOLO HEWITT

I first met Steve when he was playing with Paul (Weller) around '93/'94. Paul had told me that he had this guitarist who was from a band he liked called Ocean Colour Scene. I went to a gig at one of the London Universities, I went backstage and Paul and Steve walked towards me, and the first thing that Steve said to me was, "Is there any chance of getting the Beat Concerto book out again 'coz I love that book". He was really direct and that was something I really liked about him.

Steve also has a great enthusiasm and that I really liked too. I remember thinking that what Steve was doing with Paul might take him away from his own band but Steve is one of these guys who was able to put 100% into both bands.

As a band they had that belief about them and were like a little gang. As a group they had something very attractive. Oscar was very cool. Steve had the enthusiasm. Then you had Damon who was this half Italian, half Everton supporter and really into it and, of course, Simon who added some of the spirit.

I always liked Chris. He had that belief. Chris and the band had set their ship on a course and that was it, they were determined to get there and Chris was a big part of that. I never knew of them when they did their first album. Steve would tell me about it and how they had got fucked over by an A&R guy and what have you.

The Brit Pop thing wasn't about then. I never thought of them as a Brit Pop band. I saw them and all those other bands at that time before that stupid name Brit Pop was thought up. To me they were just good bands. In a way I was glad for them. I mean I was pleased for them when they got successful. What I knew was that once the Brit Pop thing had gone all those bands would go down with it. It's how it works. Once a fashion is over everyone moves onto the next thing. It could have been very hard for OCS to escape that thing but it turned out alright for them and it wasn't a trap.

The thing I noticed about people like Steve and Liam (Gallagher) is that they had grown up in the 80's when pop music was crap. So, quite naturally, they had gone back and discovered The Who, Dylan, Kinks and all these great bands from the 60's. And then they harnessed onto the late 80's bands like the Stone Roses and Happy Mondays. The Stone Roses album for Steve was like his Blonde on Blonde or something. The Stone Roses spoke to Steve like it did for so many of his generation. I found it interesting that Steve and Liam had this kind of 60's meets modern day pop sensibilities. For me that's where I saw a lot of where OCS was coming from. They loved the Jam but they weren't that mad on the Style Council.

I would sit around with Steve talking about all those great bands from the 60's and then the Stone Roses. Buffalo Springfield too. He was big on them. I remember that Steve once played me a beautiful song by Fairport Convention; 'Meet me on the Ledge', it's a beautiful song. Simon was perhaps more folky and Steve more R&B. The thing about OCS was that they were into songs and when the Brit Pop thing came along people were looking for Beatles references or Stones or Who, and OCS had all that. The Small Faces were a big thing for OCS too.

My first music is soul music. That's my kinda thing and Steve and the other band members were into it as well. There was a different version of Different Drum that they did with PP Arnold that I don't think ever came out. The band's studio, Moseley Shoals, was a whole play on the Muscle Shoals thing. Steve was always making me up great tapes.

Ocean Colour Scene didn't have a scene like Oasis. OCS's scene was internal and Oasis's scene was external. OCS was as much a gang as Oasis but Oasis made their gang more known than OCS's. To get to where Oasis got to they had to be so focussed and had to do certain things. But OCS were looser. They had their own studio and they just wanted to make music. And Oasis wanted to be known all over the world. OCS are still going now and they've maintained that ethos throughout. I'm sure they are happy what they are doing, whether it means playing in a stadium or to only a few hundred people. And that is to be really applauded. The other thing about OCS is that they are a force for good. Everything about them is good. What they're trying to achieve is good. Everything they're about is good. John Lennon once said that to get to the very top you've got to be a bastard and the Beatles were the biggest bastards. It's not nice but it's what you have to do. But I don't think it's in OCS's temperament to do that.

I was asked to do a northern soul show on Radio London and I invited Steve onto the show. Steve arrived and he was barefoot and completely 'up', shall we say. He played two northern soul songs and then he got out the Verve album Northern Soul. He is a lovely guy. There's no side to him, he is always up and full of enthusiasm. He is great to be around.

BRENDAN LYNCH

I started to work with the band during the making of Moseley Shoals. But I had first met them around 1990 when they were doing their first album. Jimmy Miller produced that album. They came to Paul Weller's studio, Solid Bond, in Marble Arch at a time when I was an engineer there. I think up until this point they had been working with other producers, including Tim Palmer. There was already that Paul (Weller) connection back then. Solid Bond was also a high-spec studio at the time and the fact that it was owned by Paul was an added incentive.

When I started working with the band for Moseley Shoals I had just finished working on Stanley Road. Before this Steve had already worked with Paul on the Wildwood album and I think he had started to play live with Paul too. I remember Paul saying to me "What do you think about Steve" and I said "I think he'll be great". Plus Steve was improving all the time.

Steve is an all-round musician; he really can play anything from drums to piano and a whole host of string instruments. There was one time in the studio when Steve got behind the drums and I'm not joking, he sounded like Keith Moon. His energy was just incredible. Steve could easily have been a drummer. He was a natural for it.

Simon is a great acoustic player and is great at harmonising too. Simon had sung the backing vocal in the middle-eight on Hung Up for Paul before we began working on Moseley Shoals. Oscar also has great feel for the songs. I think the best drummers play the songs when they listen to the singer and I think that's what

Oscar does. And then there was Damon who would be sitting at the back of the room working out chord charts and stuff.

In the studio it was a very collaborative working relationship. For certain songs Simon would come in and he would have them pretty much finished lyrically. Simon would write most, if not all the lyrics. Some of the more folk ones would have mostly been written too but then there were others that were pretty much written in the studio. Hundred Mile High City started off as just a riff and we carried on working on it in the studio. We didn't hear the vocal until the record was almost finished. Simon use to take the backing tape home every night and work on it at home. Then he let us hear what he had done but not until right at the end. It was exciting to work like this. I think the Riverboat Song started off in a similar way. It was a real band collaboration where they all added their own input.

I would drive up to their studios (Moseley Shoals) on a Monday and come back to London on the Friday. As a band they were very relaxed in their way of working in the studio. They were also a very close-knit group. At the time of making Moseley Shoals they were also totally broke. Every day we would sit around chatting, play cards and then, at some stage, do some work. They were also really good friends and they had a community around them. They had lots of acquaintances who were into the same things. It was a nice little culture they had going on up there.

The other good thing was that they were still doing lots of gigs. This meant that they were always pretty sharp. And they were always coming back energised. During the making of Moseley Shoals we didn't have any interference from any record company or anyone else, which was really good and made everything very positive. Everyone just felt really excited that the record was being made. There was stuff around, like thoughts of 'is it going to do well' (except for Chris who always believed it was going to do well).

At the time of making Moseley Shoals there was already that heading towards that 'natural sound'. Paul's Wildwood was like that. When you went back to the early 90's for most indie music the drums had a horrible sound, with a clicky bass drum and big, fat, distorted snare and there was loads of reverb all over the shop. But our idea for Wildwood and Moseley Shoals was to try and record the drums naturally, without any effects and not have loads of reverb, EQ and compression. We just placed the drum microphones in the right points around the kit.

All the recording was done as analogue and all the mixing was done without a computer. It was a sort of step down from the type of studios that I had been working in for the past ten years, in Solid Bond or in CBS or at the Manor, recording albums like Wildwood and Stanley Road. On the mix we would just record four bars (which may be eight seconds) and just carry on doing the mix in these sections. Doing it this way meant it took a long time but it added to the sound of the album. We were also using a sixteen track desk that the band had been given from Andy at Go! Discs. It was actually refreshing, having those types of limitations.

Steve would lay down a lot of guitar parts. We would just keep the parts that worked for the song. There would often be a lot of intricate parts on the songs and Steve did really well. Then when he played the songs live he would have to switch between the various parts he had recorded in the studio. Nowadays there is another guitar player with them on stage but back then it was just Steve. Steve always had great ideas and was such a happy character. He had real enthusiasm for what the band was doing.
I also did the Marchin' Already and One From the Modern albums. For Marchin' Already we had a different desk and tape machine to use. The tape machine was an old Ampex from the States. It was a big monster that kept on breaking and we lost loads of time trying to get it to work. When we did One From the Modern I brought in one of my own desks.

The process for recording the other albums was very different. Like I say, Moseley Shoals was very close-knit and everybody was there every day. But Marchin' Already wasn't like that. They weren't around all the time and were off being busy doing other things. In some ways I think it was a shame but it was probably inevitable. There was also more expectation and, probably, a bit more pressure too. Although they still seemed relaxed I think they must have felt some pressure. Maybe not Steve. I don't think he cared that much, he just wanted to make music.

We still needed to get some singles off the album and I think Hundred Mile High City was a good choice. There was something different about that song. It was a bit edgier than their other songs at the time. You could also hear other influences in there.

By the time of One From the Modern they had all improved so much. I think by this time Damon had started playing with Paul as well. Damon worked really hard to get into Paul's band and learn the songs. I remember he used to stay in my place in London and he would rehearse hour after hour.

I also did the Fire and Skill session that was done with Liam (Gallagher). I produced the song. Liam did his vocal part in Primal Scream's studio in London. We just got him in there for a day to do his vocals. Simon Halfon was like the executive producer for the whole thing. I think Noel joined them for a show that was filmed but he didn't play on the record. Once the song was recorded we mixed it back up in Birmingham.

RUTH WALKER (MINCHELLA)

I was only a teenager so it was okay to have posters on my wall of all the Brit Pop bands; Oasis, Blur and, of course, Ocean Colour Scene. Damon loves this story! I never got to meet the band back then. I fancied Damon but had to admire him from afar! It was only years later that I met Damon and this came about because our kids had been at the same school together, plus we knew people in the same group of friends, went to the same parties but, at that time, we never socialised together. Then I had an IPod and somehow managed to wipe all my tunes off of it. I put a post up on Facebook asking my friends 'how do I get my tunes back' and Damon replied, saying he had an IPod I could have. So we met up in the pub and that was that, it went from there and we then went on to get married.

Moseley Shoals was the big album for me. It just came at the right time. The whole feel of the Brit Pop scene was happening. The Brit Pop vibe was just great. I was at that teenage age when you're just really discovering yourself. I had always loved live music too. I grew up going to festivals because my mum used to take me to Reading.

I was from Redditch and a friend of mine (Sarah) was absolutely obsessed with OCS, we got into OCS together. We went to see the band loads of times around different venues in Birmingham City centre and some just before Moseley Shoals was released. I bought Moseley Shoals on tape when it came out. There was just something so happy about their songs. I spent loads of times with my mates just sitting around drinking cheap beer and listening to that album. It was a happy vibe that OCS had about them. OCS didn't have the 'dirtiness' that Oasis had. That appealed more to the lads really. One of my favourite gigs ever was the gig down at the Electric Ballroom. The Gallaghers got on stage and it was just wow - here are two of my favourite bands together under one roof. It was outstanding and absolutely brilliant. That gig was all about the timing for Brit Pop, the age that I was, the point I was at in my life having just left school and going to college. It was a time when people seemed completely free and enjoying every single moment of life.

TRICIA HICKLING

The release of The Riverboat Song was an exciting and fun part of my life back in 1996. My friends and I always referred to the song as an 'anthem' during the Britpop days and the new Indie scene that we were all very fondly a part of. The Riverboat also brought with it annoying, yet hilarious factors, such as my friend (in many voices and sound effects - some not even vocal!) constantly 'ding, ding, de, de, ding, ding', encouraged further by it being played loudly and representing TFI Friday at the time.

The power behind such a popular tune only pushed us along further when it was announced that Ocean Colour Scene were to play at our home town of Nottingham. The venue was Rock City on Tuesday October 8th 1996; ticket price just £10.00. Myself (the cat) amongst five blokes (the pigeons) made sure we got our tickets in advance, so as to not miss this 'big gig'.

The night arrived with much merriment, plus the usual alcohol making its mark, and so we entered Rock City to a jam-packed, sell-out audience. This mostly consisted of folks and friends that visited The Zone (Brit Pop night) every Saturday in Nottingham. It was a case of 'alright', 'how you doing?', 'eh-up duck' from one person to the next; it was a very exciting atmosphere. The crowd had already begun singing OCS songs (or in some cases, purely shouting out) warming up in anticipation of the band emerging on stage and a tension that stayed throughout the whole performance of the band.

The Riverboat Song, You've got It Bad and The Day We Caught The Train were crowd pleasers but the delivery of each song meant something to the individuals in the audience. There was, it seemed, even a sense of 'union' about the place. OCS played the track Robin Hood and, of course, dedicated it to us Nottingham folk; the crowd went crazy at this, whereas I, on the other hand, disliked the stereotypical link here, although I did enjoy the audience's enthusiasm. I most certainly appreciated seeing Simon in the flesh for the first time - he reminded me of Manfred Mann's Paul Jones!

The best part of the night was yet to follow. The venue adjacent and downstairs to Rock City is known as The Rig; this is where we carried out the rest of our evening as it was a Brit Pop night every Tuesday, which always clashed with decent bands back then. As we waited at the bar to be served, there was suddenly some shuffling of people in the dark behind the bar staff, which seemed very suspicious. Then to our surprise, we realised that it was the backstage exit door from the gig upstairs that led into the basement right behind the bar for a bands quick getaway, or so they'd hoped anyway! I'm not the sort of person to lynch mob band members and most definitely not stalk them, but I do get a little excited. We shouted to them and one-by-one, they appeared out of the shadows; Damon wearing sunglasses, Oscar in a different hat and then Simon, of whom I shouted out to and... I actually touched his hand! No Steve though? Someone had said, 'Cradock's already on his way back to Weller', but I think this was a joke. The second best part of the night was when my boyfriend stormed off and slipped on a hamburger that was on the floor in the club for some reason?! He went flying over, wiped the tomato sauce off his shirt and then humbly and quietly left the venue. The cat and the remaining pigeons danced the rest of the night away in very high spirits. The events between mid-1995 and the year 2000 were some of the best, mainly due to excellent bands that exploded on to the Brit Pop and new Indie scene. Vinyl records were back in vogue, band memorabilia, tee shirts, fan mail and fan clubs, included constant newsletters and updates, cool trainers and footwear were reborn. It was a time when you could dress 60's and 70's at the same time, without anyone daring to snigger! The OCS gig will always be a fond memory of a truly exceptional live gig, which demonstrated the enthusiasm and experience of new musicians at the time. OCS shone like a 'Big Star' that night – pardon the pun!

MICHAEL PATRICK HICKS

Ocean Colour Scene were a band I first discovered through listening to and not reading about. The music press didn't seem to have any time for them. When Moseley Shoals appeared, they were old news and the NME and Melody Maker were all about promoting the new. It seems that if these two weeklies didn't discover a band they could be somewhat hostile to them. The journalists, who would probably favour Ocean Colour Scene's music, had long moved on. The new batch of writers thought they wouldn't appeal to their readership. Their young readership! They were wrong. This type of music, songs written in the classic sense, will always sound fresh to new ears.

I was nearing the end of my school years when Moseley Shoals broke big. The album was omnipresent in the four-disc changer of my Aiwa Hi-Fi. It shared sonic space with Weller's Stanley Road and Oasis' What's The Story Morning Glory. There were a few of us who were into that type of music. As each new single from the album got airplay, our little gang got bigger. Hair got a little longer. Once slicked back – now combed forward. The back and sides were cut instead of graded. We'd have conversations about our favourite songs on the album.

They were probably the first band I was

aware of that had that heavy Mod influence. From the clothes they wore, down to the sleeve artwork. They carried that entire heritage. OK, they were not reinventing the wheel in the way Radiohead were doing, but they had great songs. Songs, which were always playing on the jukebox of the pubs, I was too young to be in. The Circle always sounded great at full volume. So did Policeman And Pirates, The Day We Caught The Train, etc. You kind of knew who was going to tap in the digits to Moseley Shoals by the way they dressed.

They were a band that, if you liked football, you wouldn't feel embarrassed in liking. Probably the same as liking The Faces in the '70s. If you admitted to liking Radiohead or Suede, some of the older lads would call you a big softie, but not in such a polite way. They were a gateway. Through OCS, a new batch of music enthusiasts backtracked and bought compilations by The Small Faces, Ronnie Lane, Free and Traffic, etc. I was one of them.

The Day We Caught The Train was also a great avenue into guitar playing. You didn't need to be a virtuoso. I flicked through the Moseley Shoals songbook, in MVC, Cardiff, to steal the chords. E minor, D major, G major. The song's opening three chords. The first three chords many guitarists end up learning. The rest of the chords didn't venture outside the fifth fret to cause a sweat-on for a novice. The Riverboat Song riff became a staple in every guitar shop you visited around that time. That, Manic Street Preachers' A Design For Life and Oasis' Wonderwall. Music was now playing an important part in my life. It had moved from the foreground. Even more than sound tracking my every move – it was shaping it.

My Adidas tracksuit top I wore to school, played host to three badges. One was an Oasis button style, another was the cherub from The Stone Roses' Second Coming and third was an OCS one. I caught them on the Marchin' Already tour in the late '90s and recently saw them on the Moseley Shoals anniversary tour at Cardiff University. The songs still sound great.

Today listening to this period of their music brings back so many memories. Singing along to them blasting from the car stereo of a friend who had just passed his driving test. Walking to school with Moseley Shoals and Marchin' Already on my Walkman and sitting in the bedroom of my parents' house learning Steve Cradock's licks and riffs. Remembrance of things past. Much in the same way as older lads, into music, introduce younger ones to bands and records, I recently told a friend, ten years my junior, to buy Moseley Shoals while visiting HMV. He bought it – and loved it. The baton was passed. It will continue to be passed.

STEVE TIERNAN - 1996

Still at school, still listing to what once someone described as a bag full of spanners falling down the stairs and it was a two week work experience in a garage. For the hard work being recognised I was given a £5 gift voucher (a lot back then). "Right" I have to spend this on the way home and what am I going to buy, "I know" something to remind me of a great two weeks. What was that song playing out for the whole two weeks that goes 'oh oh la la' I sang in Our Price. My answer from the check-out person 'new Birmingham band called Ocean Colour Scene'. That was me hooked on a new music and a new inspiration, and the want to be just like the lead singer, Simon Fowler, after seeing the video to the Day We Caught the Train. I thought 'what an image this band had' and then I got introduced to the Moseley Shoals album and the rest just follows, as all OCS fans understand.

From here on I became somewhat of a Mod and life flowed down a new avenue; learning the guitar, growing up and leaving school with a massive inspiration for music. A certain close childhood friend died at such a young age and on his headstone has the lyrics of 'Half the Dream Away' and this for me opened up a deep meaning to what Simon was doing to people, even when they passed, with an effect on how people felt to the very strong lyrics he was writing, for what Cradock once said a writer for both men and women.

Anyway from here I ended up in Exeter after meeting a piano player who I stayed with for a while, who heard this story and said to me 'one day you will meet Simon and explain this to him yourself' and I laughed it off. Around two months later I moved back to Birmingham and started a new job, in which I turned up early one day and did not fancy the premature chat so I popped down to music exchange guitar shop and saw a lad playing 'Up On The Down Side'. I went over and said "How the fuck you learn you learn that riff, it's only been out two days"? He replied, putting his head up "Just a mate of Cradock's'" and put his head back down, carrying on playing that catchy riff.

Years went by; jobs, relationships, songs written, life moving, Uni (a grey hair or two) and after my first real heartbreak relationship a friend of mine suggested 'Plenty of Fish'. "Ha" I laughed, "No way, I'm not that desperate mate". "OK" he said, "Why not try finding someone who shares your interests?" I took this friend up on this great idea and started at the OCS fan page on facebook, a social meltdown as I thought back then, but thought 'fuck it, I've got nothing to lose' and began a search.

I found my favourite pic of a Scottish lass called Michele (yes only one 'L',I hear her dad was drunk at the register office) and hit the request button to await a reply, which until now, when she reads this, she doesn't know I did not believe she ever would. Michele did reply and we started chatting for a while and this request turned into a long distance friendship, rather than a quick flutter or flirt, and we continued like this for around six months. She heard all my bad points too; the chat was always focused on OCS and our love for them, and Michele was also a massive Simon Fowler.

Anyway, I had my invite to Scotland to meet Michele and she brought me tickets to T in the Park, so I travelled up to Glasgow. En-route I spent a night (between Plymouth and Birmingham) with Liam to break up the journey (and to catch up) and continued onto Scotland the next day, getting very drunk on a bus with a bunch of Irish women and falling off the coach in Glasgow, to meet Michele for the first time. The door opened and there was a perfect, small, marriage material, Scottish bird I found as a sister and friend over those months, so I had a problem right there.

I went with my feelings and thoughts (think on your feet while you can and why you're still standing) and made a move that night and, believe it or not, got knocked back as Michele explained she did not want to ruin a great friendship if it ended in tears and my track record, which she knew, did not help I suppose.

The next day was T in the Park and OCS were playing King Tuts and I broke through a gate in the side and hid with Michele in the back of a BBC truck until OCS pulled up to go on stage. We waited there for about an hour (and held in the toilet moments you get) and then the lads pulled up, we jumped out and were tackled by the security but Simon shouted 'No they are with us' and allowed Michele and I on the stage to view the packed out King Tuts crowd from front on.

The night before this I played guitar to Michele, Get Blown Away, and that very next day, on that very stage, we sang it together to a huge, wonderful crowd in Scotland, with the band too and this was enough for Michele to accept my genuine offer of a kiss and we took off to go out with our back stage passes, enjoyed the free beer with the likes of Beyonce and Chris Martin (and many more music peeps) and went on to enjoy our first date together.

One month later Michele came to Plymouth for a second date; Mcdonald's on the Plymouth Hoe on my student loan. A year later and a few more pints with Simon and OCS, I now live in Scotland and I am happy to say that when the weather shines just for one day we will tie the knot and guess what folks, one night in Oran Mor when Simon played the 3rd Merrymouth gig, he agreed to play at our wedding if we covered the beers.

This story is real and only exists on the fuel of OCS, and my life would not have ended up in this way if OCS were never introduced, and the story of the grave stone lyrics, even to this day, are untold to Simon so this will be a first if or when he reads this.

JAMES TANNER

My favourite OCS memory was after the night they played the newly re-opened Birmingham Academy. Oscar came to the side door to say hello, wearing a pair of slippers! He got loads of stick from the fans, to which he retorted with a completely straight face "Hey these are good slippers man... they're from Asda". Oscar you are so cool you can make anything look cool mate!

PETER JACHIMIAK

I like to think that, on the evening of Monday 9th October 1995, I was one of the select few who witnessed a 'born again' Ocean Colour Scene stepping back out onto the stage – at once nervously and with total conviction. Indeed, when I saw them that evening they were very much a band in transition. Long behind them were the wishy-washy Fontana years, when they were (no fault of their own) adrift in a sea that was 'Sway' and so on. Now, having signed to MCA, in front of them was the meaty, beaty, confident bounce of Moseley Shoals.

Thus, that evening, with the release of The Riverboat Song just a few months away, myself and a girl from the Cardiff out-of-town hotel that we both worked in, were at a (then) popular live music venue close to the University, Gassy Jacks, attending one of OCS's week of 'comeback' gigs. As we walked along the dark, barely populated streets that led to the venue, we could hear clearly the signature guitar intro to Riverboat. Then, upon entering – with the place still virtually empty – there was Steve Cradock on stage, with the rest of the band nowhere to be seen, riffing and strutting away. With a stare that attempted to fixate the collective eyes of the ever-growing crowd, he seemed to endlessly play that intro to all who entered thereafter.

Slowly but surely, as Gassy's began to fill up, Cradock was now off stage, as he had joined the rest of the band in their tour van outside (to skin up?). An hour or so later, and the place was full to its rafters. Then, to the '...Riverboat...' riff once again, the band crammed themselves upon the pub's tiny corner stage and they were off. No old tunes. No looking over their shoulders. They were now, at full volume, just playing what would be, come April next year, their new album, Moseley Shoals. Yet rather strangely, their set-list sounded – at the same time – both contemporary and classic. Retro, yet modern. There was even a hint of melody and lyric in there, when sung by Simon Fowler, that reminded me of Ralf McTell's 'Streets Of London'. Jesus, it was like the Stones, The Who and Free all on stage together jamming having listened to, beforehand, a select few folk LPs over a few spliffs. Tight yet loose. Uptight Mods, yet chilled-out Rockers.

Sweat. Lots of it. Lager. Again, lots of it. Moreover, great tunes that would, eventually, transcend time. And then, after the exhilaration, it was all over. Simon Fowler, exhausted (yet as fleeting as a fox), went straight out of the door, to the respite of 'the van'. He'd probably already had enough of the adulations and falsities of fame. Cradock, beaming like a Mod Cheshire Cat, came bounding out into the crowd; Handshakes and beers all round. Damon Minchella and Oscar Harrison, like twins, stood cool by the stage, proud of what they had played, what they had achieved. Passing, and in communion, I shook their hands. We briefly chatted about the band's contribution to a just-recorded tribute LP to The Small Faces (their cover of 'Song Of A Baker' where they'd, upon recording, set the studio fire alarms off). Then I went on my way, bursting, to the basement toilets below.

Simon Fowler was seen again, just a few weeks later in November, by the faithful Cardiff crowd, as support on Paul Weller's Stanley Road. Armed with a harmonica, he belted out solo acoustic versions of OCS's songs that were then still oh-so-young. A few months later still, February 1996, and I bought my very own copy of 'The Riverboat Song' from HMV, Cardiff. The cover, with the guys in vintage Levi's jackets, corduroy trousers, Bass Weejun loafers, military badges, said it all; Mod R'n'B for the 90s. Thereafter, Top of the Pops, TFI Friday, Lock Stock..., and classic album after classic album. But, during the fag-end of 1995, things had been different, as this is what Damon Minchella had to say about that time in Johnny Morgan's Belief Is All (1997): "We couldn't get a gig outside of a shithole three months ago. We stuck at it 'cos we love it. And we've still got things to prove". So, back in October 1995, OCS still found themselves playing those 'shitholes' but, just a few months later, they were about to break out in all of their Modernist glory. And I, and a few select others, saw them 'in transition', on that dark autumnal Monday evening back in 1995.

NIC DUNNAWAY

We were at the Shepherds Bush Empire ('96) to see Paul Weller and as we entered the venue the support act, Simon Fowler from Ocean Colour Scene, walked on stage with his guitar. He sat on a stool and started to play 'Wonderwall' by Oasis. I have never seen a room react in the way it did, everyone and I mean everyone, stopped what they were doing and turned towards the stage. Now the song is a good song, everyone knows that, and Liam sings it well but Simon owned the song that night. In all the gigs I've ever been to never has a room gone completely silent when someone is on stage. It did that night and it's a moment in my life that I'll never forget.

DALE HANSON

In the spring of 1996 I bought a ticket to see 'The Scene' for the first time, at the Irish Centre in both mine and the band's hometown, Brum. The last time I'd been to the Irish Centre was for my football team's trophy presentation in 1989 when I was 10, this time round I was approaching my 17th birthday and it was a whole lot different. I remember getting off the bus, taking the short walk to the Irish Centre and seeing all these people queuing round the venue to get in, and as we joined the queue we saw Simon and Oscar walk past us.

As a sixteen year old going to only my second gig it was all just so exciting, Moseley Shoals had been out barely a month and something exhilarating was happening to British guitar music. The Riverboat Song was THE music to the best programme on TV, TFI Friday, the charts was full of good music again and Euro 96 was on the way. The gig was amazing and I remember being totally blown away by Get Away, a song that would remain the band's set closer for years to come.

Me and my mate left the Irish Centre knowing we'd seen something special, and all created by four Brummie lads to boot. Things would take off for 'The Scene' and the next time I would see them would be supporting Oasis at Knebworth in the August of 1996, was all this really happening?

The summer of '96 was a magical time and dressing like Steve Cradock was unavoidable for me. But my next date with 'The Scene' under their own steam would be in much grander surroundings, at The Royal Albert Hall in London in February 1997.

Not even 18 yet, me and a couple of mates went down to the big smoke for the weekend and took in the best mod band in the country, playing their most prestigious gig to date. Weller was there supporting, and Noel Gallagher, the Modfather himself and The Real People joined them for a couple of tunes at the end. It was all too good to be true, real music was taking over and it felt like we were part of something. We all bought a 'Scene' fishing hat and left the Albert Hall wondering where to next, Dadrock was leading the way. As we flagged a black cab to take us back to our digs for the weekend, the driver asked 'Where have you lot been? A fishing convention, we replied, nah just been to see the best band in the country play with their mates.

JOHN ROLLS

- My friend and I were waiting to see OCS at the Waterfront in Norwich 5th May 1996. We were well early, doors were not due to open for another hour or so, we were just desperate to get to the front. The lads from the band came out of the stage door, all with motorised scooters and just started larking about in the car park with us. Steve Cradock then asked me for directions down to the river, I told him and before he walked off, he thanked me and shook my hand. I said to my mate ... "he's class, he'll be up there with Weller, Lane et al, in my book". I was proven right of course!

MAX HAYES

I had done all of OCS's engineering and mixing with Brendan (Lynch). I had already been working with Brendan on the Weller stuff. But Brendan had worked with OCS back in their early days when they were with Fontana. Then Andy McDonald from Go! Discs got interested in signing OCS but for some reason in the end he didn't. Instead he gave them a sixteen track desk that we later used to make Moseley Shoals with.

There was a couple of years where OCS were just bumming about, they rehearsed and rehearsed and put down a load of demos. They were doing those demos whilst Weller also got them involved on doing backing vocals and playing on his own stuff, which at the time was Wildwood. We were recording down at the Manor. Steve and Simon came down first, the two of them would be coming down all the time, they were as thick as thieves. I remember there was one track that was really hard to record. Steve played some guitar and Simon ended up singing some really high vocals on it. It was after this that they both started to become more and more involved with Weller. Damon got involved a bit later and then, of course, joined Wellers live band.

Brendan had known OCS back when they were doing the stuff with Fontana. OCS had gone to Weller's studio to record those songs and it was then that they met Brendan. It was this connection that led to Weller hearing OCS's stuff.

Eventually it got to a point where we had to go up to the band's studios in Birmingham to work on these demos. So we went up and did the overdubs, editing and mixing. Then those demos ended up as masters and it went from there, labels started to hear them and they got signed.

When I first started working with OCS the thing I recall is thinking that their music was too clever. Their songs had lots of different time signatures and wired bits but they worked. At the time I remember thinking those songs would sell a few thousand copies but once they started to get exposure on TFI Friday and radio they went on to sell over a million. But they were shit hot because they had worked hard. They had all been on the dole together and during that time they had worked on being a band.

The band's musicianship was outstanding. That period when we were doing Moseley Shoals they worked solidly. When they weren't in the studio they were off doing something else, gigs, radio and television. They did something like a year and a half without a day off. It was mental for all of us at the time. I mean we were doing the Moseley Shoals album plus all the Weller stuff and Primal Scream too. It was crazy because me and Brendan were working with all these people and they were friends too.

What I really liked about recording OCS was that they were a really easy to record. I would set the mikes up and they would always sound good. There just wasn't one shit recording session. But whereas when we were doing the Weller stuff, we would set up the mikes and sometimes it just wouldn't happen and you wouldn't know what it was, there was something about OCS songs that meant that they always just sounded good. We put a lot of work into Moseley Shoals. We worked on it on and off for about seven months. It was all done on the sixteen track with tape edits, all mixed by hand and no computers (and all that crap). The stars lined up for Moseley Shoals. Not all bands get that but that record did, it just suddenly connected with the people.

We worked for hours in the studio and we all became friends and after the sessions, we would all go out together. It doesn't go that way with all bands. I even ended up living in Birmingham because of it all. It was quite magical. There were no egos. Everyone was just really excited. I remember everyone feeling really excited during those recording sessions of Moseley Shoals and every day something really magical would happen.

The band were at a stage where they were doing the music just because they enjoyed it and making music for the right reasons. There was an energy in that record and it had its own kind of emotion. When you put Moseley Shoals on you believe it.

I went on to do four more albums with OCS, Marchin' Already, One From the Modern, Mechanical Wonder and North Atlantic Drift. North Atlantic Drift was the last album that Damon did. Brendan's (Lynch) last album was One From the Modern. Things had been changing since Moseley Shoals. I found some things a bit weird not working with Brendan and Damon because we had all been working together. The thing was Damon wasn't just a bass player. I saw how Moseley Shoals was made and Damon had a very big input on the record. He had loads of ideas for the tracks.

As with most bands, things change. By the time we were doing Marchin' Already it was already harder to get everybody in the same room at the same time.

Chris (Cradock) was key to it all. He put his bollocks on the line for them and he believed in them. Chris was just convinced that his son had it and it was really nice to see. At the start Chris put up his house to get up the money to help the band get started. That's how we got paid. He was a bit like John Weller (but without the upfrontness). He had seen how John had operated and Chris had that same sort of enthusiasm, which is what a band wants from their manager.

The B-sides album they did was brilliant. That is what Foxy (Simon) does best. He does that sort of jangly, acoustic stuff so well. They should have made that album a full on release. If they had they would have sold three times more.

MARK HOUGH

My association with the band started way back in '96 when I met Steve at one of the many Mod nights going on in Birmingham at that time. There was a group of us that hung out at Gran Sport scooters, including Steve's then girlfriend Helen and Danny, the band's tour DJ at the time (who I first met when he was 14!). It started with me giving lifts to gigs to some of the people within this group, gradually I got to know the rest of the band, road crew and ended up attending most of the Moseley Shoals tour and Marchin' Already in its entirety, staying in some very strange places along the way!

These gigs were amazing and, to my mind, they were the best band around at the time; loud, full of energy and basically brilliant live. One gig that stands out is Glasgow Barrowlands (3 nights). That place is awesome, the building shook and to top it off Steve wore a shirt I gave him the previous night in York and what an after show night that was!

Weller also had a habit of turning up to a number of gigs around this time and even did a four song support set as a warm up for his Heavy Soul tour in Birmingham.

Moseley Shoals is an amazing album but Marchin' Already is a particular favourite for me as I witnessed the recording of most of it. People will never understand just how much goes in to making a record and just how long it actually takes. There were some great nights in the old studio with Brendan Lynch, Max Hayes and the band, plus various other well-known musicians dropping in from time to time for a chat or to put a piece down.

By now Steve had a property just down the road so we used to pop round a few times a week, always a pile of vinyl in the corner of the lounge and he used to say help yourself, which we usually did! One night in that house stands out, we arrived to find PP Arnold there, Steve took to the piano and she sang Shoot the Dove. I have never heard anything like that again and probably never will.

I still attend gigs to this day as OCS still continue to produce great music, although with a slightly different line up and are still one of the best live bands around. From Glasgow to Cardiff and Dublin inbetween, there are not too many cities/towns that I haven't seen them play. Although you can catch a gig at some point throughout the year, the intensity has died off a little, in the main due to Steve's commitment with Weller and his own growing solo career, Foxy and Ocky can regularly be seen gigging here and there, as well as more recent member Andy, who seems to be keeping busy also. Thanks for the memories lads.

1997
MARCHIN' ALREADY

1. Hundred Mile High City
2. Better Day
3. Travellers Tune
4. Big Star
5. Debris Road
6. Besides Yourself
7. Get Blown Away
8. Tele He's Not Talking
9. Foxy's Folk Faced
10. All Up
11. Spark and Cindy
12. Half a Dream Away
13. It's a Beautiful Thing.

Even though there was a sense of 'levelling off' for the sussed, Oasis remained a popular band. Their album Be Here Now was received with mixed blessings. By the time of the release the Spice Girls were massive. The Prodigy attracted conflicting media attention with their Smack My Bitch Up but the headlines were stolen by the death of Diana, Princess of Wales. Elton John performed his old classic Candle in the Wind and then his record company reissued it. It sold over four million copies. The best film and soundtrack of the year, without a doubt, belonged to Trainspotting.

1997 did, however, give us two other brilliant albums alongside Be Here Now (that included D'you Know What I Mean); Urban Hymns by the Verve (that included the inspiring The Drugs Don't Work) and Marchin' Already by Ocean Colour Scene, but this year also took away Ronnie Lane, who died aged 51 on 4th June.

Side A of Marchin' Already opens with the frantic and energetic Hundred Mile High City. There are instant echoes of the Riverboat Song with its unusual time signature. Paul Weller doesn't make an appearance on this album but if he did he would have been quite at home with his Rickenbacker on this song. What is highlighted is that Cradock's years of performing and recording with Weller are now quite set in. In fact the whole band are on a roll and the listener is going to need much more than a car to keep up. Welcome to Marchin' Already and flash-fast-forward to track two.

Better Day is eased in with a gentle piano intro. Fowler is soon to join in before he invites the rest of the band. This is going to become an OCS anthem; something to sing-along with in the car or in the crowd. The world may be falling down outside the band but inside the circle they are going from strength to strength. The middle-eight on Better Day is the first hint that the band's Kinksy influences are not far away.

Next up and sign off side A comes Harrison's rising drum beats that gradually evolves into a familiar northern soul four to floor beat. Then comes an R&B piano and all the band are in. The image of Danny and Rachel performing their northern soul steps in the video springs to mind.

Then as if the song is not delivering enough 'enter the stage' the first lady of Immediate herself, P.P. Arnold. She of course sweetens the song. This is rock and soul at its British best. There are also comparisons to be made here when we are reminded that the Small Faces were PP Arnold's backing band for a chunk of the 60's and that OCS have, by this point, become Wellers backing band (with the exception of Steve White on drums rather than Harrison). Travellers Tune is Simon Fowler proving his worth in his abilities as a blue-eyed soul artist too. This track is a reminder that 60's soul is a constant in the band members' lives. Remember also, the album sleeve with its picture of Diana Ross and the Supremes.

Travellers Tune also serves as a refreshing distraction from the laddish culture that Oasis had been spearheading for the past three years. By this time the 'scene' was cooling off a bit and Oasis were levelling off a little. Knebworth brought Brit Pop to a sudden end and the media that had created it waved it goodbye. OCS were, however, still rising. Thus ends side A.

It is the sweet vocal from Fowler and a friendly acoustic guitar that introduces side B. The band's nod to the feel of records made in America's West Coast is evident here. Many years after this record was made I watched Steve Cradock's solo band sound-checking before a gig in London's 100 Club. Afterwards I told Steve that some of his songs had that West Coast feel. He agreed and commented 'it just comes out that way'.

Debris Road is a reminder that this band are British. It has all the trademarks of the Kinks. Much of the album does as compared to Moseley Shoals that had more Small Faces and Who reference points. This is British music and OCS are keeping that torch of the British preservation society burning.

Side B ends with Besides Yourself. It's dreamy and sweet. Again the band need only acoustic guitars and percussion and a strike on a deep sounding tom tom. Fowler delivers a fine vocal and Cradock's style of playing would reappear often in the albums to follow and especially in his own solo work.

Get Blown Away is the first song on side C. The song is introduced by a brilliant sounding guitar that is up there with the guitar intros on How Soon is Now and All Tomorrows Parties. The band are gradually faded in and then Fowler joins the rest of his gang. There are also some great piano and guitar parts in this mysterious song.

Tele He's Not Talking and Foxy's Folk Faced include a mixture of sounds and instruments. The bands 60's roots are obvious and there are flavours of country folk rock too. If EmmyLou Harris should ever cover an OCS song it should be Foxy's Folk Faced. Her beautiful warm country soul voice would do the song proud.

Then it's All Up. Here are the band working with the Lynch Mob again to create an authentic 60's soul feeling number. There are of course, naturally, hand claps and a piano part that is more Ramsey Lewis than Booker T. It is a rare instrumental performance from the band, with Harrison returning to a northern soul stomp and Minchella driving the rhythm along. It's a great song to dance to. Pleasing in every way.

Spark and Cindy kick off the next section and it's a reminder that if Moseley Shoals was more Small Faces, then Marchin' Already is more Kinks. But then the unexpected happens and there's the reggae feeling Half A Dream Away. This must have put a smile on Harrisons face and his days with Echo Base must have seemed like a lifetime away rather than just a dream away.

To give the song that seal of authenticity and approval the trombone solo is played by the legend that is Rico Rodriguez. Rico would have dropped onto the band members' radars during their teenage years when Rico performed with the Specials and was part of that Two Tone and late 70's ska chapter. Half A Dream Away is a suitable wind down before the final song on the album reintroduces PP Arnold.

Beautiful Thing offers a delightful blend of PP's and Fowlers vocal supported by a perfect piano part. The video for the song had the band playing on a cold winter's day in a barn. They are all wearing thick fur coats.

There is an almost choir like delivery from PP Arnold that only PP Arnold could deliver and Fowler is at his strongest. Then just as the song appears to be signing the album off it evolves into an instrumental section that is as long as the vocal part of the song and could have been a song in its own right. By the time the song fades to its end the listener is assured that this band is a band that will stand the test of time. They certainly went on to deliver many more superb albums and outlived the majority of their 90's peers, including Oasis!

PETE KELSEY

I was the head of the art department at MCA/Universal at the time. Despite the success of Moseley Shoals, the band wanted a new direction for the first single from the new album, Hundred Mile High City. We were asked to put together some visuals to show the band and given a pile of studio pictures. We produced a series of cover options and I went up to Birmingham to meet the band and show them what we came up with. They loved the collage version that became the single cover and the basis for the album campaign, so we got the commission to produce the rest of the campaign. It was quite a big deal for us - in-house graphics teams tend to lose out to the bigger agencies on the prime jobs, so it was pretty special to be working with a band at the height of their success.

I was a fan of the band anyway, but when you work for a record company your judgement gets skewed a little by the fact that you want your label's bands to do well. The period 1995-98 was a good time to be working in the music industry, probably the last of the good times in retrospect. But yes, I was a fan of the band, particularly live, where I must have seen them 10 or 12 times.

I guess as the designer you get to do most things associated with the visual marketing of the band. It helped that Tony (Briggs) was, and still is, a good friend, so we worked pretty closely together on most things. In addition to the single and album covers we did all the posters, adverts, special edition releases, tour programmes, t-shirt designs and other merchandise. Probably lots of other stuff too that I can't quite recall.

Regarding the location details of how we set up Marchin' Already: We set up a few shots which we'd intended as cover images, 2 or 3 different set ups, and then we had agreed to do a series of individual portraits in the doorway. We didn't have a lot of time, an hour or two max, and a wedding was going on in the hotel so we kept getting interrupted. These were pre-digital days so we didn't really know what we'd got until the contact sheet arrived a few days later.

I did some layouts with the 'cover' shots we'd intended to use but none of them were really coming together. I didn't want to do a collage but it seemed we had four great individual portraits, so we stripped these together as an initial visual, with the intention of comping it together as a single image if the band chose it - it was still a 'filler' visual at this stage and I thought that the band would go for one of the set-piece shots but when they saw the first draft they unanimously chose that composite image.

In those days we used apple macs to put the artwork together, but the final file was then 'recreated' at hi-resolution in a reprographics studio. When we went down there I had intended to comp the four of them together into one shot, as if they were all standing together. But, once we started with the hi-res images in place I decided to leave it as it was, so you can see the edges of each image. I'm happy I did as I think this feature gives the cover some character. You only discover its four separate images on closer inspection. We used the proposed cover shots on the CD reverse and inside shots.

We then spent the next week or so putting together the finished artwork for the album, including the inside spread collage for the booklet, plus the other formats; gatefold vinyl and cassette. The band wouldn't have seen anything since the initial visuals so I arranged to meet them in Ireland where they were playing the Galway Arts Festival. I went over alone with all the artwork, expecting a lot of problems with certain images and prepared for having to redo much of the work although we were up against a tight deadline. As it turned out, the band were good as gold and approved pretty much everything. They played a great show and we had a long, raucous night. I remember borrowing some golf clubs the next day from the hotel and playing a round of golf, everyone else was in bed, but I was relieved and elated in equal measure that the campaign had gone so well.

It was a great time, and I was lucky in that I got on well with band and they liked what we were doing. I remember one evening, not long after I'd met the band, I was talking to Steve. He asked me what other bands I was working with - I used to work on The Stone Roses and then post-split with John Squire and the The Seahorses. Steve got really excited and asked if it was possible to meet John, he was one of his heroes. I said no problem - in those pre-mobile phone days you couldn't just fire a message off, so by the time I'd got back to the office and contacted the manager, the Seahorses had decamped to LA to record their album... I never did arrange that meeting.

Another time I came to Birmingham wearing a brand new pair of Adidas Samba's. After a few drinks Steve got sight of them and insisted we swapped - I came out of that deal pretty badly, the shoes I got in return were a knackered pair of too-small desert boots. Still, rock-star shoes I told myself, as I shuffled off to the station the next morning. Finally, after my golfing exploits in Ireland Oscar told me he was a keen golfer. OK, I said, I'll bring my clubs next time we meet up when you're on tour and we'll have a game. The next time was in Scotland for T in the Park, there was no course for miles around so we had a long driving competition instead, firing balls off from the hotel garden and over the heathland below. The result of the competition remains a mystery even to me.

WEZ GIBBONS

I got involved with the band because I was working with Tony (Briggs) when he had his studio in Rivington Street, London. I joined Tony just around the time of Marchin' Already. The first time I met the band was while they were filming the Hundred Mile High City video and then I spent the next year with them doing the festivals and so on.

I remember the Electric Ballroom gig when Liam sang with them. This gig really was electric. That was a special night.

My most clear memories are of the festivals. We did Glastonbury and it was the same year that Radiohead played. There was something special about that gig. Ocean Colour Scene really caught the crowd. They got the atmosphere going. The sun was just going down and everyone was singing along with the words to The Day We Caught the Train.

It was one of those really muddy Glastonbury festivals too and you just couldn't move about. We had to be driven everywhere by tractors. The back-stage area was covered with hay to help you stop sinking in the mud. Everyone had their wellies on. I remember being at the side of the stage with Tony, watching the band and they were so brilliant and so on fire. I'm surprised they could even stand up because we had all had a heavy night the night before. Earlier in the morning they couldn't string two words together but on stage every note was pitch perfect and every bit of playing was spot on.

One of my great images that I've always held onto was the look on their faces. They all looked like six year old boys. They were all excited and their faces were all flushed. It was totally different to Radiohead, who looked all sullen and serious... like they had just run over a cat or something.

We bumped into Ray Davies backstage too. I think he had played earlier in the afternoon. I think having people like him and OCS around, in many ways, kinda summed up what the feel of that festival was like. They kinda epitomised that sort of Britishness at the time. They were like the direct defenders of bands like the Kinks, then into Weller. The mood, the atmosphere, the lighting over the fields on that summer's day was very English. It captured what the scene was like at the time, along with that whole mod resurgence. OCS really took the whole mod thing by the scruff of the neck and took it forward.

T in the Park was another great festival gig. We were there because the band were shooting the cover for Marchin' Already. I think the plan was to do the shoot in some place of historic interest, such as a castle, but that fell through. Instead the shot was done in some old, derelict Abbey that was in the grounds of the hotel we were all staying in.

I just remember that everyone was in such high spirits. The album (Moseley Shoals) was doing well and the band were topping the bill at festivals. It was great. On one occasion we were all playing football. Damon especially loved his football. I think he may even have had trials for Everton at some time. He was a good goal keeper. Anyway whilst playing football I kicked the ball, I mean really fuckin' punted it at the goal and it hit Damon's hand but pushed his thumb right back. I just remember thinking shit 'this band are at the top of their game and I've just killed the bass players hand'.

I remember going back to the hotel after the gig. That turned into a wild night. We all gathered in one of the bars and made it into our after-show party. Paul Weller was there getting pissed with everyone. In one of the other bars there was a wedding going on. It was full of burly Scottish geezers all dressed in their kilts. I don't know what happened but Steve almost started a fight with them and he was tiny compared to them. The whole thing was like a clash of cultures with these biscuit tin, Kilt wearing, Scots on one side and a rock and roll band on the other.

Doing the video shoots was also great days. I have fond memories of doing Better Day in Steve's house. By this time I had seen them several times live and they always had a great live sound. They were definitely one of the best live bands around at the time. But whilst doing the video shoot they would just sit around and sing or play acoustically - Simon picked up a guitar and started singing and I remember how all the hairs on my arms stood up. His voice was just so brilliant and, up until then, I had never really experienced being that close to such a talented singer. He was singing so naturally and relaxed. It was a brilliant moment. So yeah, doing the video shoots were great for those type of moments.

Some of the other videos were more difficult. The video the band did with Pat Arnold was more difficult because it was outside and it was cold. The one big memory I have from that day was trying to get the band up in the morning. Trying to get them out of bed was one of my jobs. And it was never an easy job trying to get a rock and roll band out of bed at 8 o'clock in the morning.

There was something about OCS that generated the feeling of goodwill from the crowd. Not all bands can get it but OCS did and still do. Every time I saw them they were note and pitch perfect, and I always got the impression that if the stage or sound collapsed or something, the crowd would keep them going. You just felt the crowd would go on and sing every word to The Day We Caught the Train. OCS have that connection with the crowd. It's as if the crowd performs with the band.

At the time, when you had bands like Blur and Oasis, you also had OCS and they were a big part of that Britishness and if anything, at more of an underground level. OCS certainly connected with that time and the crowds and when I used to stand on the side of the stage I used to see it all the time.

LIAM GARLAND

I was 7 years old, playing on the streets of Ladywood , Birmingham, along with my friend (Ricky) and we went inside an old looking building looking for firewood for a bonfire but we were kicked out. But Steve Cradock was absolutely amazing to us and took us inside. He gave me an electric guitar, a lead and a little tiny Marshall amp. Then he showed me some chords and sent me away. I'm now 27 and still speak to them and go to see them regularly. We have even supported OCS and Steve's solo stuff with my own band, Little Liam.

My first gig was October 1998, the Marchin' Already Tour at Manchester Apollo theatre. I remember it so clearly because, again, I'd been bugging Steve and the band in the studio to see 'what they do?' and 'when do they do a gig?'. I was very young but Steve sorted a chauffeur to pick me, my sister, Ricky and his sister up from the studio and take us to the gig and it was amazing. I'd been ringing Chris Cradock almost every day saying 'please can you not forget us about coming to a gig'.

When we arrived they took us in through the guest list area and straight through to the back where the band was having pre-gig sesh and yes, it was amazing. We sat at the side of the stage on a flight case and watched the gig. After the gig Oscar let us tear into some massive boxes of bootleg merchandise, which had been seized and said we could take what we liked, we did just that, I think we even took the empty boxes.

There are way too many brilliant songs to pick a favourite but the two that I always find myself playing are The Circle (acoustic) and Foxy Folk Faced which, funnily enough, only three weeks ago we played at a festival with my band Welfest and Simon came and joined us on stage and we performed both these songs. Dreams do come true.

JOHN ASHTON

Ocean Colour Scene first came to my attention after I purchased a Huge Hits 1996 CD. I was just starting to get into music seriously and The Day We Caught The Train was on there. I instantly loved it. It was fresh sounding, different to anything else around at that time and unique, yet it had a retro quality feel to it. That same year I had another compilation album which featured The Riverboat Song. After playing these two songs endlessly I decided the next best thing to do was to go and buy Moseley Shoals. I remember OCS being talked about a lot by people at my high school and a bunch of people owned the album already. I will always remember getting Marchin' Already the following year before my friends and them asking me during an art lesson what it was like. Naturally I bigged it up and told them to go and buy it. I loved the dress sense they had as a band, as they looked so different and out of sync with everything else, in a cool way.

My first time seeing the live OCS experience wasn't until October 2003. Funnily enough I'd never seen a band live up until this time so I decided it was time to start seeing my favourite bands live. I remember as my brother and I were standing at the back (we had seats but never sat in them during the gig) I saw Damon Minchella sitting alone a few rows ahead of us. After a while I plucked up the courage to approach him and get him to sign my tour booklet. I wasn't sure if you were allowed to take photos in venues, as I had no experience of live gigs before, so I told my brother to follow me and while I talked to Damon he was able to get a sly photograph, although sadly the quality wasn't amazing. I recall by the time the band had ended their set the crowd were incredibly loud in calling them back out for an encore and I even saw a few people with broken seats hitting them on the floor to make more noise. It was awesome.

Most people will say Moseley Shoals is their favourite album and I guess I'm no different but North Atlantic Drift, for me, is up there in a tie with Moseley Shoals. There isn't a weak song on the entire album and the sound ranges from loud raw guitars to beautiful lush string sections, it's a really underrated and underappreciated album. Asking someone to name one favourite song by a band is a near impossible task as it changes pretty much every time I listen to an OCS album, as I'm sure it does for anybody listening to music in general. At a push I can just about narrow it down to a top five (in no particular order whatsoever); The Day We Caught The Train, She's Been Writing, Village Life, So Low and Up On The Downside.

I've been a fan since 1996 and have never looked back, buying all of their albums and a bunch of their singles on various formats. I own everything in their back catalogue in terms of studio albums, live albums, live DVDs and various compilation albums. I will support the band in any way I can and forever spread the word of Ocean Colour Scene. As a fan it frustrates and saddens me that they don't receive the radio play they deserve, especially when it comes to new material they release.

I remember one gig in 2010 when my brother and I went to see Simon and Oscar playing a live show in Leeds. After the show I caught up with Oscar outside and asked him whether there would be anymore singles taken from the current album at the time, Saturday. Oscar replied and I quote "I don't know I'm only the drummer. Drummers never get told fuck all, man!", I thought it was a humorous but honest reply.

PAUL 'FISH' BURFOOT

I first met OCS through Tony (Briggs) Briggsy and we had a few beers out with them. Then Simon and Damon started coming to have their hair cut. I don't think Steve had much at the time. This was around the time of the Riverboat Song.

I opened Fish up in 1987. We had a bit of mod culture around us anyway. Much of this was based on my own musical influences and style. At the time it was all rave curtains so I started off the Soho crop, which I put on the map and got a bit of media attention. A bit after that I did another cut, a look I modelled on the look of Tony Montana from Scarface, which was taken up by the Brit pop movement. That got really popular too.

I had been doing Paul Weller's hair since his solo days and there was a bit of a scene around. I had met Weller at a London Records party. We got chatting and I told him that I had a barbers shop in Soho and, if he was in the area, he should pop in. Then the next day I was in the staff room and one of the girls come out and she could hardly speak but said 'you ain't gonna believe this but Paul Weller's in the shop'.

So he used to come in regular and give us tickets for gigs. I remember one time he said 'do you wanna come to a gig? We're doing the Royal Albert Hall'. So I said 'yeah nice one, if you got a spare ticket.' Anyway he booked us a box and all the staff went. We also did the cuts for his Paul Weller album and he gave us a credit in the sleeve notes.

People wouldn't just come in for a haircut, they would drop in just for a cuppa tea. I mean if Damon was shopping (and he often was) he would just drop in. Fish was a bit of community centre like that. It was a nice vibe. And sometimes the band would pop in and want to go out but they didn't want to always go anywhere too glitzy, so I would take them to some nice quieter drinking dens around Soho. There's a nice photo of Damon sitting on my

Vespa outside Fish. The picture was used in one of their tour programmes.

One night I was at a Power Minds do in Brixton. It was only a small do above a pub. I got a phone call from Damon asking where I was and what was going on. So I told him. I think they had been playing at the Brixton Academy. Damon says 'okay we're coming then'. I explained that it was a small do but he still wanted to come. They always liked just mixing with normal people. The next thing is my mates telling me that I need to sort something out. What had happened was that Damon had brought the rest of the band and the tour bus with him and this massive tour bus was parked outside the pub blocking the street. They all came in, were drinking and all that and weren't interested in moving the bus.

There was another time when I got a call from Simon telling me he needed his haircut for Top of the Pops because they were doing the Riverboat Song. So I say 'yeah okay when?' and he says 'now'. So I say 'fuckin' 'ell, OK but just make sure my names on the door 'coz I don't want to come down there and have all that aggro of trying to get in. .Anyway I got down there and, of course, my name's not been sorted out. But it got sorted and I'm in the dressing room. They're all mucking about. Weller is in there because he was also doing a song on the show. They were all like kids, it was chaos, they were grabbing my scissors and trying to cut each other's hair and fight each other.

Doing The White Room was a funny occasion. I had some tee shirts made up with Fish on them and asked the band to wear them but they wouldn't 'coz they're all quite moddy. Plus they said we can't anyway because you're not allowed to wear labels on the tele. But Oscar said he would and he put the tee shirt on. Then just as he was about to walk on there was these two floor managers trying to stop him and flapping about, but it was too late and Oscar was on and sitting behind the drums.

Simon was smashing. He was quiet, very funny with a dry sense of humour. A great singer too. Damon was a lovely lad, the boy next door type, a real good laugh, likes a drink and his football. Steve always seemed very focussed and very driven, a bit like Weller. I mean, if you was in a room with them the two of them they would just talk about a pair of shoes for three hours and nothing else. Steve is very natural and down to earth. He's the type that probably doesn't get any nerves before he goes on stage. I think OCS didn't lean towards the commercial market like bands like Oasis did. They had a different type of soul in them. They seemed comfortable in their own skin, a kind of 'well this is my job and I'll carry on doing my job whether it means playing in an arena or in some small pub'.

RACHEL MULLEN

I first met Steve and Simon in the Jug of Ale pub in Moseley. There was a big gang of us that used to live and drink in Moseley at that time (1990's) and we all became good friends with the band for many years. As the band got big, looking back now, I consider myself very privileged to have been a part of it and the many gigs and events I attended.

My all-time favourite gig(s) has to be in January of 1998 - it was my birthday. Me and some others went on the tour bus for two nights. PP Arnold was on tour with them at the time (Marchin' Already tour) so to meet her was a dream come true. My birthday was at a gig in Plymouth and during the show PP Arnold came on the mic and wished me a happy birthday. After the gig we were drinking at a hotel bar and PP and Simon sang songs on the piano. It was a great way to spend a birthday and gave me memories I'll never forget.

The Travellers Tune video was shot in the old library in Digbeth next to the Custard Factory. Danny Turner and I were asked by Steve to go down and dance, as they wanted a northern soul background to the video/song. It was a great day and very hot. We threw down some talc and just got dancing, it took a few hours and there was much sweating. It was such a fun thing to do! I think we went to the pub after for some well-earned pints, ha! I remember seeing the video for the first time and feeling really honoured to have been a part of it. I remember joking, saying that's one to show the kids. Now 15 years later my two boys think it's cool.

SARAH FERGE

I'm from Redditch and they (OCS) had a very loyal fan base in the area. I first got into them after a friend gave me a copy of Moseley Shoals. From that day on I was obsessed with them. I had always liked my guitar music rather than dance, so OCS were it for me. Their songs hit you because they were catchy tunes.

Then I started going to see them and, up until then, I had never been to a proper gig. It was magic and I remember I couldn't sleep for days before I got to see them. My first gig was at the Birmingham Academy. There was some sort of problem and they all walked off stage. Only Simon Fowler was left. Although I think I heard that the reason they had walked off stage was because Simon had lost his voice (but I also heard that he had just got really pissed). But Damon came back on stage and offered everyone free tickets for another gig. So I got to see them twice for the price of one. Not having been to a gig before I just remember it being complete mayhem. I didn't know what to expect and I got completely crushed. It was just brilliant.

Being Birmingham based we felt like they were our band. In the way Manchester do Oasis. But it sort of felt like a small but dedicated fan base. I once saw Steve in the balcony at the Academy (Birmingham) but I was too shy to approach him. I got to meet Damon later on because my best mate started seeing him.

So many of OCS's songs bring back memories. I still get butterflies now. OCS have so much to do with the younger me. Robin Hood is one of my favourites. It's just amazing. It's the main song that I wait for when I see them live. But they have so many brilliant songs and it's just amazing when the crowd chant along with the words.

The thing about OCS was that they didn't offend anyone. They were never pushy and putting themselves out there in that arrogant way. They didn't need to because they were good at what they were and didn't need to prove anything to anyone. Their music spoke for itself. I still think that they are one of the most under-credited English bands and I hope that one day they'll get the credit they deserve.

ALICE BRIGGS

I do remember the first time I met them, with Tony (Briggs) when he was doing his first pictures with them at Holborn Studios (I had seen them play at an earlier industry showcase though and had been aware of them for quite a few years beforehand). I had never seen anything like it – the four of them came in very quietly and all set up individual ironing boards and started ironing their shirts etc – not a word was said. It was a bit intense! They did warm up a little bit, but not much, during the session. I felt that they were quite an insular little unit, not incredibly press friendly…

I did get to know them quite well over the years and they were always very, very nice. They were a fantastic band to shoot – looked good and so into what they were doing. Our dog (Steve the Dog*) even became a sort of mascot and popped up on quite a few covers and videos. One of my favourite memories was Steve and Sally's magnificent wedding at Merlin's cave in Tintagel with a Wizard vicar… I think they'd had to get a civil ceremony done beforehand and Tony had to lend them the fee because they weren't carrying any money. The sight of Pat Arnold, Mick Talbot and a load of music industry wankers (I include myself) climbing down a long, tricky path carrying amps, keyboards etc to the cave in their fancy London outfits will never be forgotten. The party afterwards was very, very messy. Our taxi driver back to the station the next day hated us all, I think he probably represented the majority view.

*Tony told the band that the dog was named after Steve Marriott, but I always said it was Stevie Nicks… This is the power of a wife to embarrass their other half – I also threatened to tell Paul Weller that Tony had a cat named after him…. I'd always been a bit more of a 'rock chick' and in no way mod and I remember Sally Cradock saying sort of the same thing about going to Northern Soul nights on their honeymoon on the IoW and feeling like a hopeless hippy (Tony and I were also there – why?).

Which does remind me of another moment – on said honeymoon we (Steve, Sally, Tony, me and no doubt the dog) were travelling in a camper van on the IoW. There was a scooter run on and the look on everyone's faces when they realized that Our Lord Steve Cradock was travelling alongside was a great moment – very reverential, we parted the scooters like Moses. Brilliant reflected glory.

I don't know too much about the row with Damon which led to him leaving or, more likely, I've forgotten. What a shame though. I saw them at this year's V festival in Chelmsford and really missed seeing him there (it had been a long time since I'd seen them play). Actually, I really missed his hair! Which is a weird 'bird' thing to say except that Tony says there are always loads of online comments about how Damon's hair was an integral part of the band and sadly missed.

PAUL BRACKEN

Myself and my mates were at the Olympia. I had a pain in my arse along with everyone else getting to meet the band over the years, so I had a plan. As soon as the gig was over I had heard Simon would often get a chipper or a sneaky pint in Brogans bar next door to the Olympia, so myself and my mate Graham went hunting.

Anyway there was no sign of him and I was pretty pissed off as I was almost certain to see him. Next of all there was Oscar. We went straight over to him but didn't know what to say to him, so I asked him any chance of a pic. He was actually loading up a van with the equipment from the gig. Graham took a pic, I was ecstatic so I then took the phone off Graham to take a pic of Oscar and him but I didn't have a clue how to use the camera and Oscar was obviously in a rush. So Oscar says to Graham 'will you ever show that fella how to take a pic' and he goes back inside.

Next, lo and behold, Oscar comes back out to us and says 'right lads are you ready for this pic'. JACKPOT! We were very happy lads and for the rest of the night we were talking about how much of a gent Oscar actually was.

MICHELE O'HAGAN

Not really having any experience with OCS, more like life changing moments is what I recall because music, certain music can do that. Having listened to some of their tracks before I had never really paid attention until my ex-mentioned them until going to watch them at Barrowlands. For the first time my opinion changed. I loved them. Oscar stood behind us in the crowd for a bit before they went on stage and as he squeezed by I felt I was getting my money's worth to pat him on the back.

So many more concerts after, I was hooked and we revelled at the sight of Cradock in Dunoon having a curry next to the Queens Hall with Oscar, again, being cool beside him but we never got a glimpse of Simon.

A few years on and a while after I had my second child and things got a bit rocky in my relationship I found myself escaping to the edge of the Clyde in my not so new car, drowned in thoughts of depression. All I could think of was my girls, then there was a song that I tuned into on the CD player in my car… the lyrics went through me like a thunder bolt and into my head. This was my life and I had to change. So from here on, grabbing every opportunity to see the OCS boys was my highlight. Concerts, festivals, travelling 6 hours to Dumfries to Wickerman. Good times, then I overheard one night they were playing in my town! The gig was amazing as per but standing meters away from Simon, my idol, and watching him get emotional I think I cried a bit myself.

My mate had disappeared for a while then came back with a pass saying she was outside having a smoke with Oscar and she was going back to their hotel to have a few drinks. So I followed on shortly after with a kind invite and sat up most of the night in the bar. What a night! Fast forward a few years and my nephew and a few people were at my house, he was straight out of army training and declared he was reactivating his Facebook page. Well after a few vinos and curiosity I asked what it was and within minutes I was signed up to OCS. This was my band. A couple of years on and one guy had requested to be my friend. My instant thought was 'don't know this guy'. That was until I found the connection - we both liked OCS. So I accepted Steve and we got talking, talked through Facebook a lot, spoke to the wee small hours; confiding, becoming best friends and then we exchanged numbers.

A few months on I asked him to come

to T in the Park and he accepted! Pure platonic friendship and the love of Simon Fowler was all I was after! Ha! My heart jumped out of my mouth when we met for the first time, as he came off the coach! Trying to keep cool I never let on, we had a great night and the sparks flew whether I wanted them to or not and having that first kiss I was nervous as hell!

We went to T in the Park and we took a wee chance squeezing through King Tuts tent on the Saturday to get backstage. Before I knew it I was heading on the stage with OCS and the guys saying to security 'they're with us'! Wow you could have blown me away but the moment you stand next to your idol on the side of a stage with a massive crowd chanting in the background was, indescribably, one of the best moments. And what do I say to Simon, my big chance to speak to him my biggest idol of all time! 'HI'! That's it! Ha ha but we did get to spend all day backstage, so beat that for a first date!

CRAIG LEE BARDEN

I can fondly remember the first time I heard the music of Ocean Colour Scene. Being the son of a man who classed himself as a rude boy, I grew up listening to a variety of top superb bands such as Madness, The Specials and Bad Manners. Like always in life, times change when you least expect them to and you find yourself drifting into a new segment of something you enjoy and, in my case, this something was music. I heard The Beatles song "With a little help from my friends" and became completely obsessed with the four mop tops from Liverpool. From that moment on, I knew that music had a special power beyond anything I could ever have known.

Eventually, I found myself taking a turn for the whole "mod" subculture, which interested me greatly. I discovered bands such as The Who. The cool Roger Daltrey standing in the front of the stage accompanied by the angry playing of Pete Townshend, the imageless picture of John Entwistle playing bass like I have never seen it played and the phenomenal shenanigans of Keith Moon bashing into his drum kit. What a bloody combination The Who were. This sudden realization that there was a vast sea of different artists out there, waiting to be heard hit me real hard and my ears were now open to everything. The Kinks, The Yardbirds, The Jam, The Style Council, The Rolling Stones, David Bowie, Led Zeppelin, The Doors, it was as if the sounds from the musical geniuses were locked behind a door that I had just unlocked!

I remember one day about six months ago when I was playing around with my Fender Telecaster guitar, playing some Beatles and some Who when my dad came into the room. "Haven't you ever head of a band called Ocean Colour Scene Craig", he said questioningly. I searched my brain for any music that I might have heard of the group and the results came back negative. "No, I can't say I have. Why?" I responded. "There quite a good group and a lot of mods listen to them. You'd like them, definitely" He simply said. I sat there, continuing to play my music, thinking of how I'd never heard of this band, if they were supposedly good as my dad had described them. Eventually, I decided to have a search for the group named Ocean Colour Scene and threw them into YouTube. I clicked on the Riverboat song and waited for the track to play. I was absolutely blown away. The quality of the track was absolutely amazing. The slightly crunchy guitar, mixed with the strategically thought out drums, the top notch vocals and the overall feeling of the song combined together to form a cocktail of musical goodness for me. That of which, I swallowed without hesitation. I repeated the track until I had realized that I had idiotically journeyed into the late hours of the night, which caused me to get to bed quickly.

I began listening to the Ocean Colour Scene regularly. The Day We Caught the Train, The Circle, Better Day and Beautiful Thing were all tracks that heightened my love for the band. I was quick to tell my group of good friends about the band. My friend Stephen (with whom I shared a fierce passion with for blues) had already heard of the band and we talked of the pure awesomeness of the group for ages. Another friend, Tommy, wasn't familiar with them and when I showed him, he was as equally impressed by them as I was.

When the band released their newest album (Paintings) a few months ago on February the 11th I was blown backwards by the set of recordings. With tracks like We Don't Look In The Mirror, The New Torch song and my personal favourite, The Winning Side, it led to me constantly asking myself "Why aren't this band given more credit for what they have achieved?"

I am still a massive Ocean Colour Scene fan and I am continuing to be astounded by their works of art. Hopefully I can get my dad to take me to see the group pretty soon, as it'd be a bloody brilliant night out! Even if they aren't the most famous group in the world, Ocean Colour Scene will continue to do one thing for people and that is make them happy. Their music always feels as if it has been carefully constructed from the heart, which is something that they will always be proud of. At the end of the day, if music doesn't connect with you, then there is no point of creating it or playing it for that matter. I'm fifteen now and I'll have many more years of listening to The Ocean Colour Scene to come and I know that wherever their career may take them, they will always leave behind a lasting legacy of musical masterpieces. So for that, thank you.

JAMES PYATT

Before I found OCS my taste in music was predictable and questionable. Jungle to Josh Wink, Kriss Kross and Prodigy was about as good as it got. Then one night, while being intoxicated and so forth, beyond belief it all changed. Moseley Shoals was left on repeat at a party and being in the state I was, it had the chance to sink in. From then on I became hooked on guitar music.

I have fond memories of Cofton's party in the park. I remember the police trying to get a bloke down who had climbed on to the speakers with his sun hat in tow, showing them two cold fingers and then dancing away. I thought if he loves it that much it's gotta be good. I then decided I wanted to play the Riverboat, Got it Bad, The Day We Caught the Train and so on myself. My own music was born from that desire. I followed OCS to many places for gigs and always caught the Brum shows, Blackpool, Leicester, Wolverhampton and the N.E.C of the Marchin' Already tour.

I've bought every album and most singles and vinyl releases. They opened my mind up to Rock and Roll, Tamla, Stax and Atlantic label type music and guitar greats such as Free, Clapton, The Doors, Hendrix, The Spencer Davis group, Traffic, Jimmy Page, Paul Weller and all British invasion type bands, even Black Sabbath. Going to watch OCS was a real buzz as they are a real Rock and Roll band, looked cool, sounded great and were off their nuts most of the time. I have massive respect for the whole band, but it was Simon's singing and Steve's playing especially, that captured my imagination and heart.

Being a Mod or following that way of life for me means something and it's down to them, it gives a young British lad identity within a music scene. Basically if that night's enlightenment had never happened I'm sure my life would have been completely different today. It made music the most important thing. My own playing eventually got better and I put a few bands together, which then led to finding Liam Garland on Myspace. Upon meeting with Liam I found out he had grew up around the band and that Steve and Simon had mentored him from the age of 7. Within a matter of 12 months I was jamming and performing with Liam, with him supporting my band, Copious.

On about our 5th gig we opened for OCS on their 1st night of thier Saturday tour. It was immense to see Steve and Simon in a reverse role watching us. Their set was top and it was the first time I'd heard Policemen and Pirates live in The Rainbow in Digbeth (our drinking and stomping ground). It was great to see them in a small venue and intimate gig situation. The place was jammed packed and you could barely move.

There have been many highlights at gigs, basically dreams came true and I have got to drink and chat to with my idols on more than one occasion, which only strengthens my love for their music, my music and music in general. Music and OCS without doubt is the core of my life and without it, life would be very different. So OCS were pop stars when I was cutting my teeth on music and their last album, Painting, was still as exciting to explore as Moseley Shoals, except I'm not listening to it in Maths lesson, I'm listening to it washing up, working, chilling or drinking with friends.

Mine and Liam's love for OCS, folk & rock music has led to us gigging as an acoustic duo for two years or more. We supported The Jam DRC one night where I met my fiancée, Ange Lloyd. She played keys and trumpet for them, she now plays keys, trumpet and sings in Little Liam. We supported Steve (Cradock) on his solo tour and, more recently, Simon (Fowler) got up for a couple of tunes on our set at Welfest 2013. It's amazing to have such opportunities, considering Simon's stature. In my eyes he is a very humble, friendly, hilarious bloke whose talent is off the scale.

OCS to me are what The Beatles, the Stones, the Who, the Small Faces and Bowie were to my parents. Merrymouths album is very moving, as are Steve's solo albums. It seems that as I have grown up their songs have too, in the sense that they are still very relevant to my life now. Family is the most important thing when it comes to it because 'ya can't party happily when things ain't right'.

Being an OCS fan to me signifies being truly British too, as it's built on British music history and they've also helped sculpt the last twenty years of British guitar music. In my eyes they deserve any future recognition they get and I get this feeling they will do. They are very underrated and most original fans don't even know half the albums they have released. The die-hard following are a testament to their quality however. That is my musical Magic Carpet Ride to date so far, in a nut shell.

1999
ONE FROM THE MODERN

1. *Profit In Peace*
2. *So Low*
3. *I Am the News*
4. *No One At All*
5. *Families*
6. *Step By Step*
7. *July*
8. *Jane She Got Excavated*
9. *Emily Chambers*
10. *Soul Driver*
11. *The Waves*
12. *I Won't Get Grazed*

1999 was a big year for Norman Cook (AKA Fat Boy Slim) with his hit album You've Come A Long Way, Baby and single Praise You. He also picked up the Brit award for Best Dance Act. This year also witnessed the Spice World falling apart. Geri Halliwell had left at the end of '98 and the remaining four had a Christmas hit with Goodbye… for most of us it was good riddance. However '99 couldn't quite shake off the dribble from the boy bands and Five, Boyzone and the Back Street Boys continued to swoon teenage girls' hearts. Thankfully, Eminem was parachuted in from the States to shake things up a little. He would dominate rap culture for the next few years.

The big screen of 1999 gave us tears of sadness with Titanic and tears of laughter with Austin Powers The Spy Who Shagged Me. A decade on and underground mod clubs would be frequented with Austin Powers lookalikes… some pulled it off, most didn't.

Y2K was on the doorstep. Some stocked up with rice and tins of beans, awaiting the digital fall out. They woke up on News Years Day with hangovers and their computers working okay!

2001
MECHANICAL WONDER

1. *Up On the Downside*
2. *In My Field*
3. *Sail On My Boat*
4. *Biggest Thing*
5. *We Made it More*
6. *Give Me A Letter*
7. *Mechanical Wonder*
8. *You Are Amazing*
9. *If I Gave You My Heart*
10. *Can't Get Back to the Bassline*
11. *Something For Me (UK bonus track).*

2001 would be the year that the world would change forever. The events of 9/11 horrified and shook the world in such a manner that couldn't be compared to before. The war against terror took on a whole new meaning.

The musical backdrop was often equally as shocking, with the charts being dominated by the likes of Blue, Westlife, S Club 7, Atomic Kitten and Shaggy. Destiny's Child also arrived on the scene. There were okay albums in David Gray's White Ladder and Dido's No Angel, both albums producing some excellent singles. And the Brits were all about Robbie Williams and new comers Coldplay (who had a decent debut album in Parachutes).

2001 was also the year (with so much to answer for) that gave the British public their first real taster of the pop talent shows. Popstars gave the public something to do on a Saturday night and, at the end of the competition, Hear Say were crowned popstars. Like most who would be dragged into this and similar television shows over the next decade they were quickly forgotten.

2003
NORTH ATLANTIC DRIFT

1. *I Just Need Myself*
2. *Oh Collector*
3. *North Atlantic Drift*
4. *Golden Gate Bridge*
5. *Make the Deal*
6. *For Every Corner*
7. *On My Way*
8. *Second Hand Car*
9. *She's Been Writing*
10. *The Song Goes On*
11. *When Evil Comes.*

2003 was all about Justin Timberlake and Christina Aguilera. The sexy Girls Aloud also burst onto the scene. Radiohead achieved their fourth number one album with Hail to the Thief and the Christmas number one slot was filled with a version of Tears For Fears 80's classic, Mad World.

Beyonce made a passable appearance in Austin Powers Goldmember and 2003 saw the arrival of a new festival… the Download Festival. The landscape of the music industry was changing fast. Love it or hate it, if you wanted to sustain a career in the industry you had to be in it. Many of the old guard resisted, some held out for as long as they could but a decade on, even Paul Weller was releasing download singles.

2005
A HYPERACTIVE WORKOUT FOR THE FLYING SQUAD

1. *Everything Comes at the Right Time*
2. *Free My Name*
3. *Wah Wah*
4. *Drive Away*
5. *I Love You*
6. *This Day Should Last Forever*
7. *Move Things Over*
8. *Waving Not Drowning*
9. *God's World*
10. *Another Time to Stay*
11. *Have You Got the Right*
12. *Start of the Day*
13. *My Time.*

Each week between January and May an Elvis single was released to celebrate the 70th birthday of 'the King'. But mostly the charts were packed tight with soulless drivel. There were a few outstanding tracks of note, such as Dare from the Gorillaz (featuring Shaun Ryder) and Push The Button from the Chemical Brothers. But 2005 belonged to the Arctic Monkeys and it was the best thing that had happened to the British music industry and scene for several years. The Arctic's stormed in with I Bet You Look Good On the Dancefloor and hope for British music was reignited - thankfully!

By 2005, downloads were very much a part of the industry and, in this year alone, allegedly 96% of people downloading were male. This was something the industry set their minds towards addressing. But what was for certain, downloading was now a part of our culture.

2007
ON THE LEYLINE

1. I Told You So
2. On the Leyline Waiting
3. For Dancers Only
4. Man In the Middle
5. I Just Got Over You
6. Go Ton Sea
7. These Days I'm Tired
8. You'll Never Find Me
9. Don't Get Me
10. Loneliest Girl In the Whole Wide World
11. Mr Brown
12. Two Lovers
13. Daylight.

This was the year that The Who played Glastonbury on the Friday night and the Arctic Monkeys headlined on the Saturday. The Spice Girls announced a reunion tour. We laughed. In July Wembley hosted a Concert For Diana. Duran Duran, Tom Jones and, of course, Elton performed. Some would have preferred a concert for Factory Records big cheese Tony Wilson, who died aged 57. This year Radiohead released an album inviting buyers to pay what they considered the album to be worth.

2010
SATURDAY

1. 100 Floors of Perception
2. Mrs Maylie
3. Saturday
4. Just a Little Bit of Love
5. Old Pair of Jeans
6. Sing Children Sing
7. Harry Kidnap
8. Magic Carpet Days
9. The Word
10. Village Life
11. Postal
12. What's Mine is Yours
13. Fell In Love On the Street Again
14. Rockfield.

2010 was a year of Brit pop reunions with Pulp, Cast and Suede tuning up their instruments again. Further Brit Pop recognition for Oasis too when (What's the Story) Morning Glory was given the Brit Album of Thirty Years award. The Spice Girls got the Brits Best Thirty Year Performance Award for Wannabe. Paul Weller received the Ivor Novello Lifetime Achievement Award and Johnny Marr the Inspiration Award.

Glastonbury of 2010 was headlined by Motown star Stevie Wonder. Take That reformed and were joined by Robbie Williams and in April the world said goodbye to Malcolm McLaren, who died aged 64.

2013
PAINTING

1. We Don't Look in the Mirror
2. Painting
3. Goodbye Old Town
4. Doodle Book
5. If God Made Everyone
6. Weekend
7. Professor Perplexity
8. George's Tower
9. I Don't Want to Leave England
10. The Winning Side
11. Mistaken Identity
12. The Union
13. The New Torch Song
14. Here Comes The Dawning Day

In this year both JLS and Girls Aloud announced they were to disband… were they ever a band! The year was all about Adele though. The Brits Best Live Act went to Coldplay and the Global Success Award fell upon the heads of One Direction. Thankfully Shane Meadows put together a Stone Roses film to coincide with the bands shows, one of two, of which were held in London's Finsbury Park on the 7th and 8th June.

May was a sad and horrific month following the shocking news that soldier Lee Rigby had been attacked and murdered by Islamic terrorists in the streets of Woolwich. The nation rallied, right wing groups made their presence felt but could never overshadow the British spirits that make this nation great.

129

Ocean Colour Scene
Provisional ~~1999~~ release time plan
2000

✓

FINISHING TOUCHES

Phone someone who gives a shit

W/C		
Mar 1	Master/artwork 1	
Mar 8	Shoot video 1	
Mar 15	Band Rehersals	
Mar 22	Band Rehersals	
Mar 28	Video Delivery	
	UK Tour Commences	
Apr 2	Hereford Leisure centre	(2400)
3	Crawley Leisure Centre	(2400)
4	Southend Cliffs Pavillions	(2000)
Apr 5		
6	Swindon Oasis	(2400)
7	Truro & Cornwall	(1650)
9	Jersey Fort Regal	(2500)
11	I.O.W Ryde Arena	(2400)
Apr 12	Folkeston Cliff Hall	(1400)
13	Kings Lynn C.Ex	(1200)

THERE ARE OVER 550 EDITS ON THE FINISHED ALBUM - IT'S (MOSELEY SHOALS) A GREAT LISTEN ON HEADPHONES. **BRENDAN LYNCH**

131

They were happy times for us all I think. Everyone was learning and that knowledge was a shared experience. These were positive and creative times and I'm glad I witnessed it **PAUL WELLER**

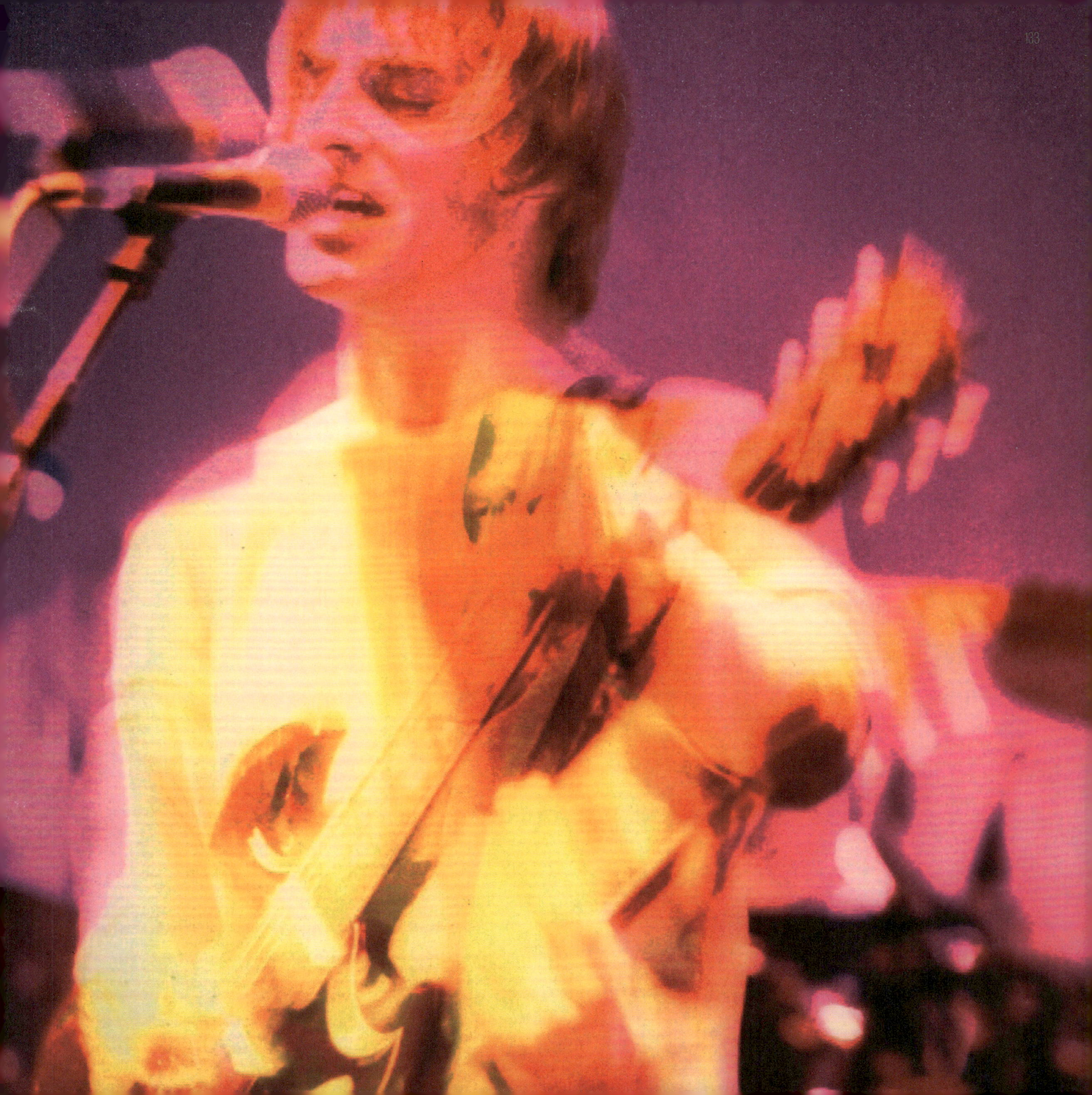

134

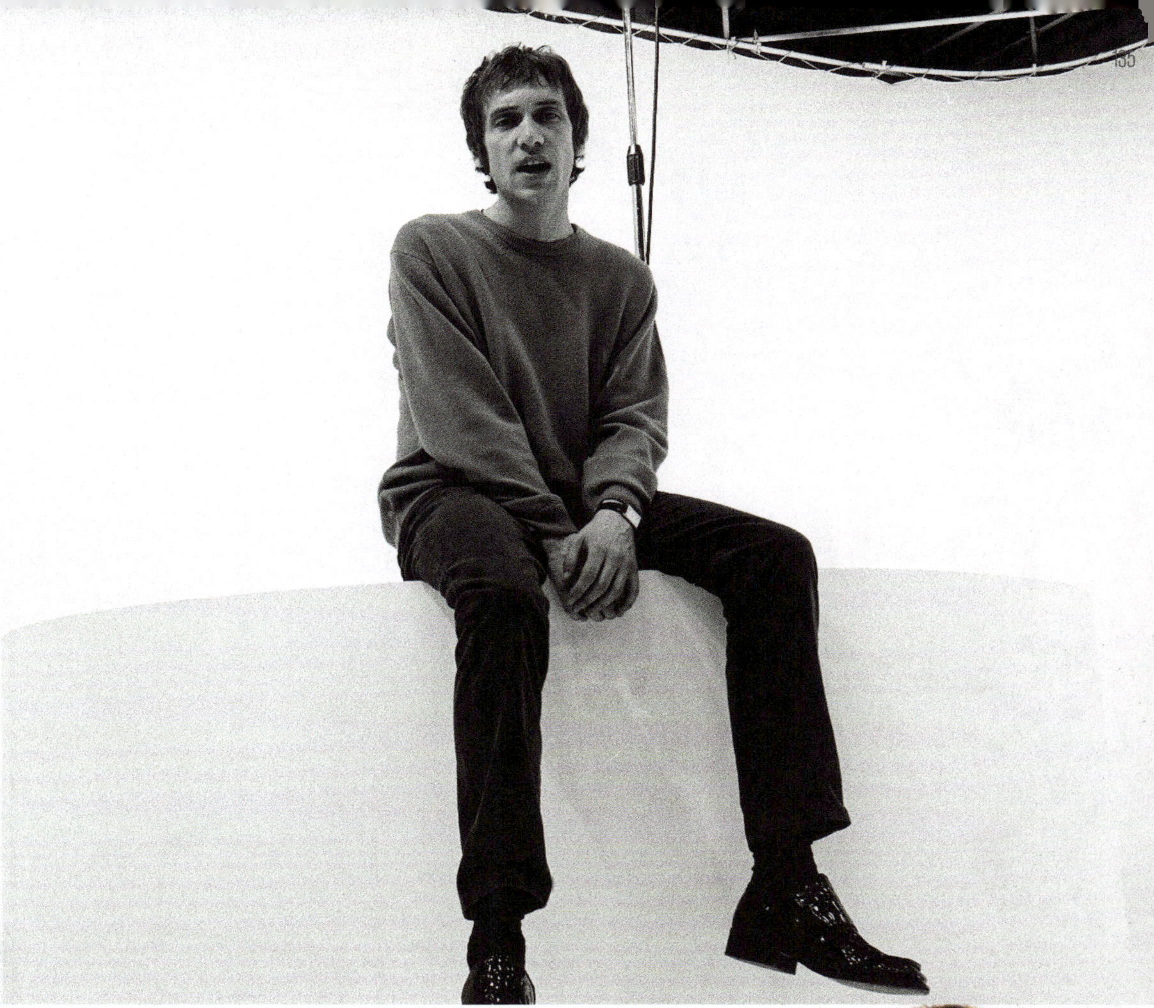

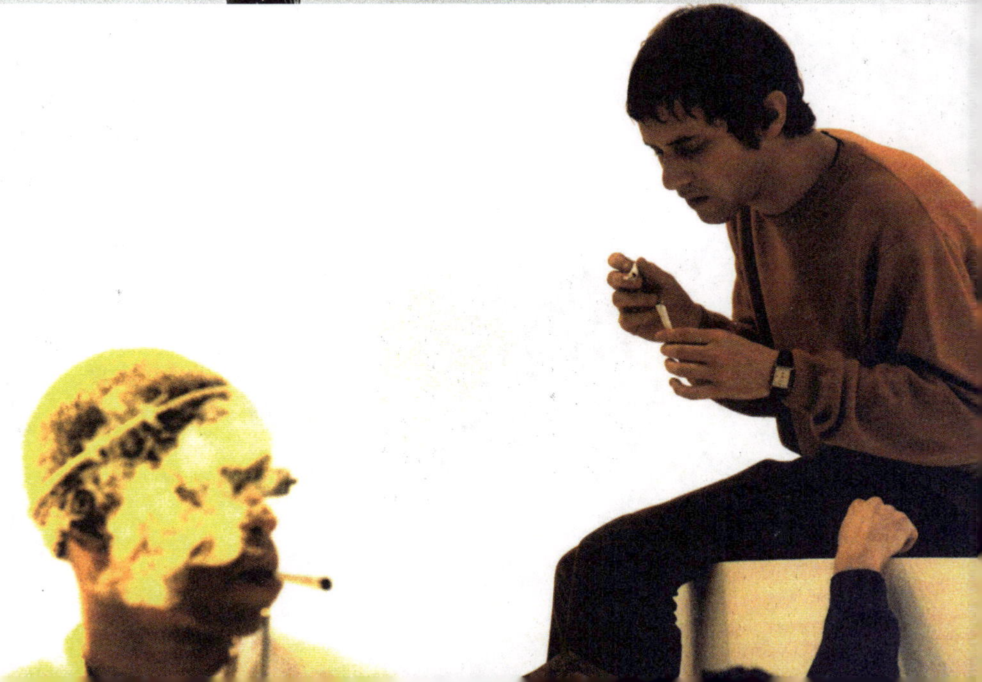

136

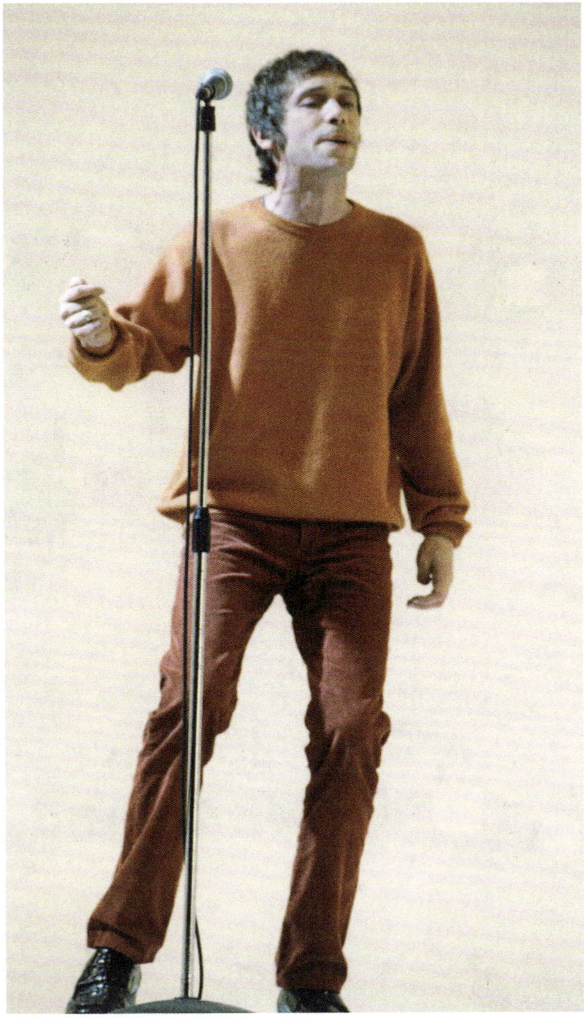

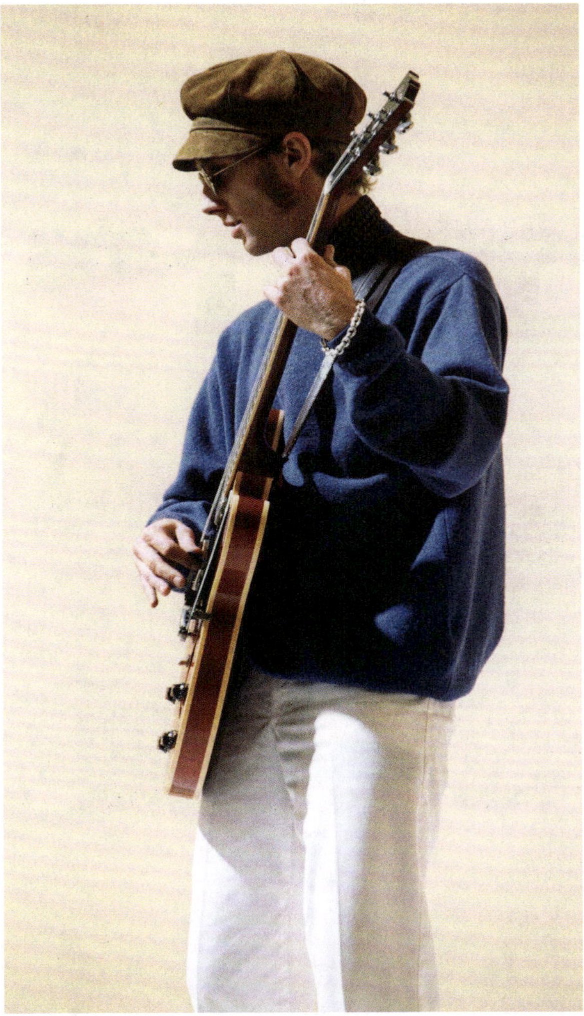

138

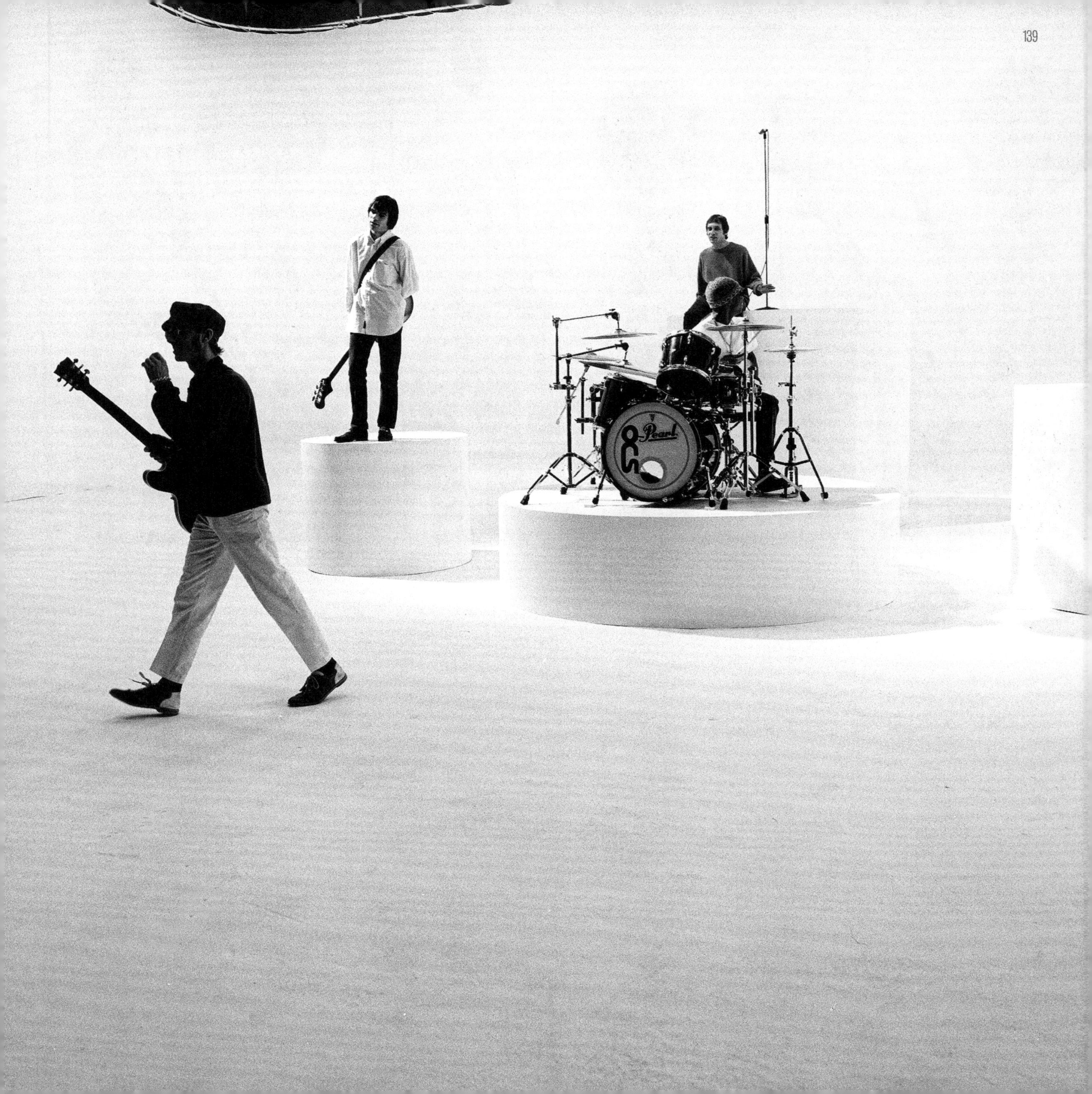
Pearl

140

WE WERE IN MADRID FOR A SPANISH MUSIC FESTIVAL WHEN WE HAD THE IDEA FOR THE HUNDRED MILE HIGH CITY VIDEO USING WHITE PODIUMS. WELL I NICKED THE IDEA OFF AN OLD WHO ALBUM COVER. I SHOT SOME GREAT STILLS FROM THAT SESSION, A FAVOURITE BEING THE COVER FOR THIS BOOK. UP UNTIL THEN ALL THE BANDS' VIDEOS WERE DIRECTED BY DOUGLAS HART. I CAN'T REMEMBER WHY BUT HE PASSED ON MAKING THE NEXT VIDEO SO THE RECORD COMPANY WERE SHOWING THE BAND NEW DIRECTOR SHOWREELS. IT WAS WHILE ON TOUR ONE DAY WE WERE SITTING IN SOME HOTEL ROOM WATCHING A VIDEO OF REEF (THE ONE WITH THEM BOUNCING OF THE WALLS) AND THE IDEA WAS TO HAVE THE SAME DIRECTOR SHOOT THE NEXT OCS VIDEO. BUT STEVE DIDN'T LIKE THE VIDEO AT ALL, HE PRESSED THE EJECT BUTTON ON THE VIDEO MACHINE, TOOK OUT THE VIDEO AND SMASHED IT AGAINST THE WALL AND THEN TURNED AROUND AND SAID TO THE MCA LOT THAT "BRIGGSY WAS DOING IT". THIS WAS THE FIRST I HAD HEARD ABOUT IT AND STEVE JUST WALKED OUT. **TONY BRIGGS**

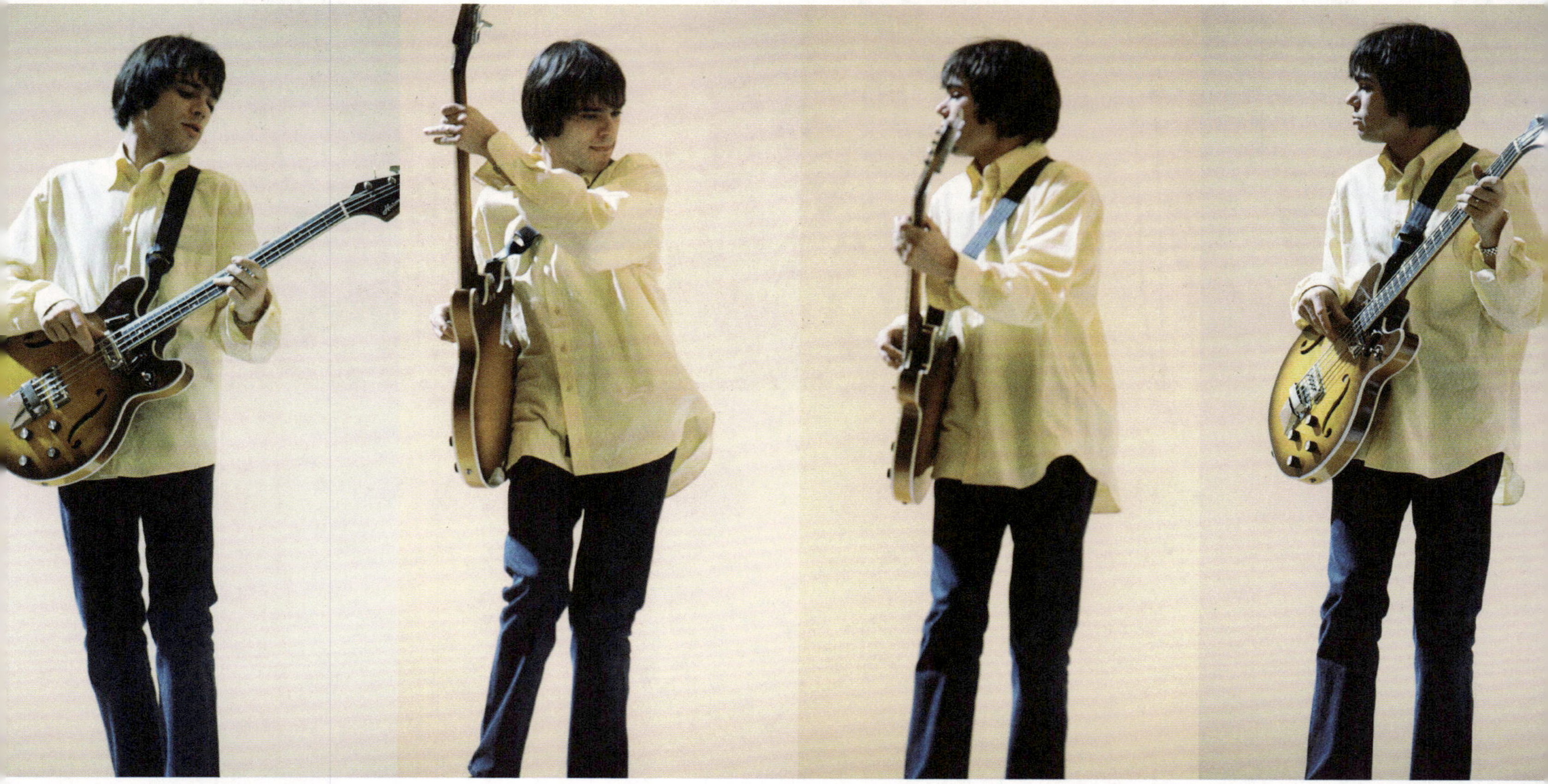

143

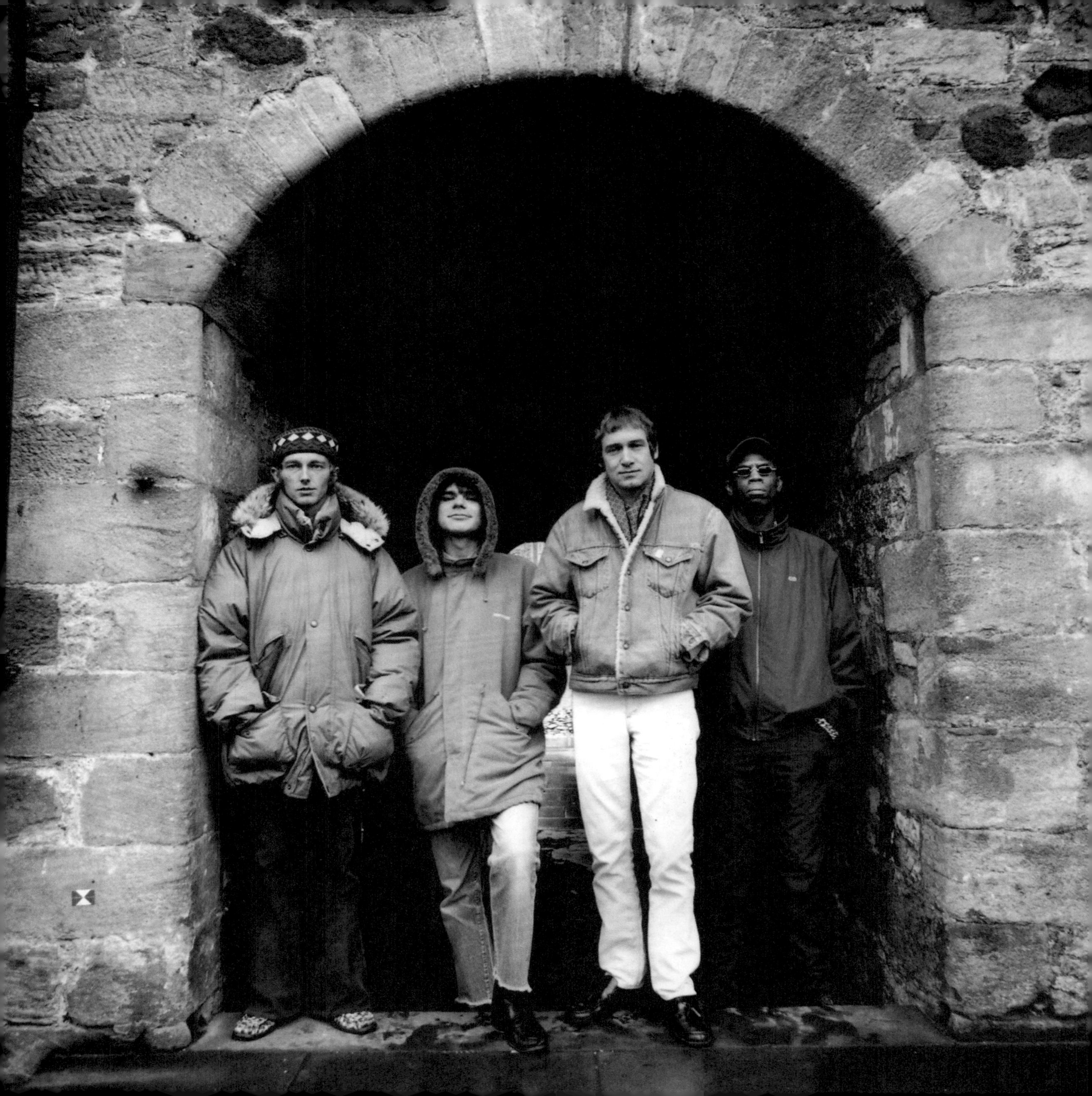

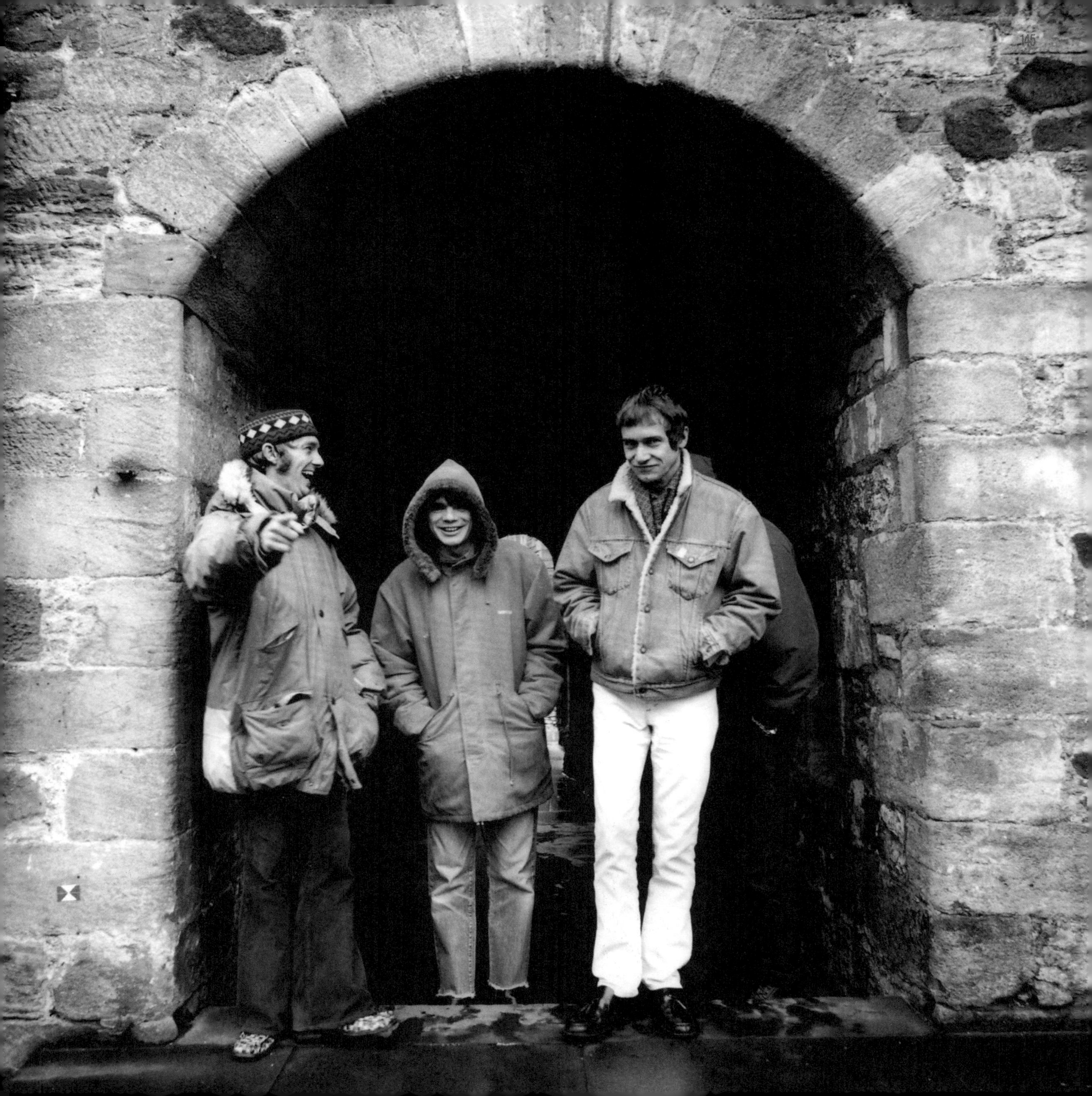

ANOTHER FAVOURITE GIG WAS STIRLING CASTLE, THEY PLAYED THREE NIGHTS SOLD OUT IN THE CASTLE GROUNDS. THEY CALLED IT THEIR 'SALUTE TO SCOTLAND'. I GOT SOME GREAT SHOTS ON STAGE AT THE END OF OSCAR WAVING A HUGE SCOTTISH FLAG. THEY HAD BAGPIPERS WITH FIREWORKS AND IT WAS QUITE EMOTIONAL, THE BAND HAVE A HUGE FOLLOWING IN SCOTLAND. I REMEMBER CHRIS WATCHING THE FIREWORKS WITH ALMOST A TEAR IN HIS EYE. I QUESTION IF HE WAS FEELING 'EMOTIONAL' AND HE SAID FUCK OFF, THAT'S TWENTY GRAND JUST GONE UP.
TONY BRIGGS

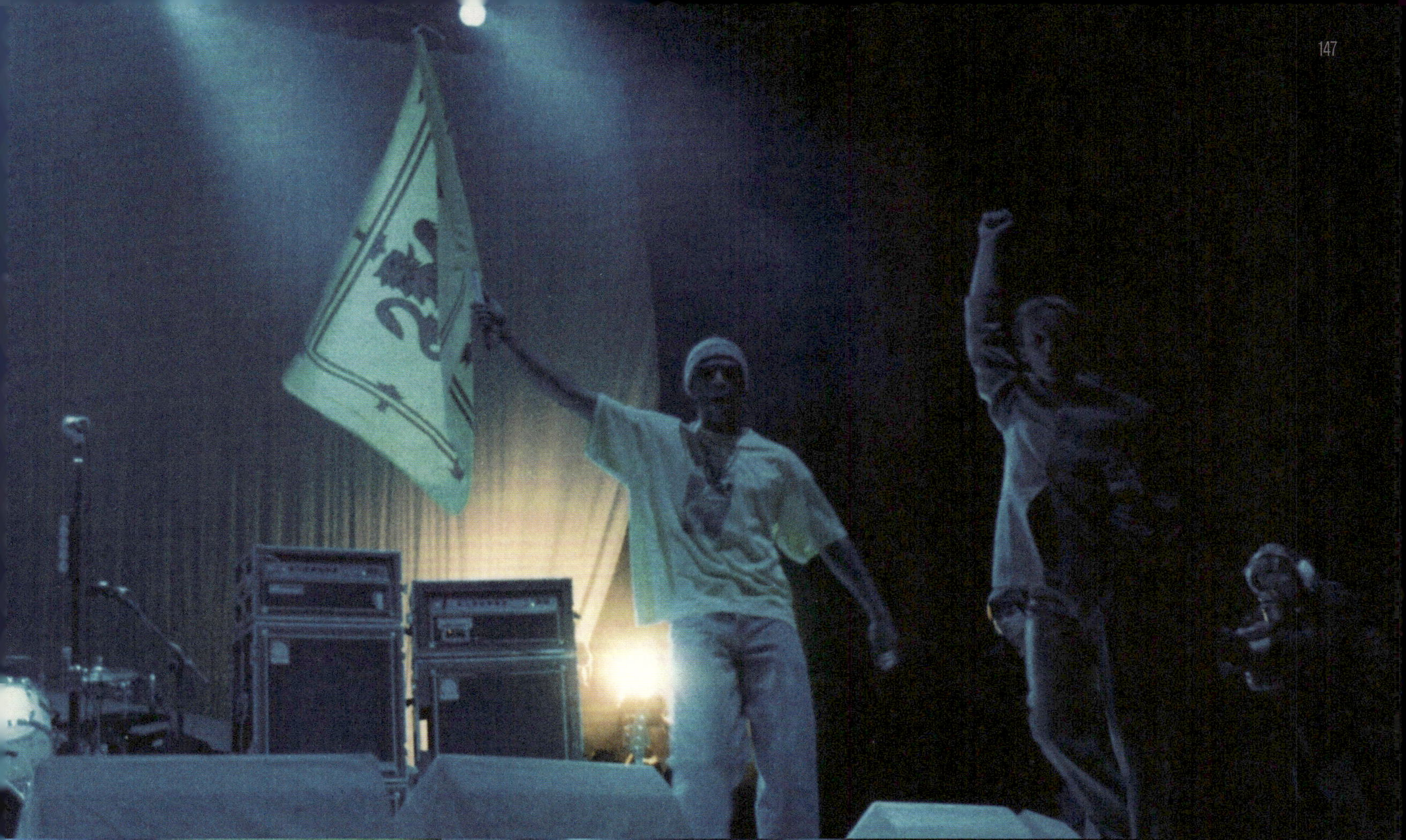

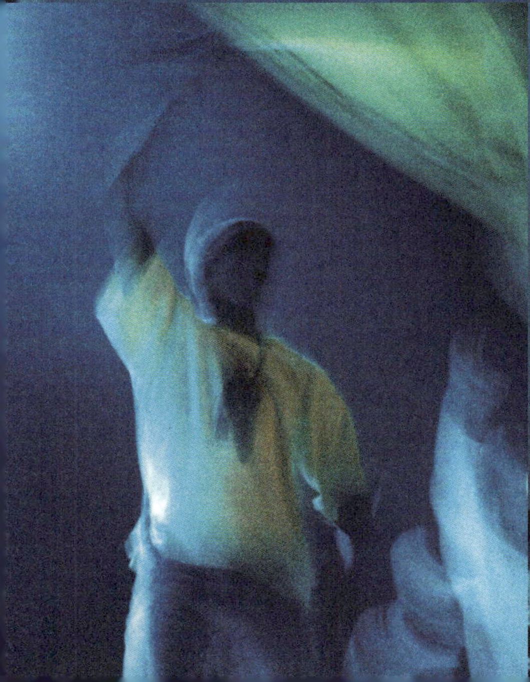

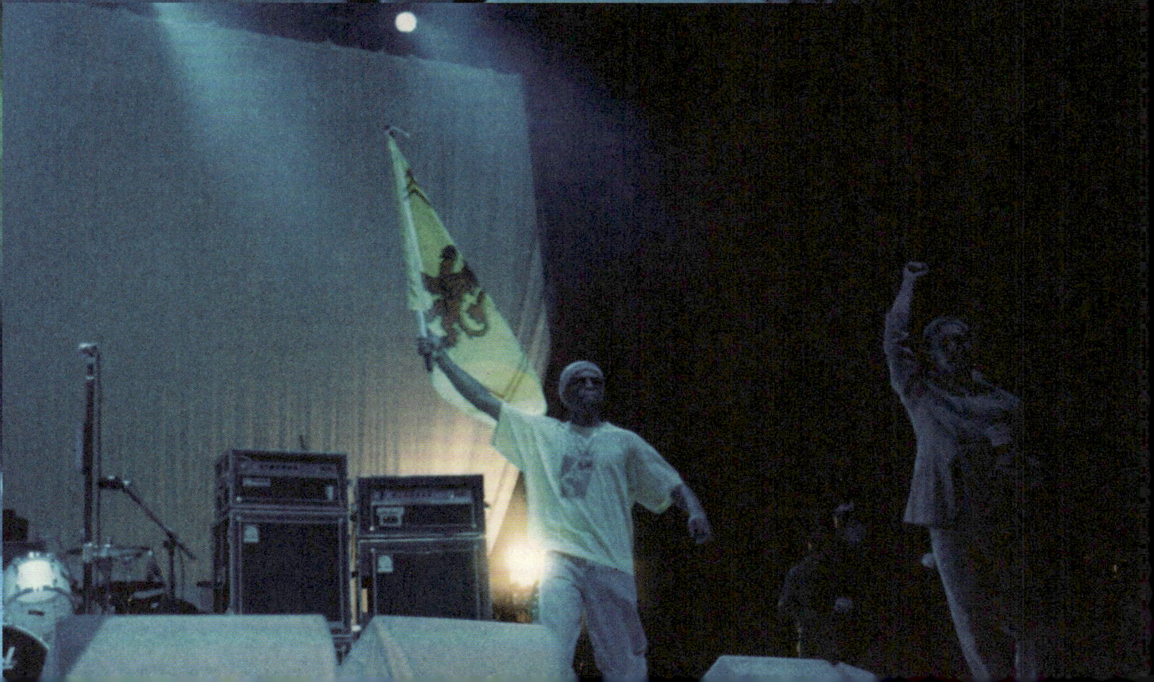

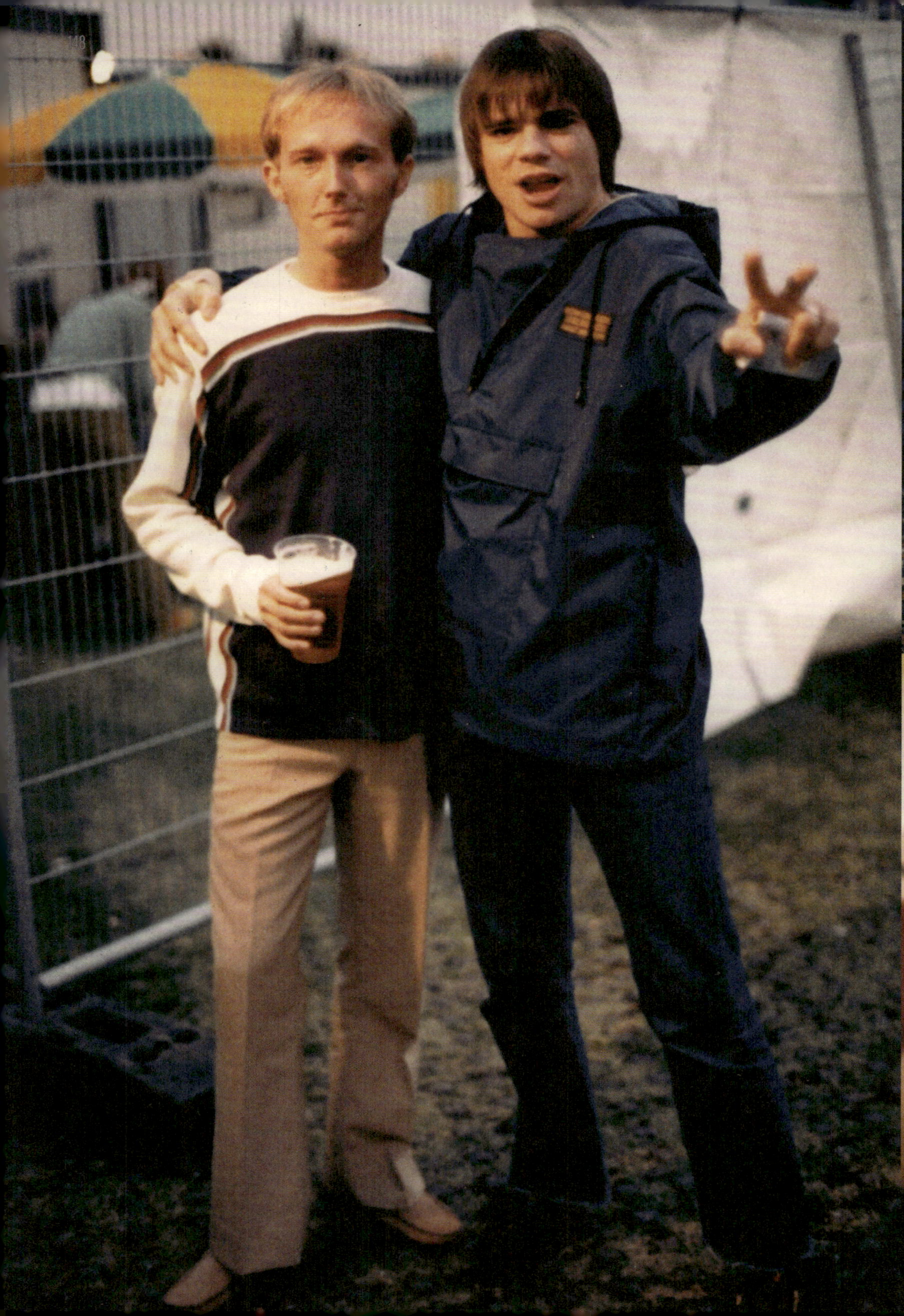

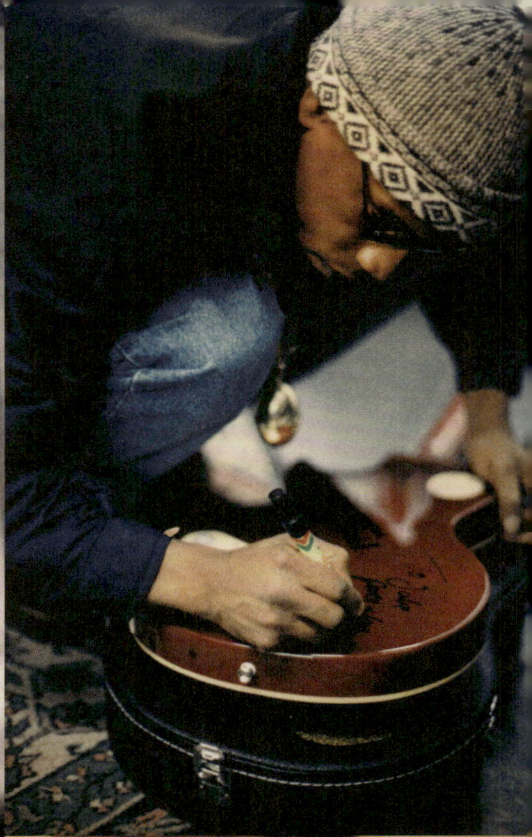

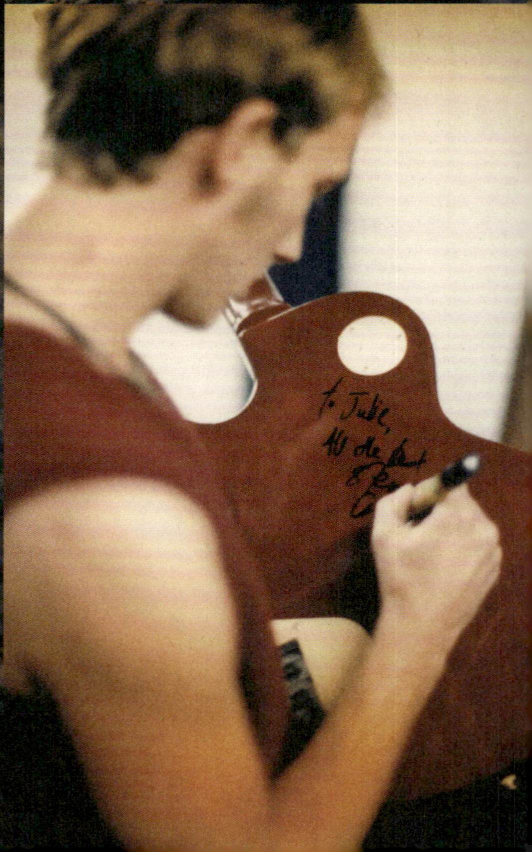
To Julie,
All the best

149

150

ANOTHER OF MY FAVOURITE PHOTO SESSIONS OF THE PERIOD HAS TO BE FOR 'BEAUTIFUL THING', FIRSTLY BECAUSE ALICE AND I SHOT THE SESSION IN OUR LOFT STUDIO WE LIVED AT IN SHOREDITCH. IT WAS VERY PURE, VERY 60'S. JUST ME, AL AND WEZ AND THE BOYS, BLACK PAPER, ONE BIG LIGHT AND HALF A DOZEN ROLLS OF 120 BLACK AND WHITE THROUGH MY OLD HASSELBLAD AND A 80MM LENS.

THE BEAUTIFUL THING VIDEO WAS SHOT IN A BARN NEXT TO THE STUDIO WHERE THEY WERE RECORDING DOWN IN SUSSEX. I THINK IT WAS NEW YEAR'S EVE OR SOMETHING (IT WAS WET AND FREEZING) AND WE HAD TO RUSH TO GET THE VIDEO DONE BECAUSE THE RECORD COMPANY WANTED IT BY A CERTAIN DATE. THE BARN WOULDN'T HAVE BEEN MY CHOICE FOR A LOCATION BUT IT WAS ALL WE HAD AVAILABLE. WHEN MATT AND I RECCED THE BARN IT WAS EMPTY SO WE HAD TO FILL IT WITH THE HAY. PAT ARNOLD WAS THERE FOR THE DAY AND SHE SANG LIKE AN ANGEL AND THE BAND (WHO ALWAYS REFUSED TO MIME) PLAYED LIVE, SO WE ALSO HAD TO DRAG IN ALL THE KIT, AMPS AND INSTRUMENTS AND MATT EVEN HIRED STEVE A MINI WHITE GRAND PIANO. **TONY BRIGGS**

THERE ARE NO SPECIAL EFFECTS, NO TRICKS OR GADGETS, JUST STORY TELLING. BLACK AND WHITE MAKES IT MORE INTERESTING, MORE INTENSE, ADDS GLAMOUR, A NOSTALGIA FOR THE PRESENT. **TONY BRIGGS**

153

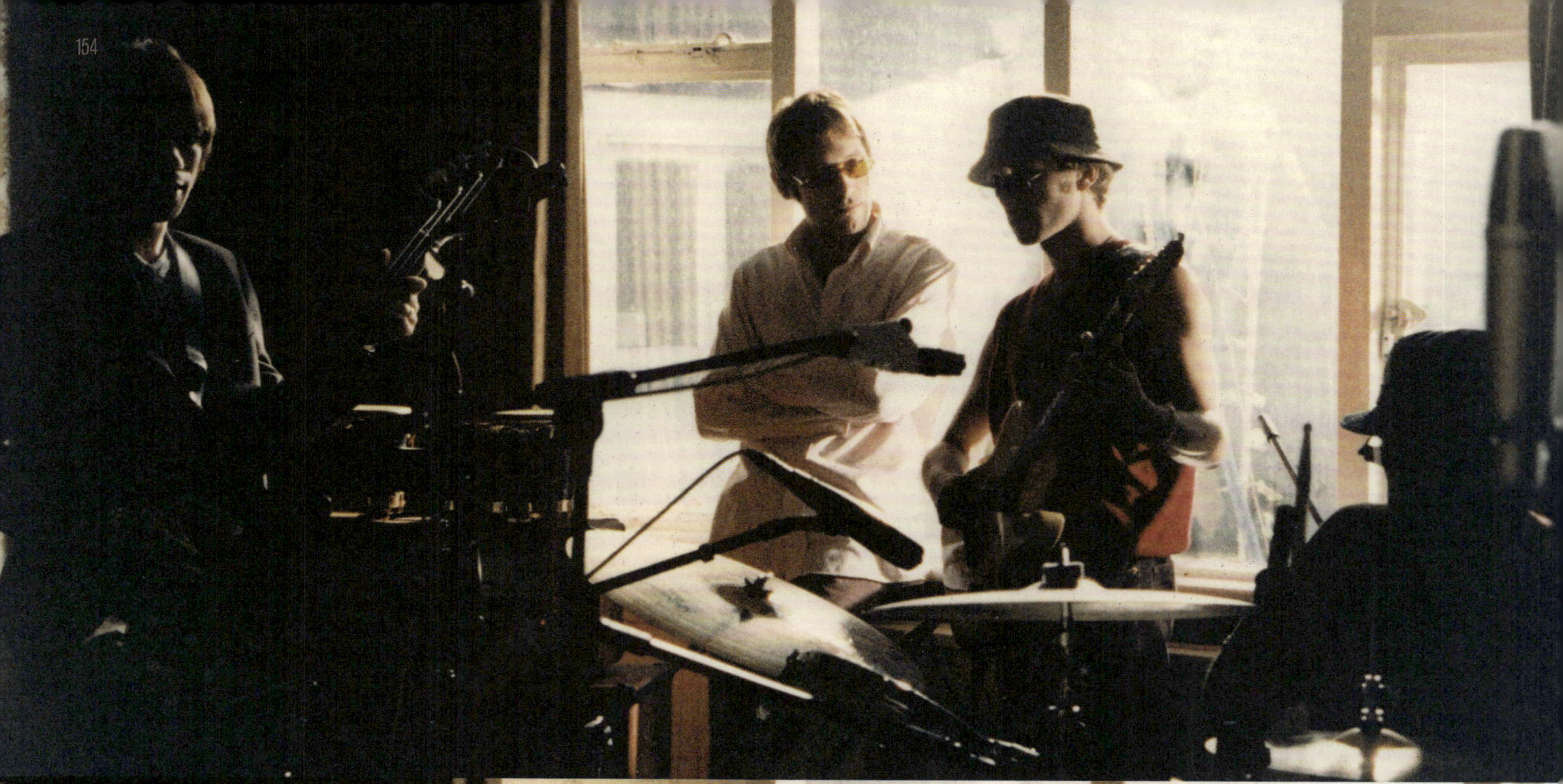

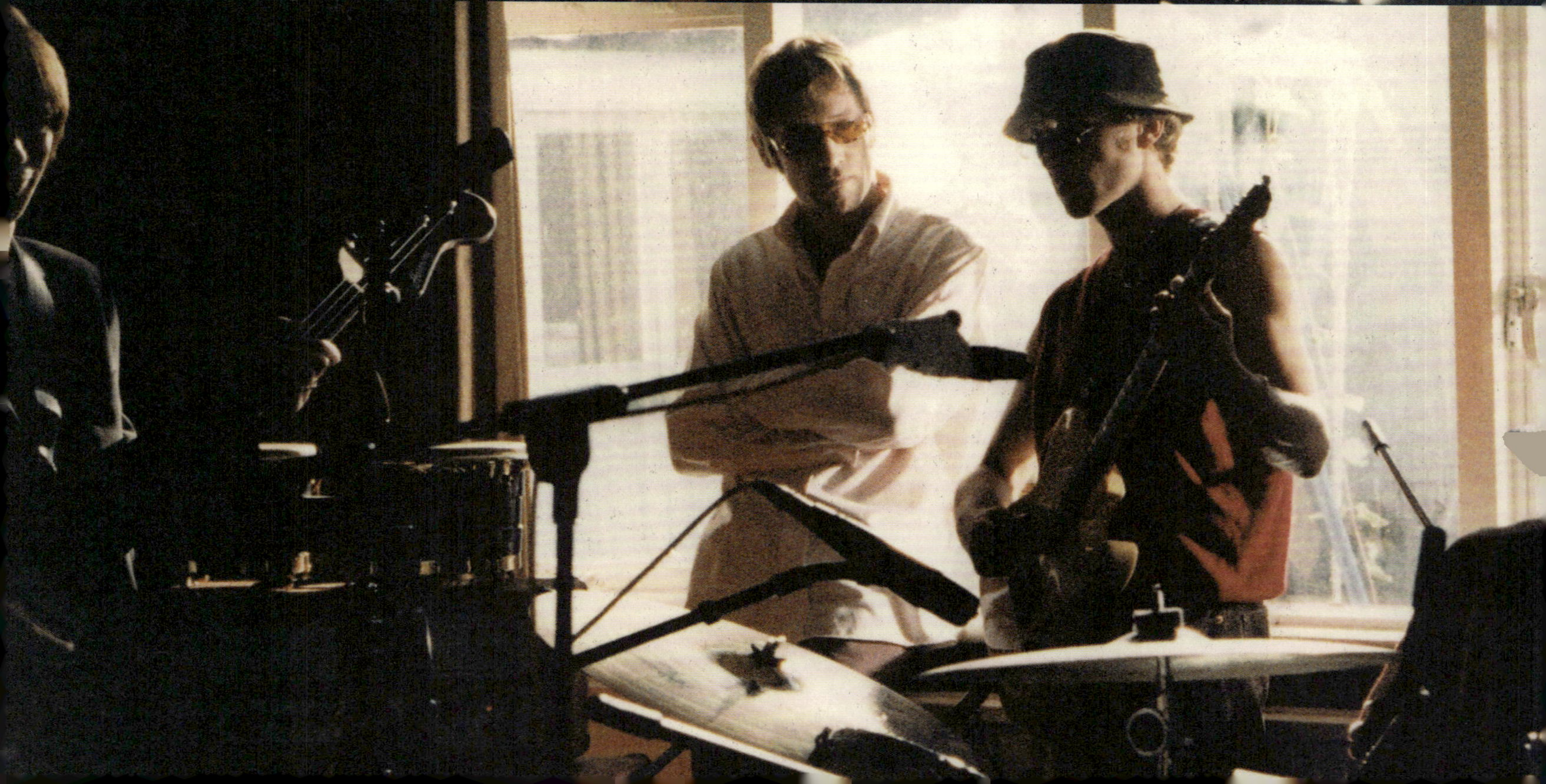

BETTER DAY WAS MY FIRST ALL-OUT BIG BUDGET VIDEO. WE FILMED IT AT STEVE'S HOUSE IN EDGBASTON. I LOANED SIMON ONE OF MY SHIRTS TO WEAR BECAUSE HE TURNED UP IN HIS USUAL STRIPY THING AND I TOLD HIM THAT HE COULDN'T WEAR IT IN A VIDEO AGAIN. WE HAD VARIOUS PEOPLE HANGING ROUND THAT WE MANAGED TO GET SHOTS OF, MY MISSUS ALICE (SITTING UNDER THE DRUMS WITH OSCAR), BERTIE DUNN (DRUM TECH) AND STEVE THE DOG (AGAIN). A LOT OF PREPARATION WENT INTO THAT SHOOT (THANKS TO MATT BUELS MY PRODUCER AT THE TIME).

ALICE ACTUALLY SHOT THE SLEEVE PICTURES FOR BETTER DAY, AL SHOT A LOT WHILE I WAS WORKING WITH THE BAND, WHILE I DISTRACTED THEM. WE ARE A GOOD DOUBLE ACT, ALWAYS HAVE BEEN. ALICE HAS A GREAT EYE FOR LIVE AND DOCUMENTARY SHOOTING AND SHE PRODUCED SOME BEAUTIFUL WORK WITH OCEAN COLOUR SCENE. FILMING BETTER DAY, STEVE ACTUALLY THOUGHT IT WAS A REALLY LUCKY SUNNY DAY. HE DIDN'T REALIZE THAT WE HAD TWO TRUCKS OF 5K LIGHTS IN HIS BACK GARDEN (BEHIND THE BOUNCY CASTLE). HE THOUGHT THE SUN FELL OUT OF THE SKY WHEN WE TURNED THEM OFF. IT WAS ALL SHOT ON A 35M FILM STEADY CAM. IT LOOKED VERY CINEMATIC. BUT MY BIGGEST WORRY WAS ALWAYS HAVING THE BAND TURN UP, FOR ANY SHOOT, WHICH IS PART OF THE REASON I SHOT IT AT STEVE'S HOUSE. I SOMETIMES FELT LIKE I WAS BEING PAID JUST TO SHEPHERD THEM INTO A ROOM. MY TRICK WAS TO BE ABLE TO GET THEM TO SIT STILL TOGETHER LONG ENOUGH TO HAVE THEIR PICTURES TAKEN. BABYSITTING BASICALLY, WITH A FILM CREW. **TONY BRIGGS**

THE DOG YOU SEE ON THOSE PICTURES WAS MINE AND ALICE'S DOG STEVE. STEVE CRADOCK USED TO THINK THE DOG WAS NAMED AFTER STEVE MARRIOT BUT AL SAID ALWAYS SAID HE WAS NAMED AFTER STEVIE NICKS. HE WASN'T, HE WAS ALREADY CALLED STEVE WHEN REECE GAVE ME HIM AFTER A LOADED MAGAZINE SHOOT. **TONY BRIGGS**

157

HAPPY BIRTHDAY OSCAR...

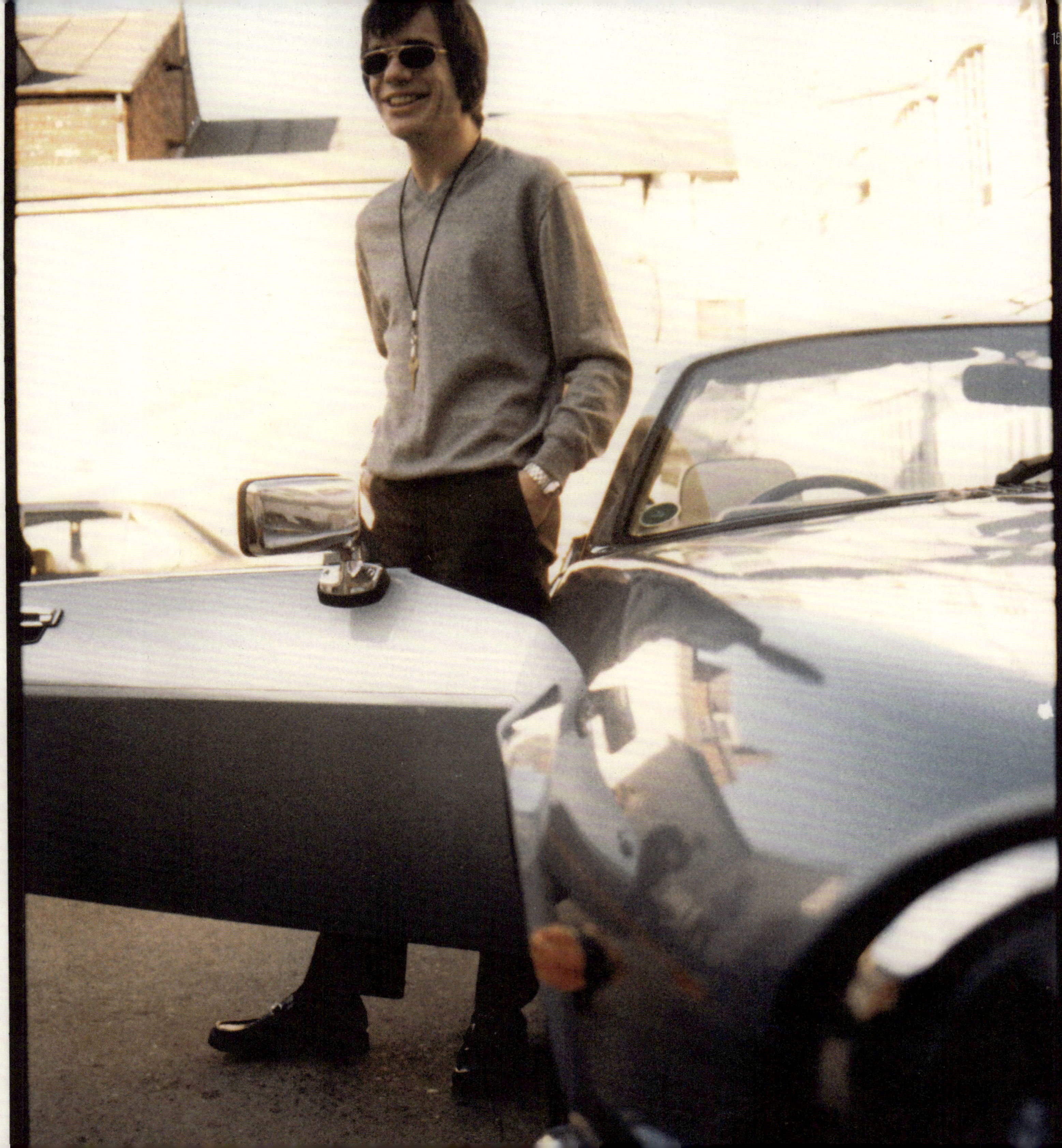

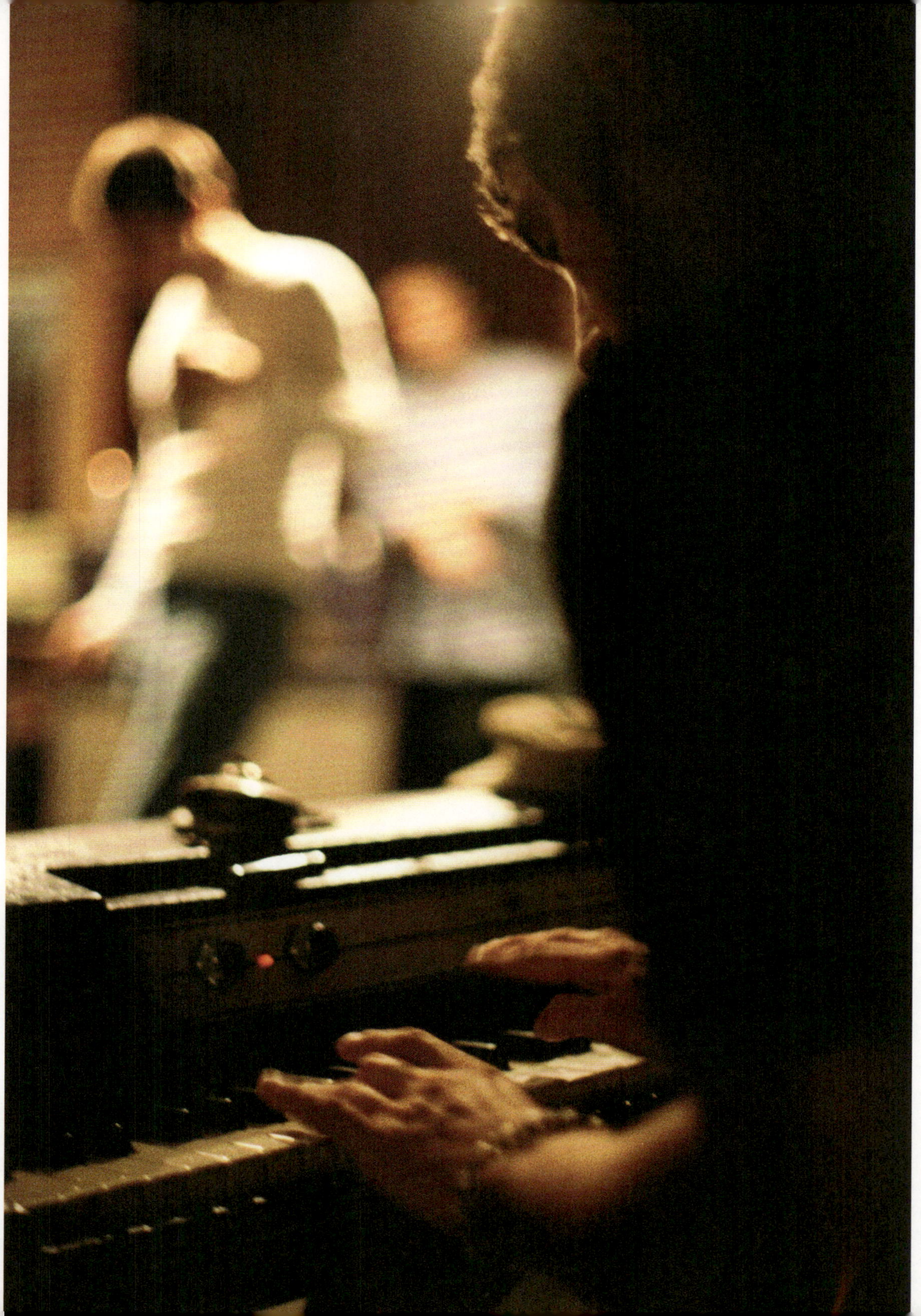

I'D MET PAUL WELLER ONCE OR TWICE OVER THE YEARS, WITH PAUL AT FISH BUT I STARTED SEEING HIM AROUND MUCH MORE WITH OCS. I REMEMBER HIM SAYING ON MORE THAN ONE OCCASION THAT OCS WERE HIS FAVOURITE BAND. IT WAS AMAZING TO ME TO PHOTOGRAPH AND TO SPEND TIME WITH A CHILDHOOD HERO. PAUL IS ONE OF THE MOST CREATIVE PEOPLE I'VE EVER MET. **TONY BRIGGS**

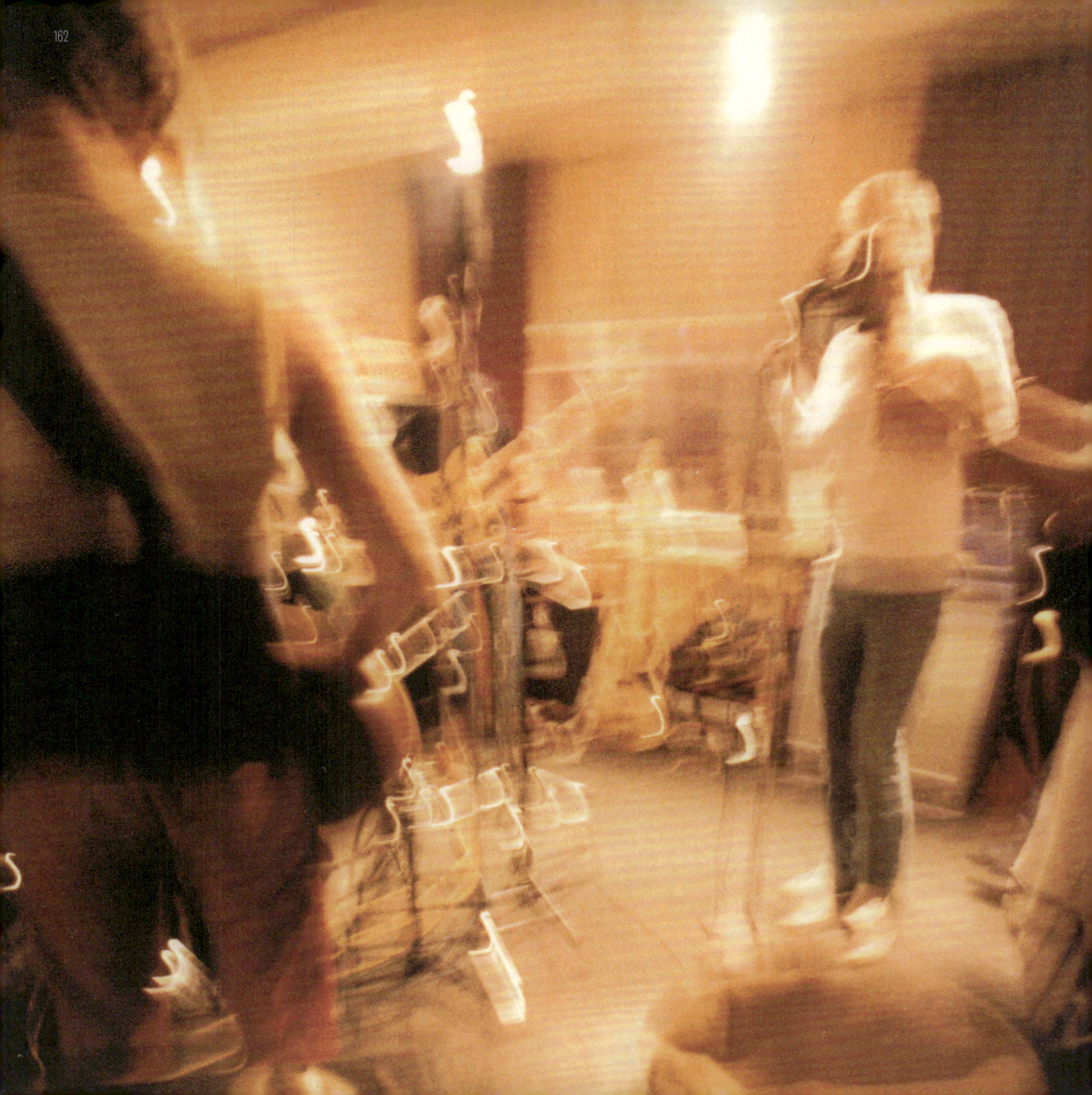

TONY REALLY GETS UNDER THE SKIN OF HIS SUBJECTS. THESE AREN'T HALF-HOUR PRESS SESSIONS, SNAPS FOR POSTERS. HE SPENDS DAYS, WEEKS EVEN MONTHS TO TELL THE WHOLE STORY. **DOMINIC DELANEY**

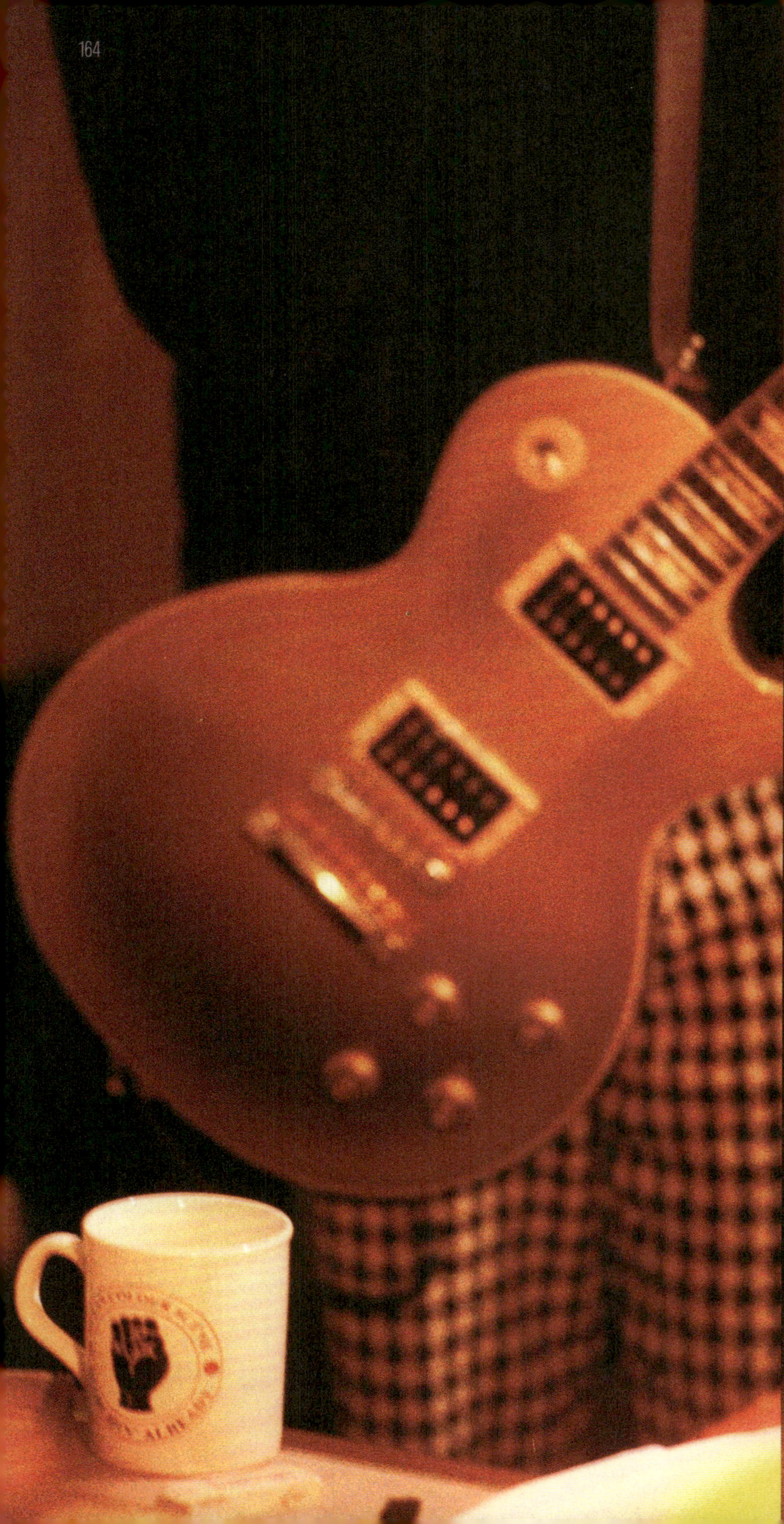

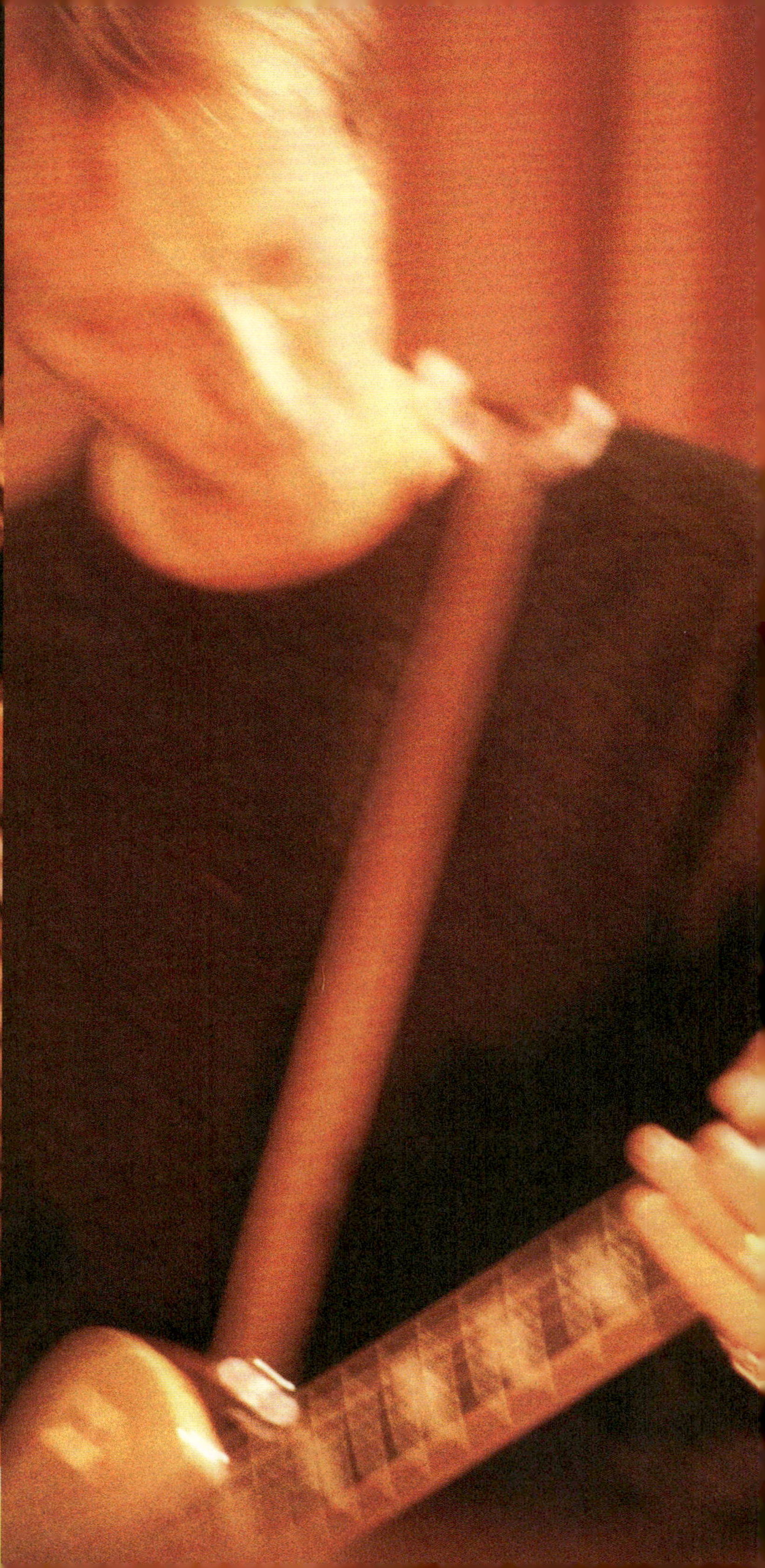

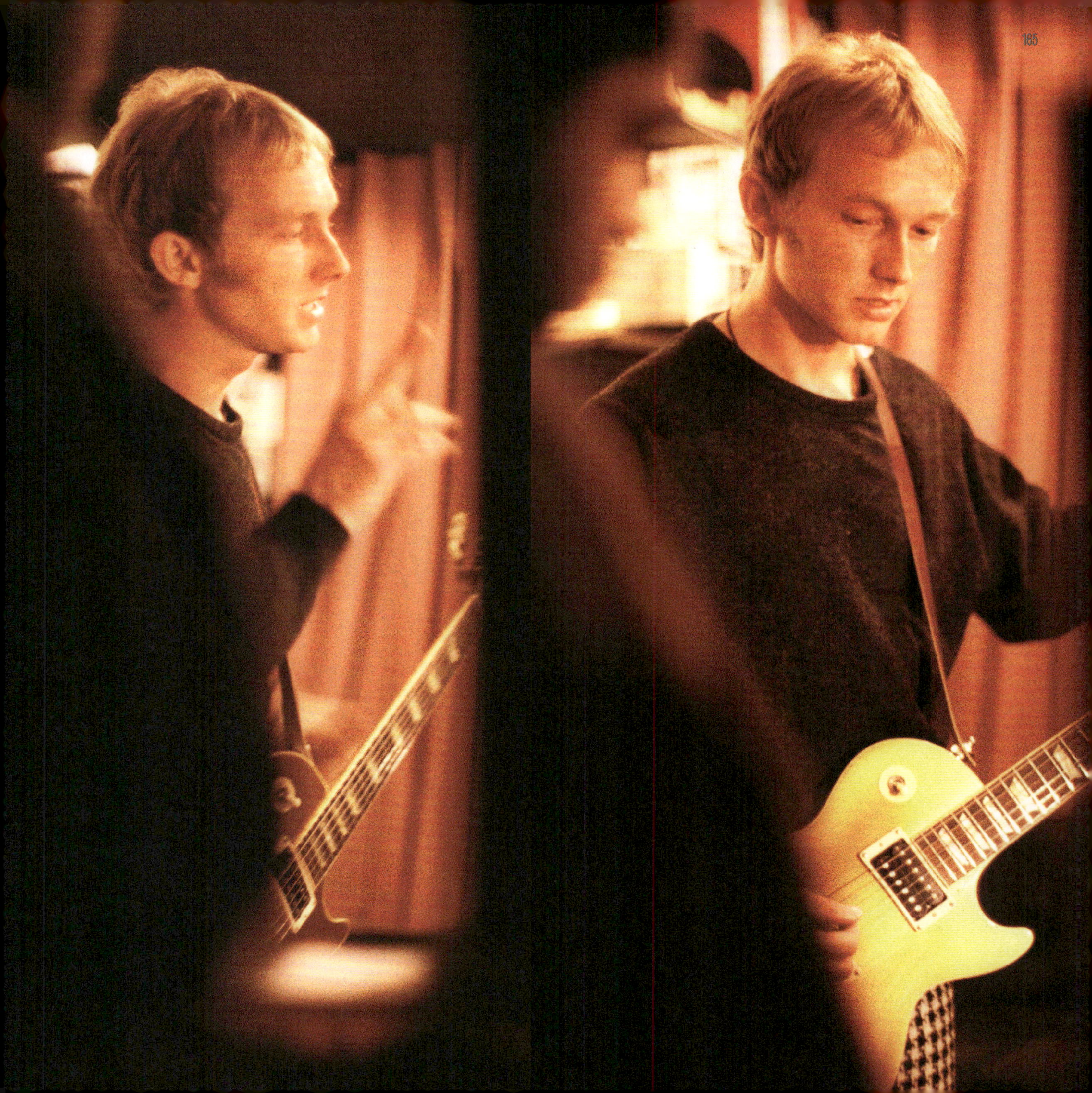

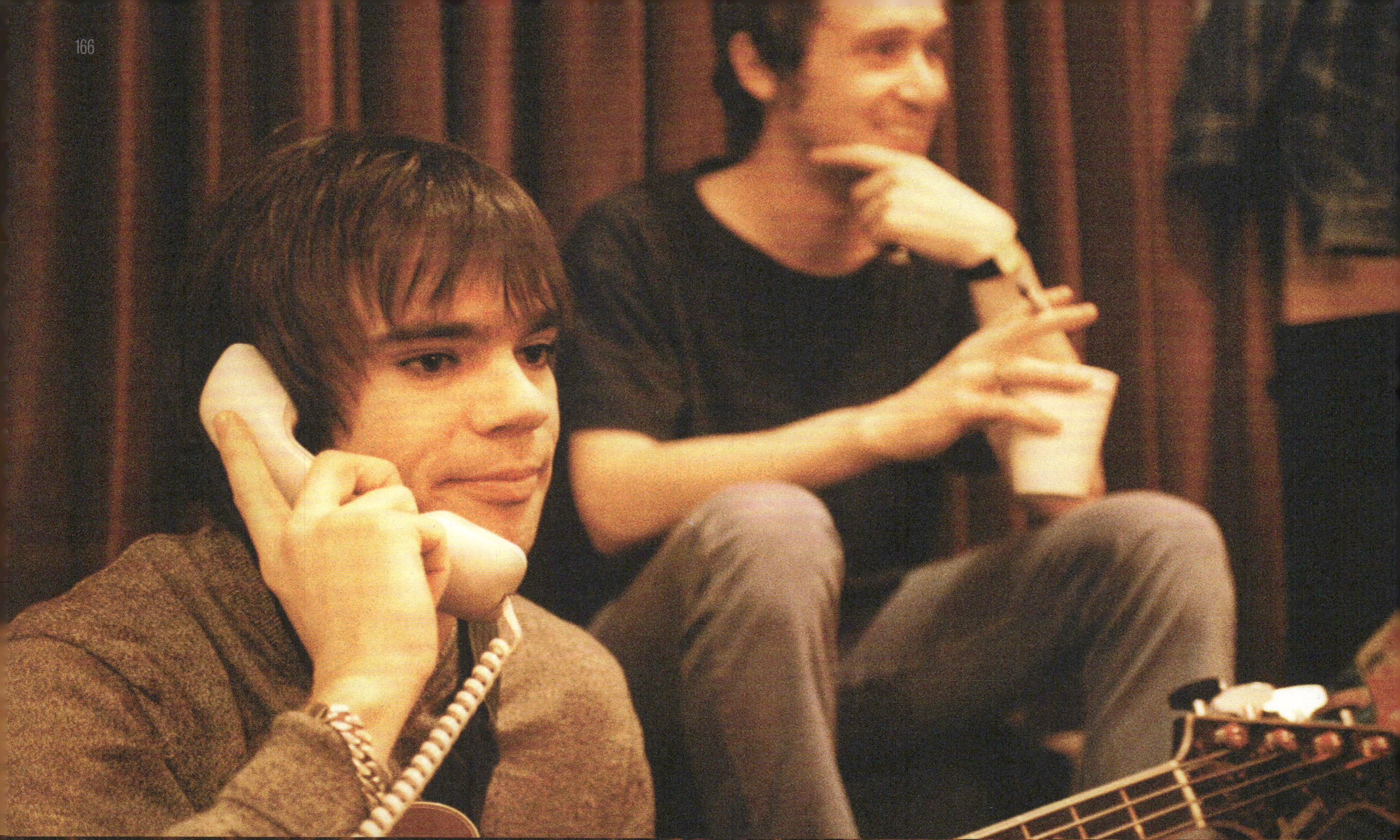

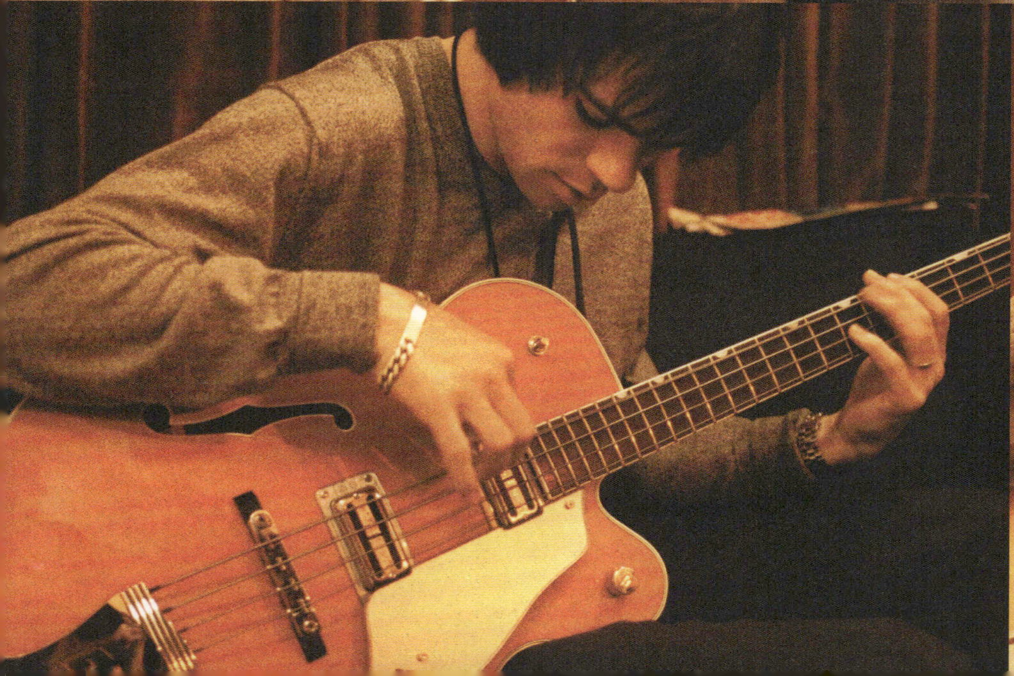

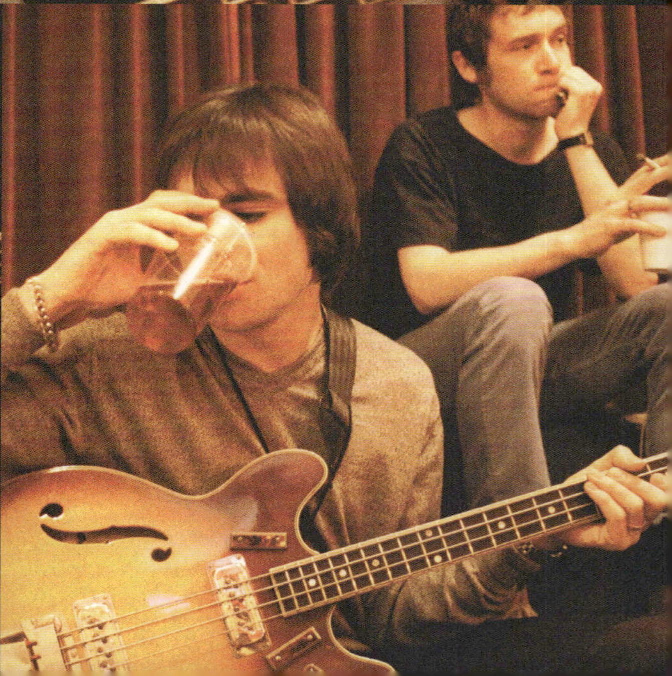

167

168

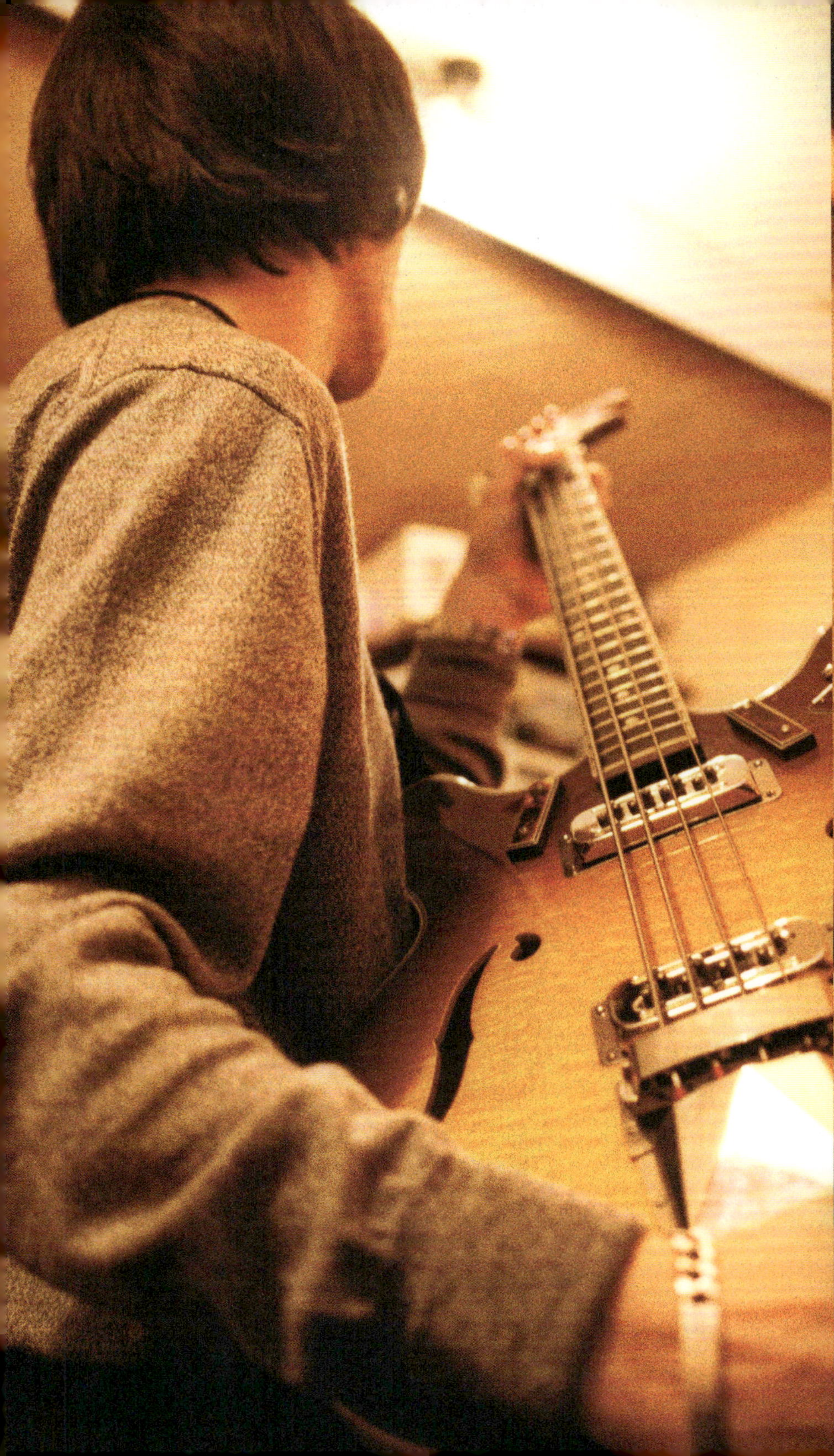

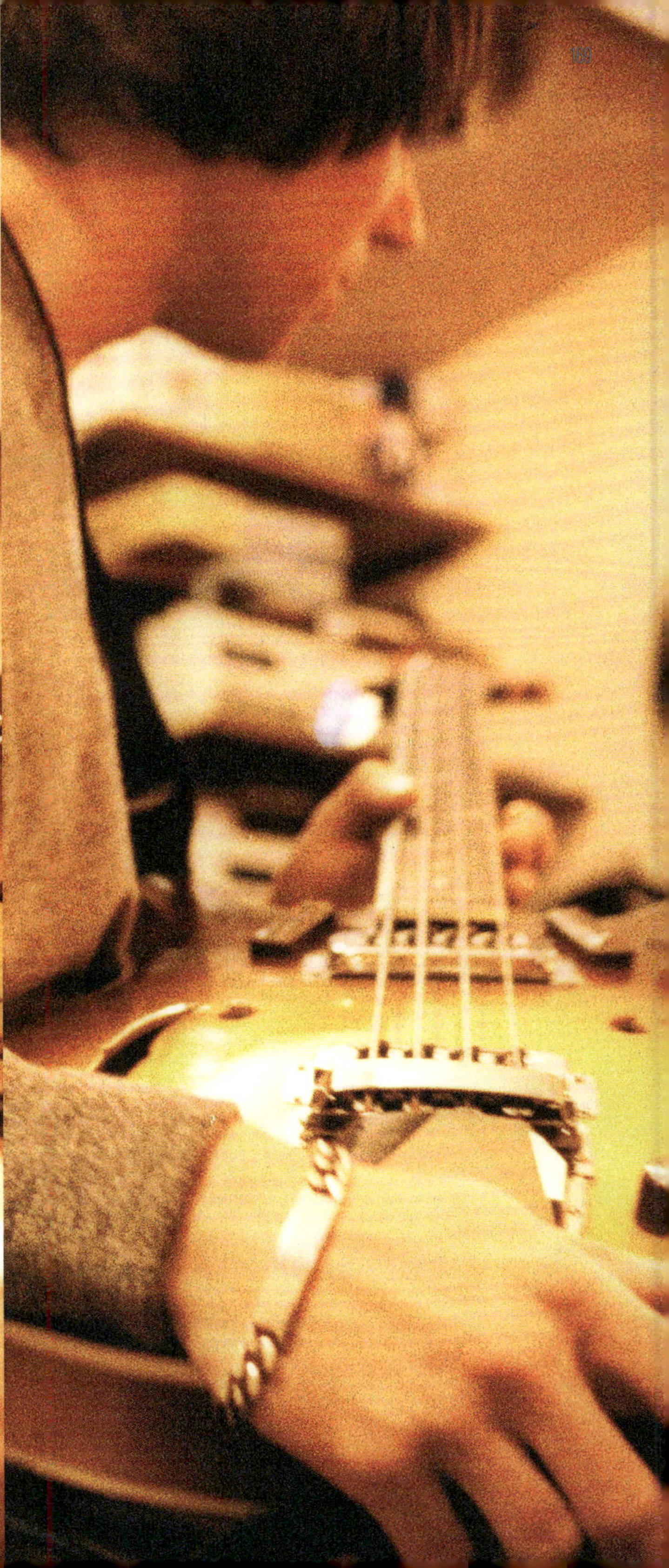

170

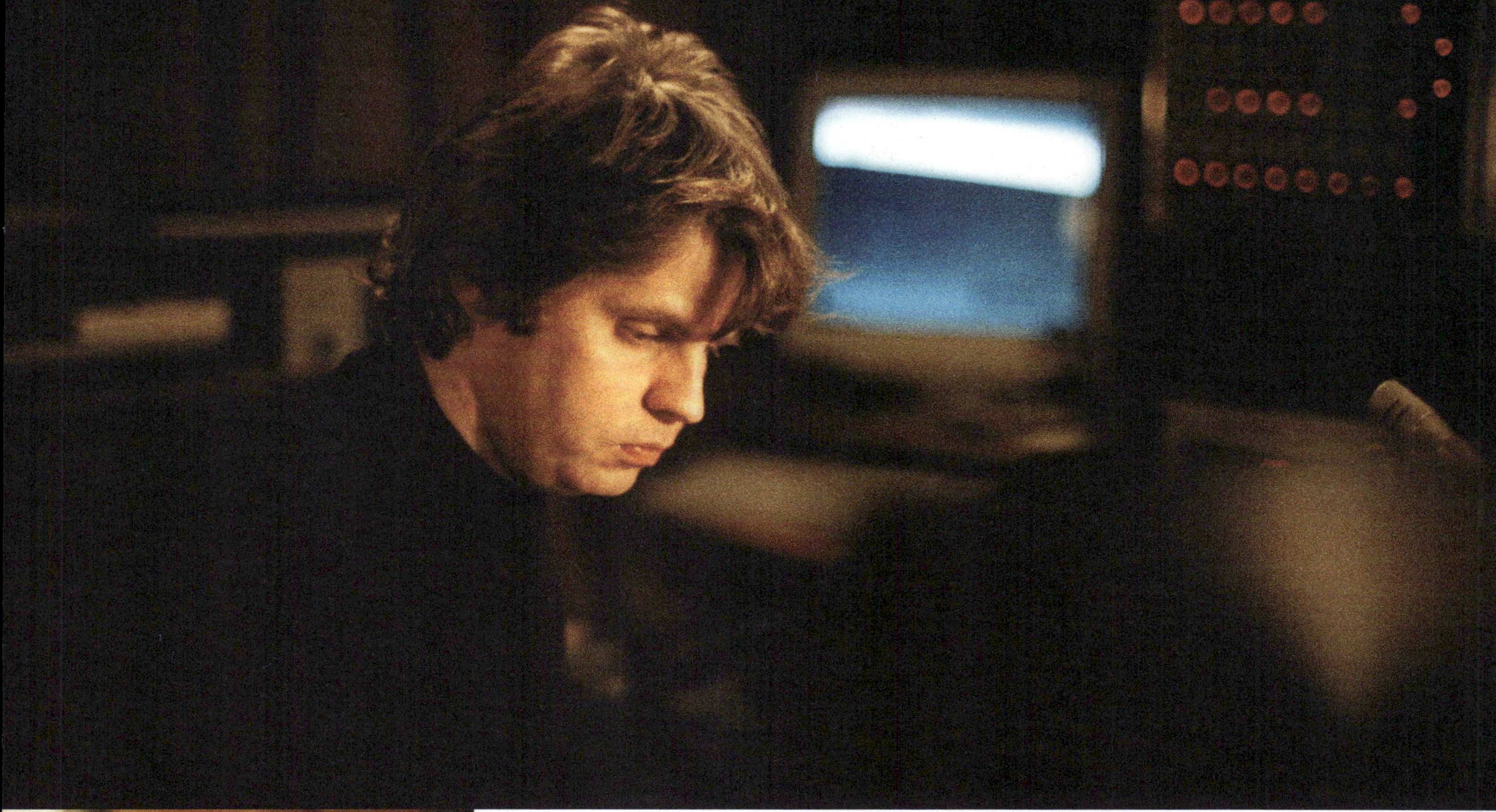

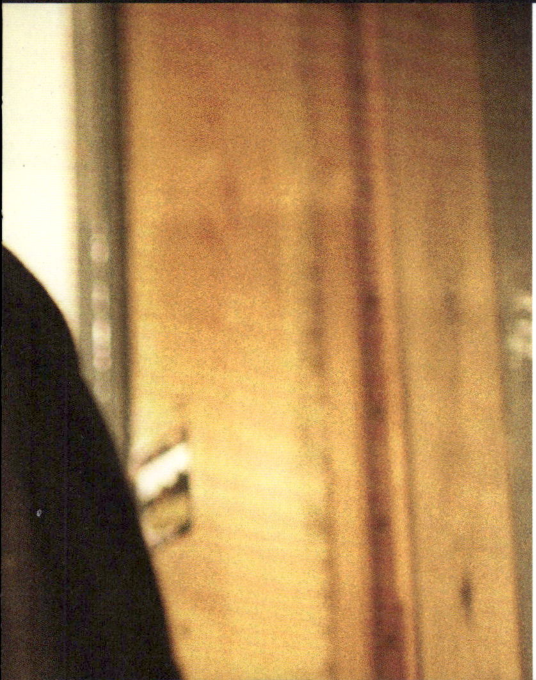

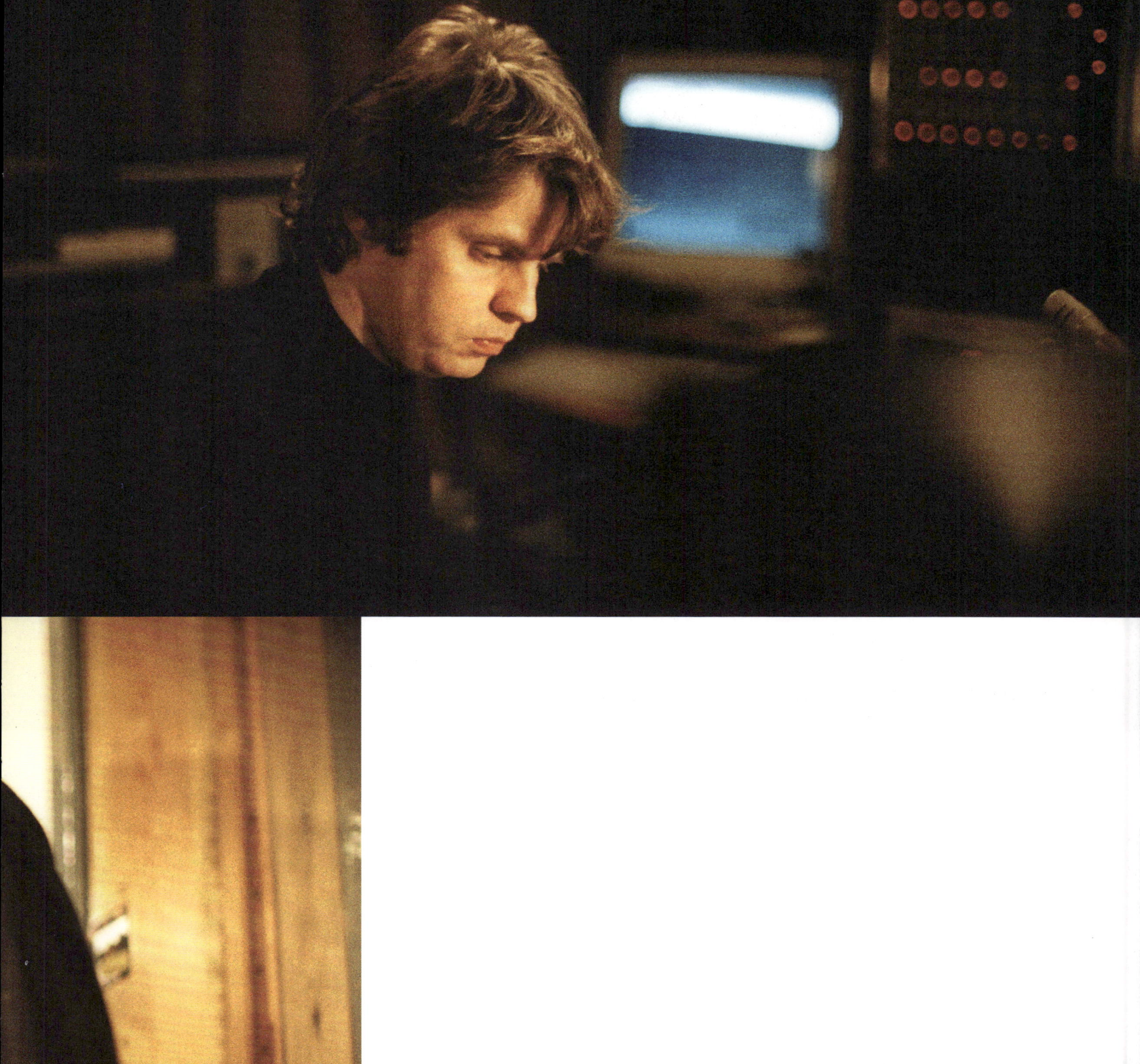

172

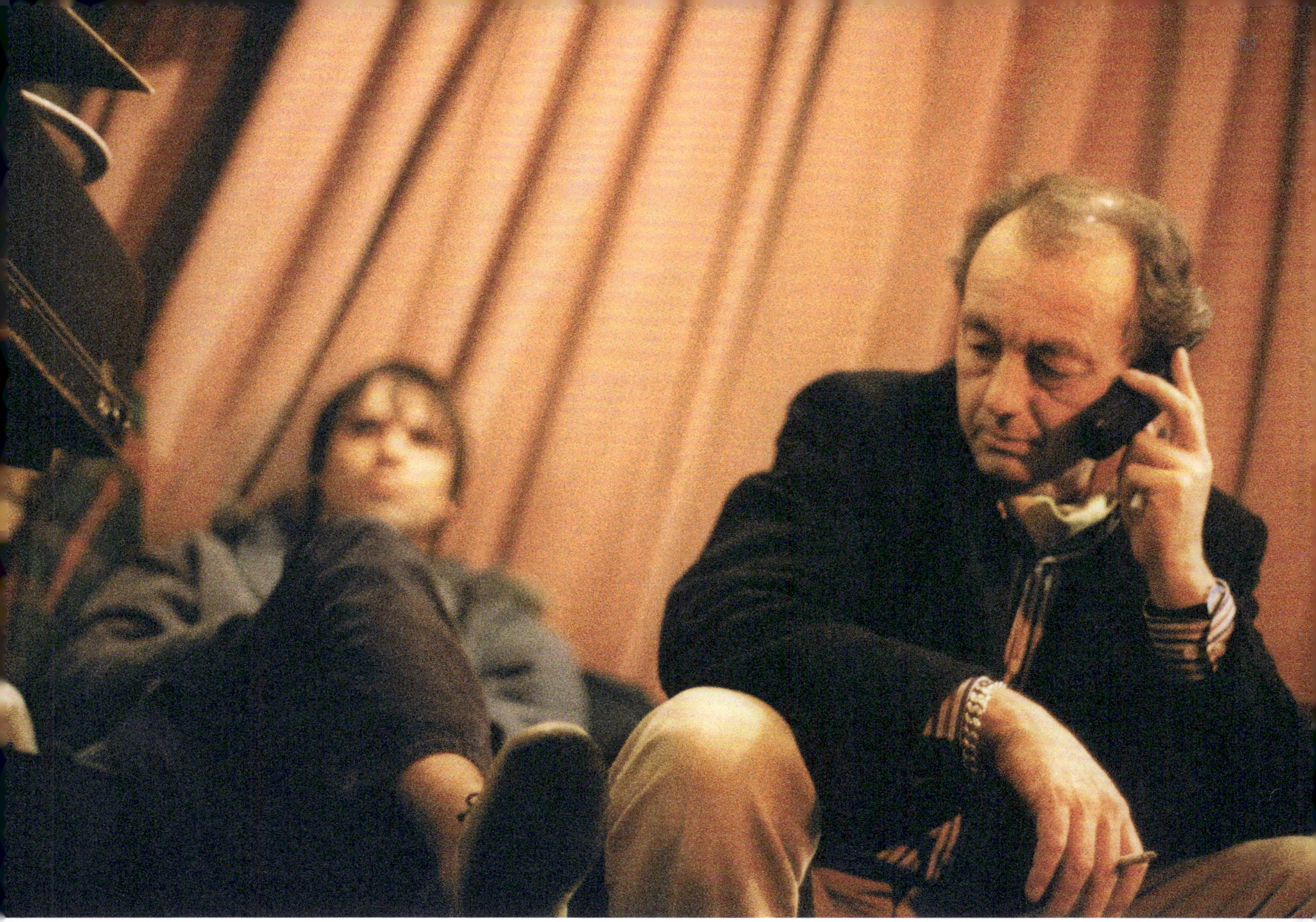

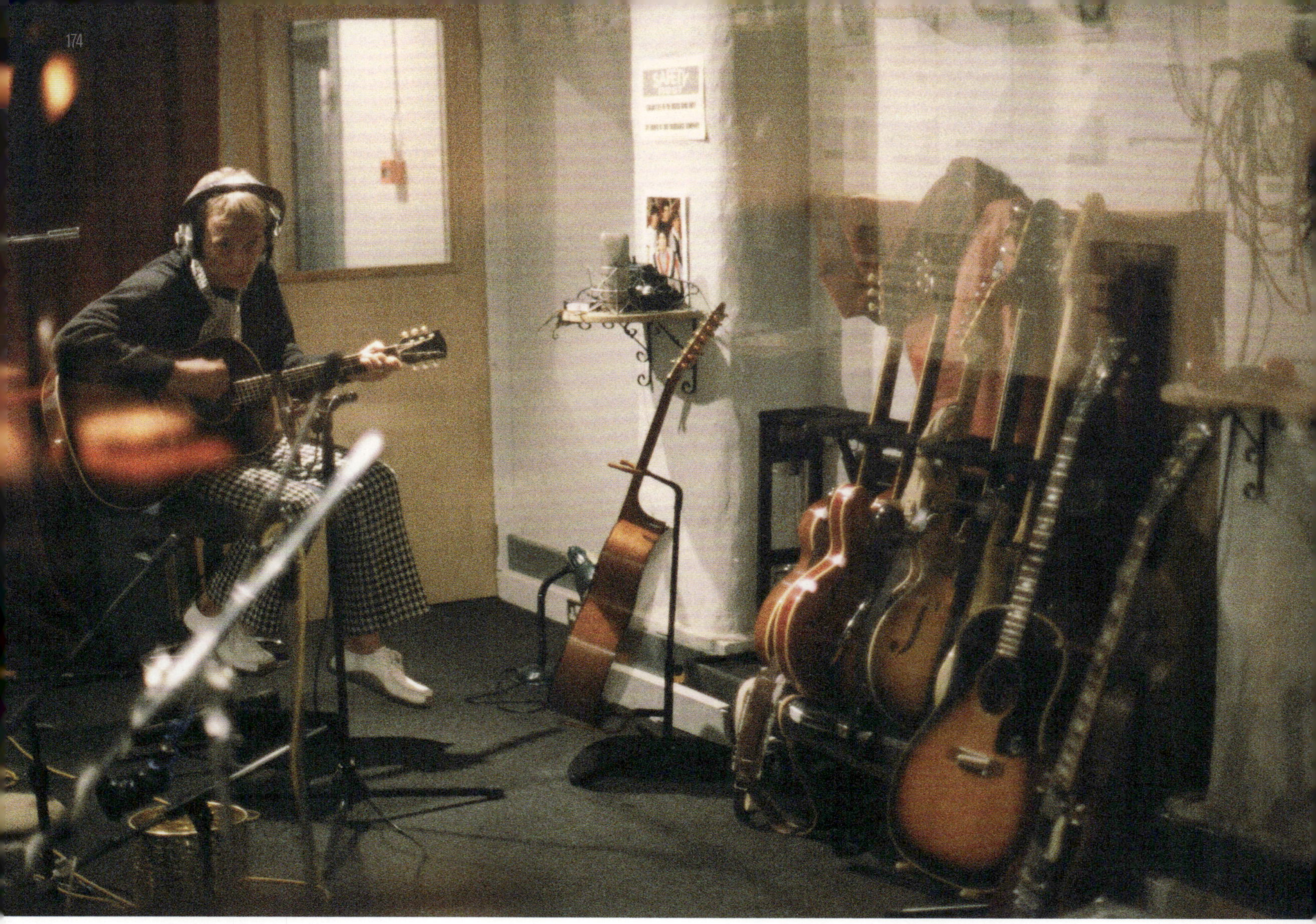

175

I REMEMBER PAUL CALLING ONCE ASKING IF HE COULD HAVE THE DAY WE CAUGHT THE TRAIN CANVAS WE HAD MADE FOR THE BACK OF A STAND UP PIANO FOR TOP OF THE POPS. THAT WAS NICE. **TONY BRIGGS**

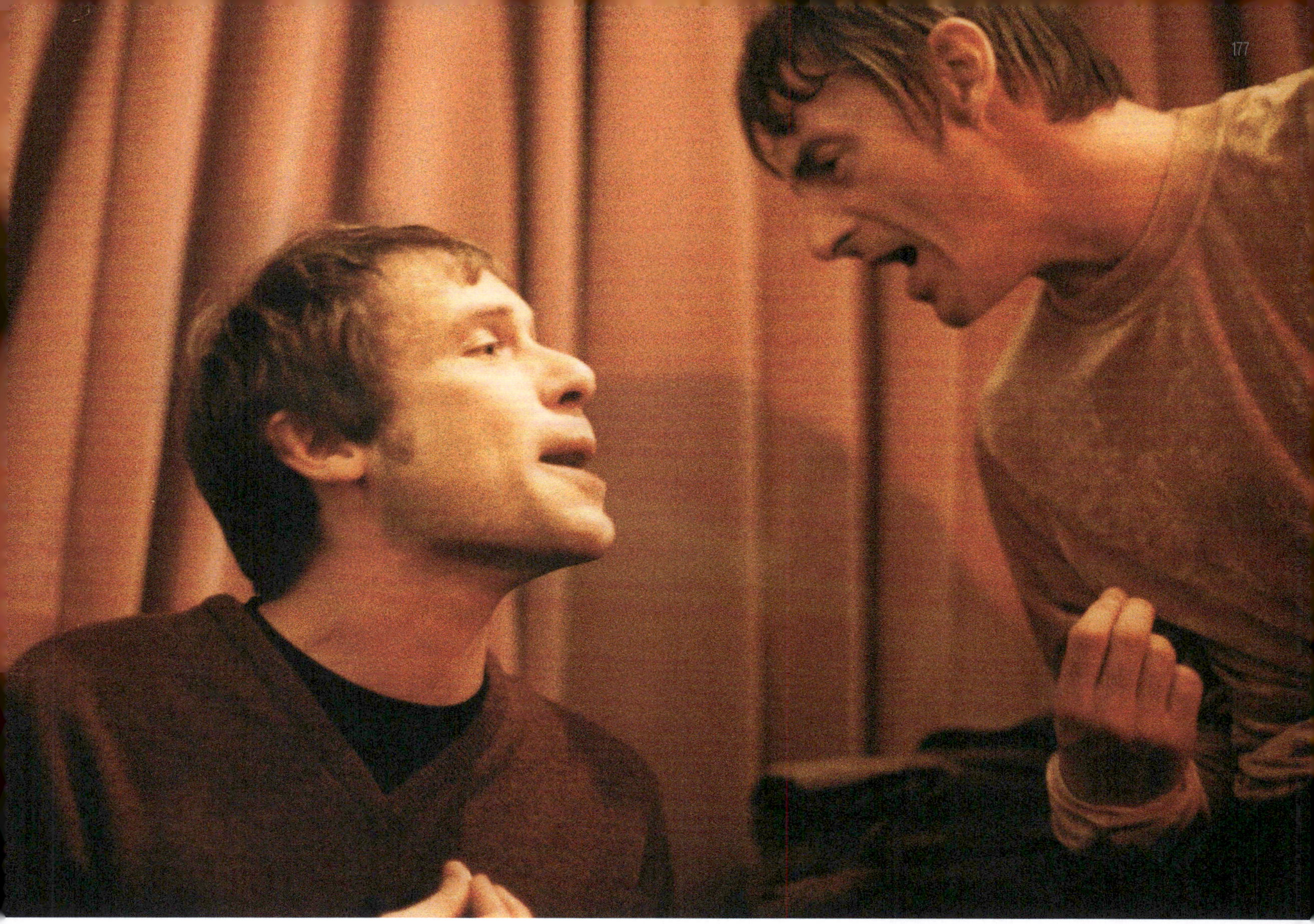

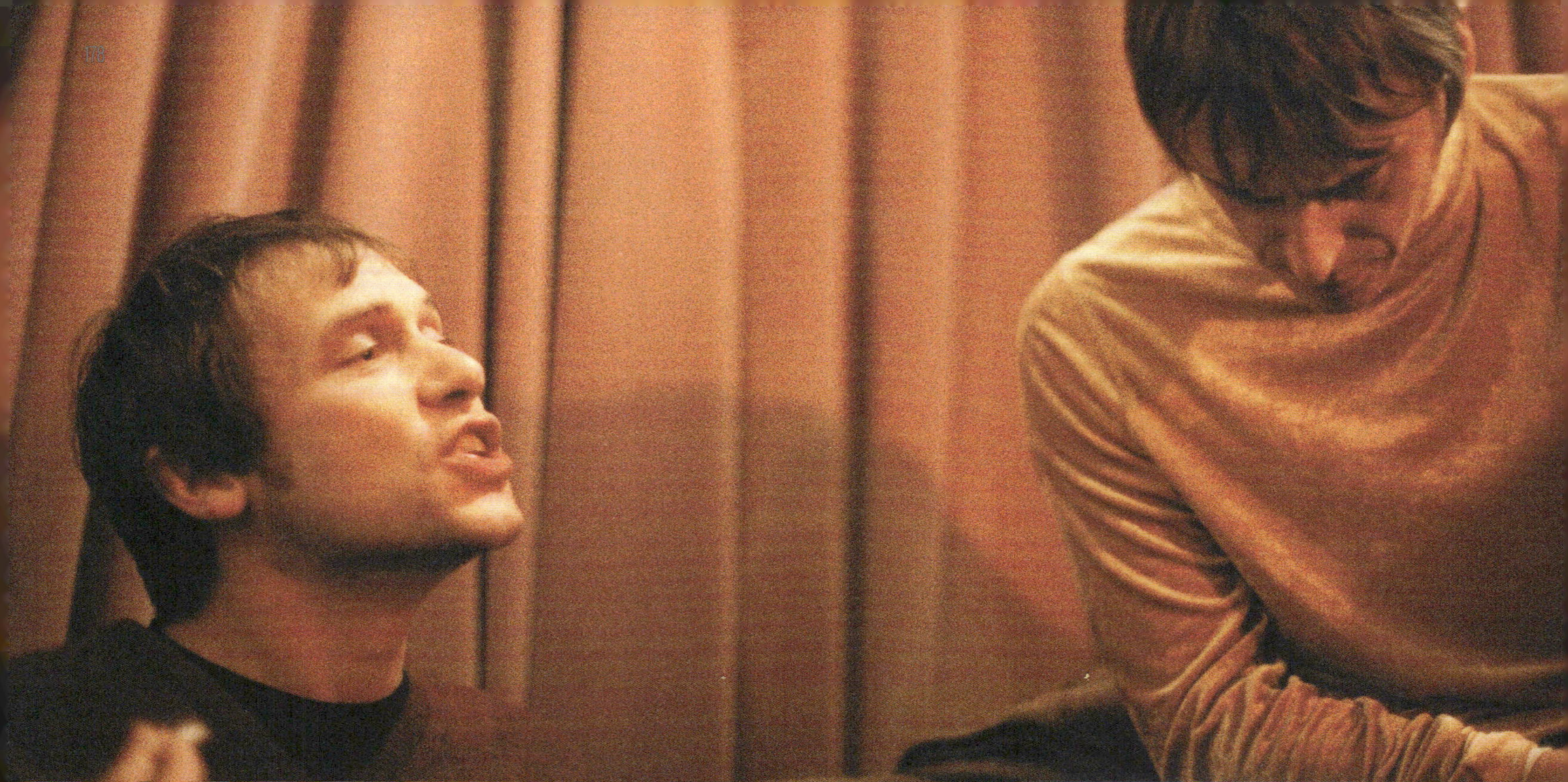

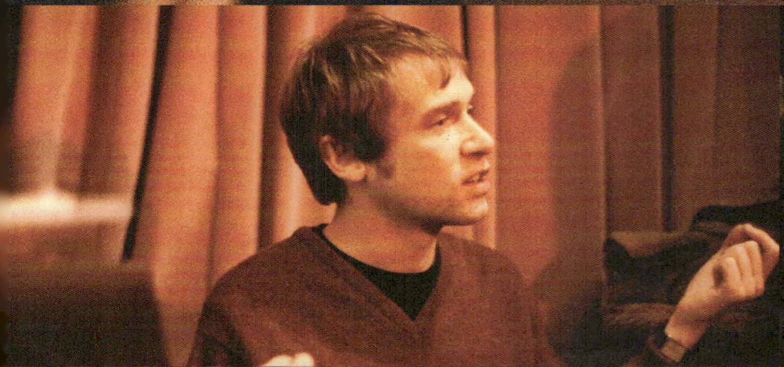

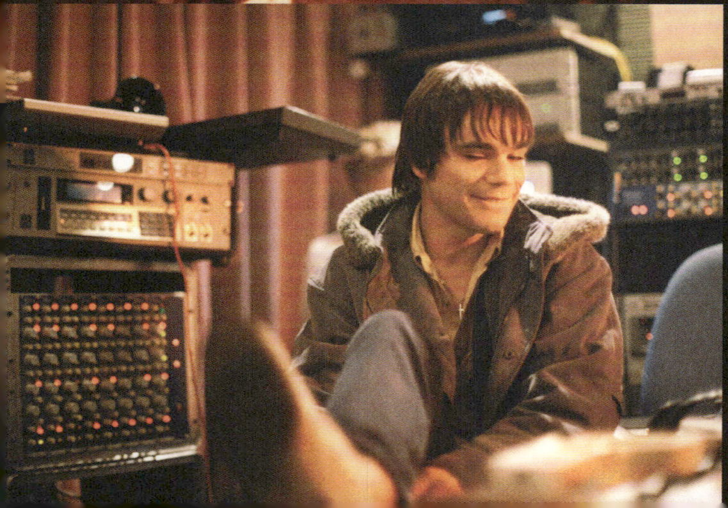

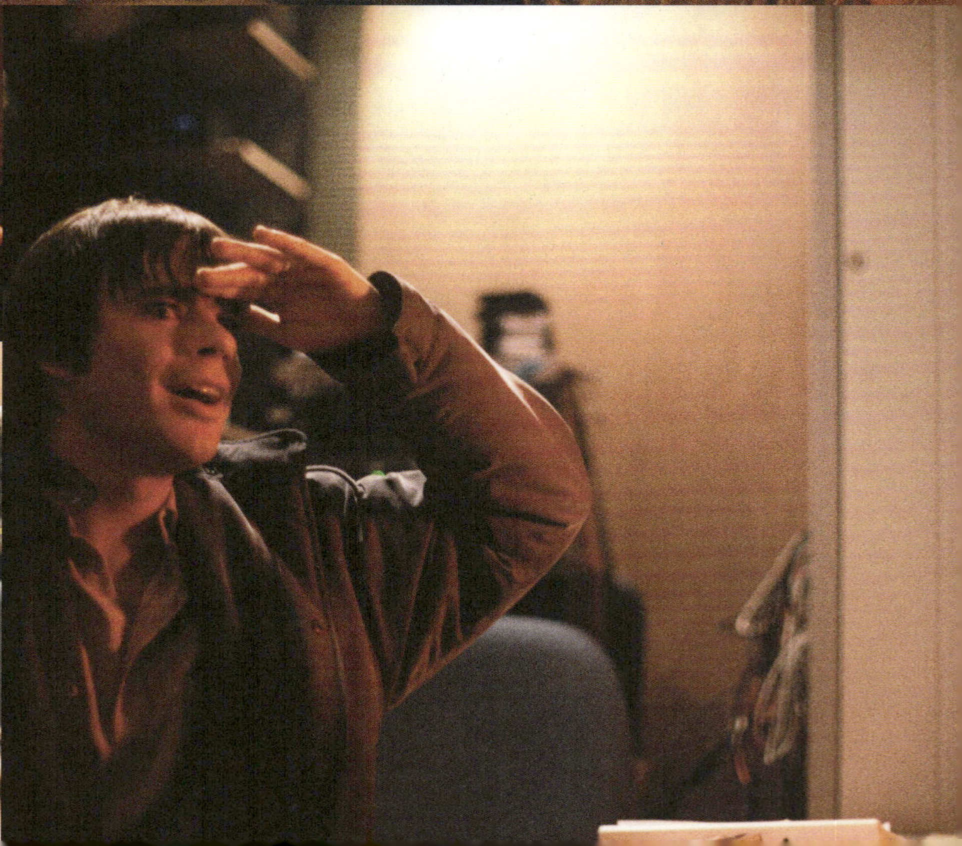

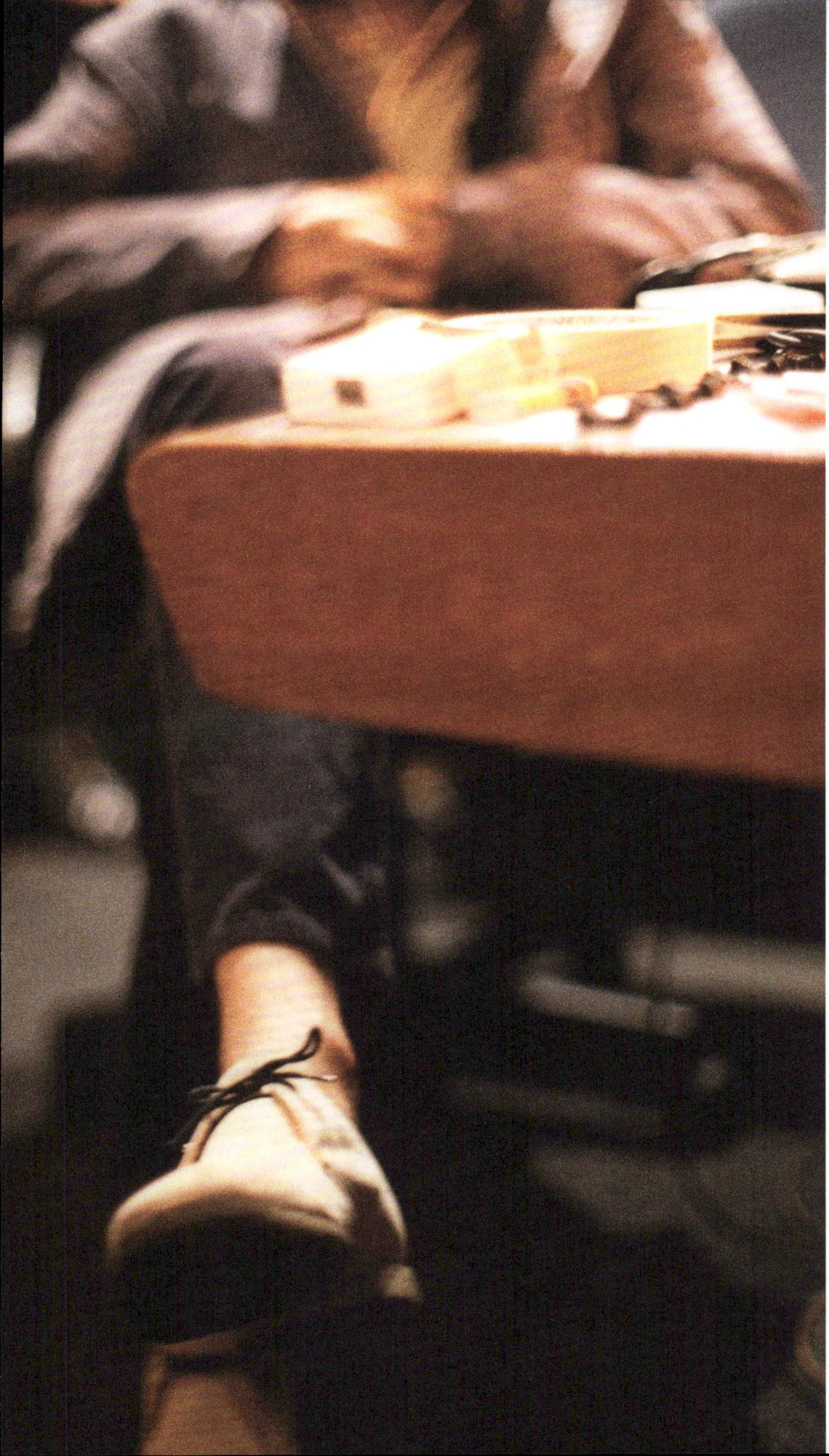

180

181

A LOT OF MY PICTURES OF THIS PERIOD ARE SELF PORTRAITS, THEY'RE HOW I SEE MYSELF. **TONY BRIGGS**

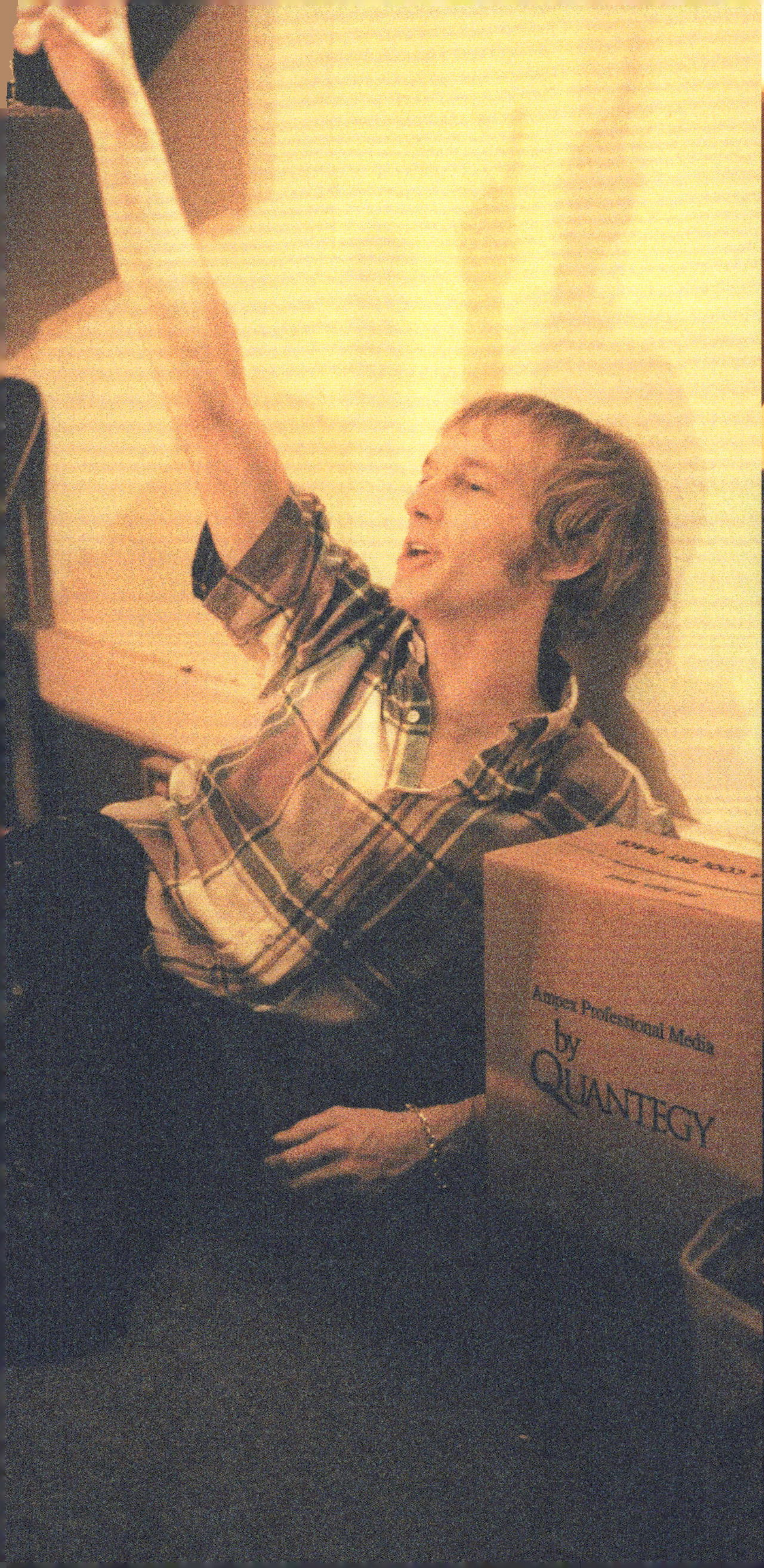
Ampex Professional Media
by
QUANTEGY

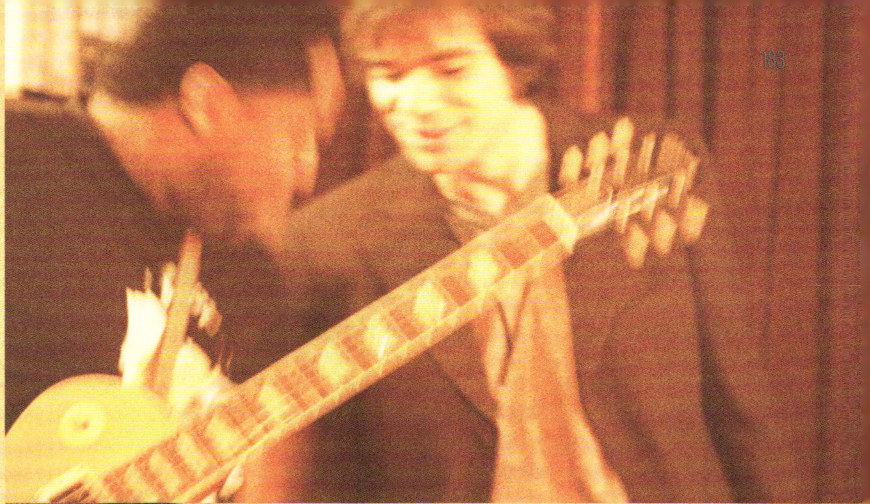

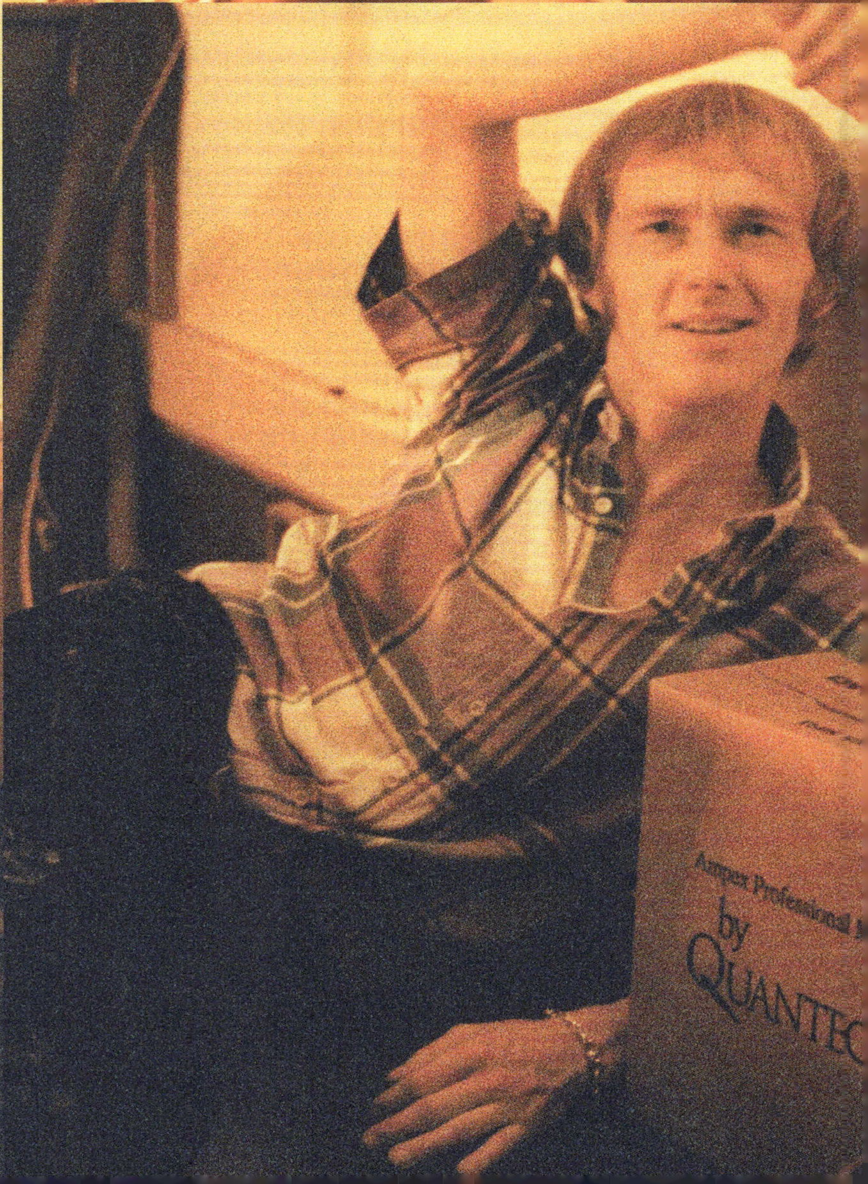
by
QUANTEG

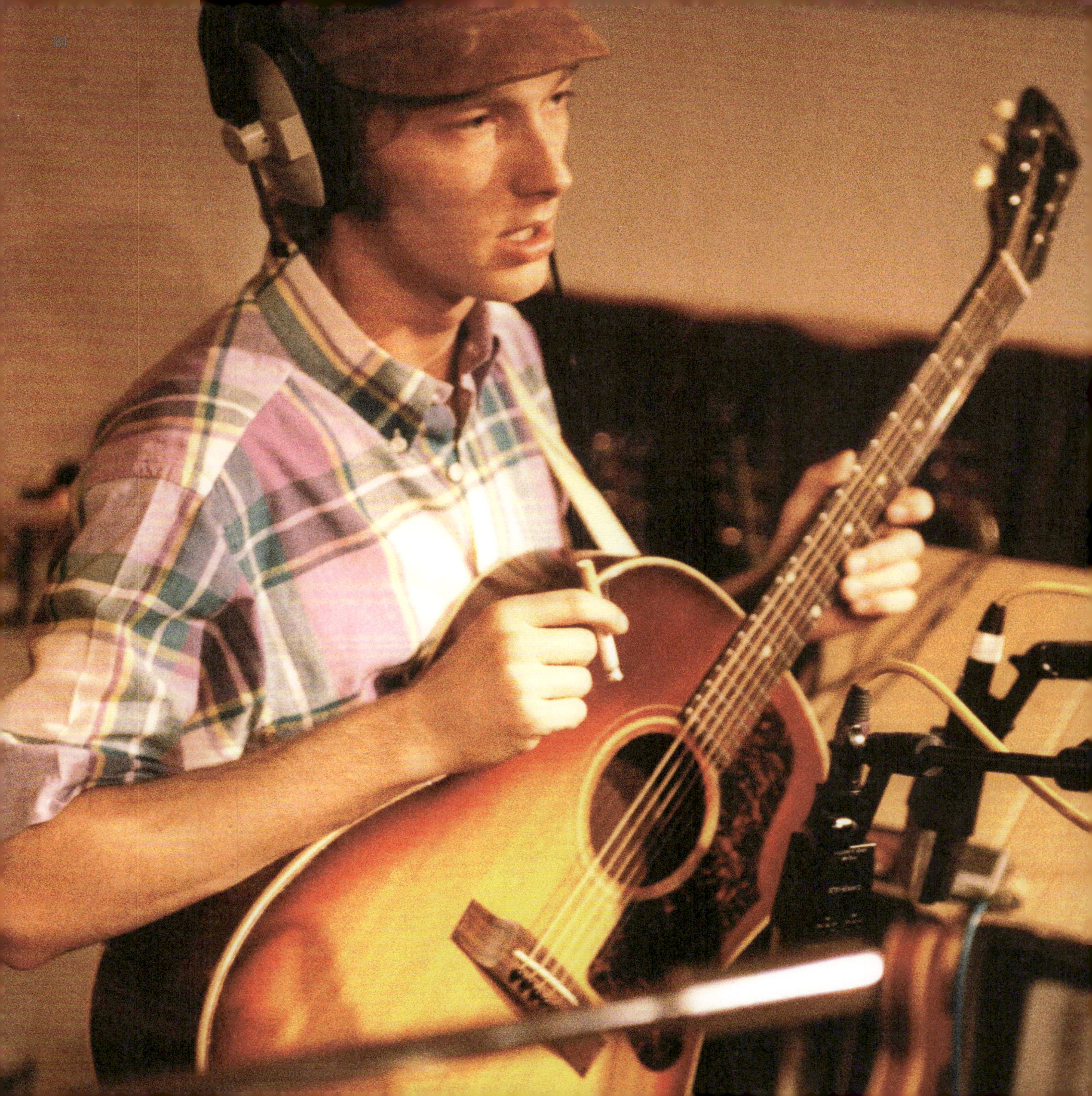

185

186

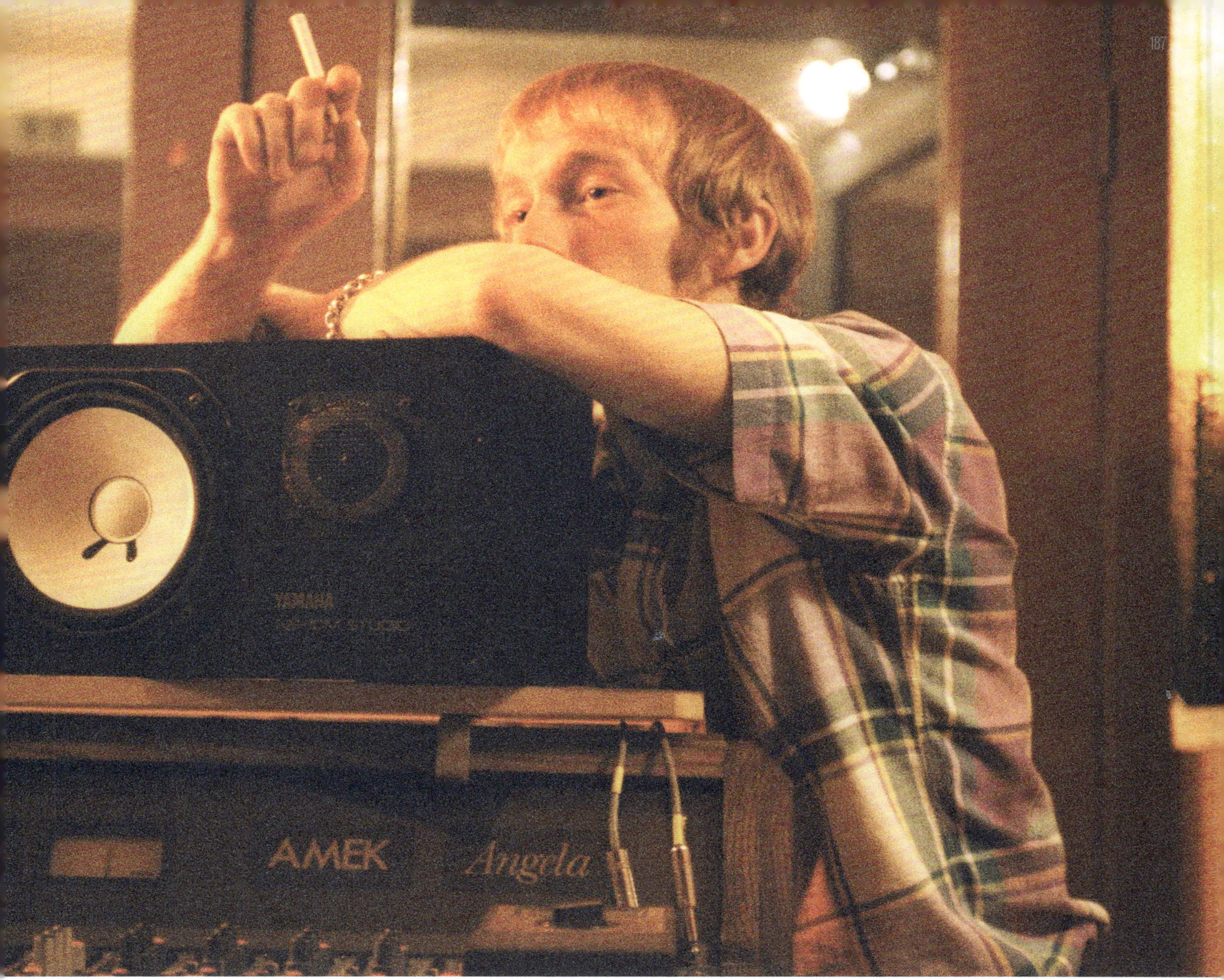
AMEK
Angela

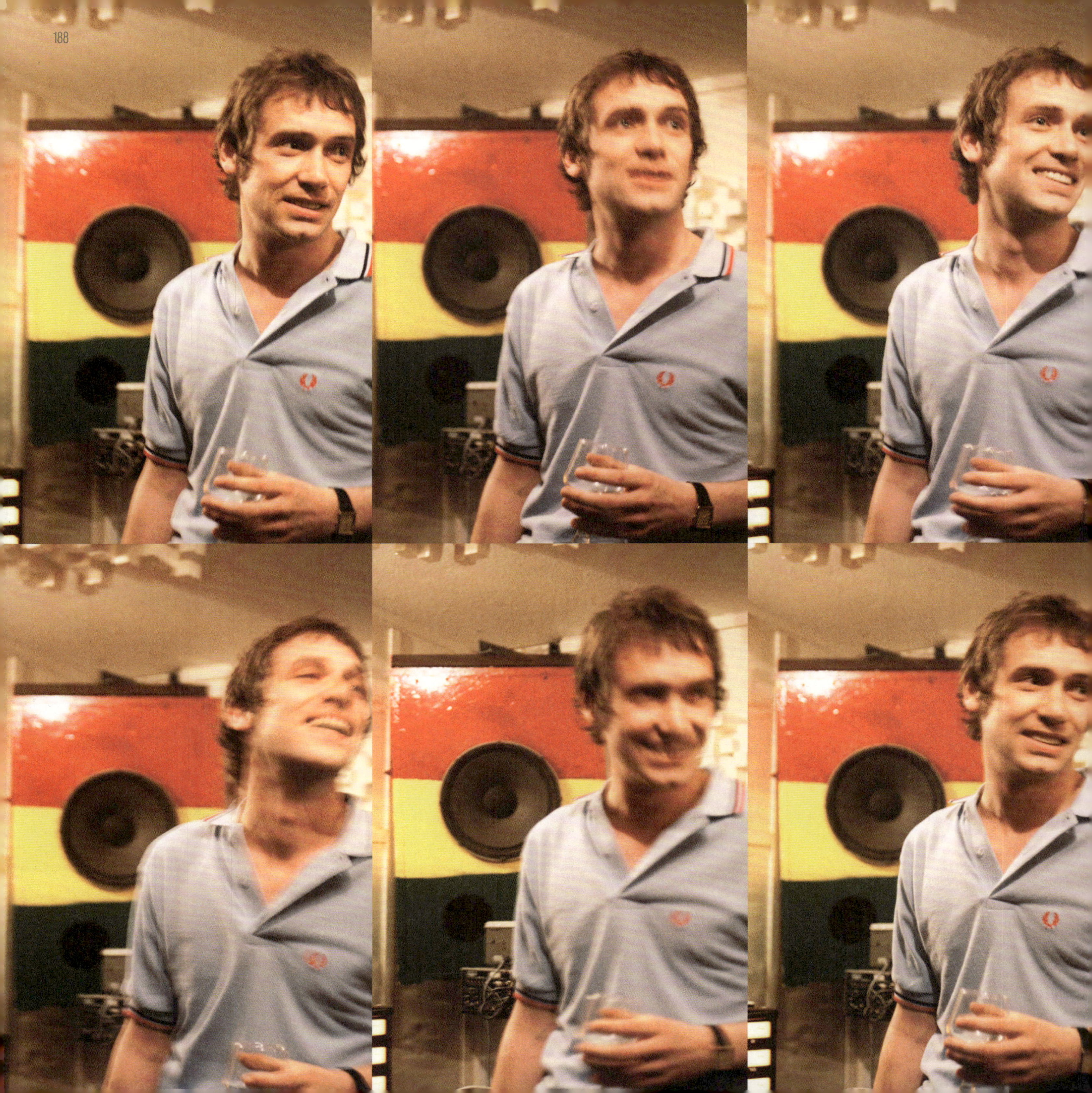

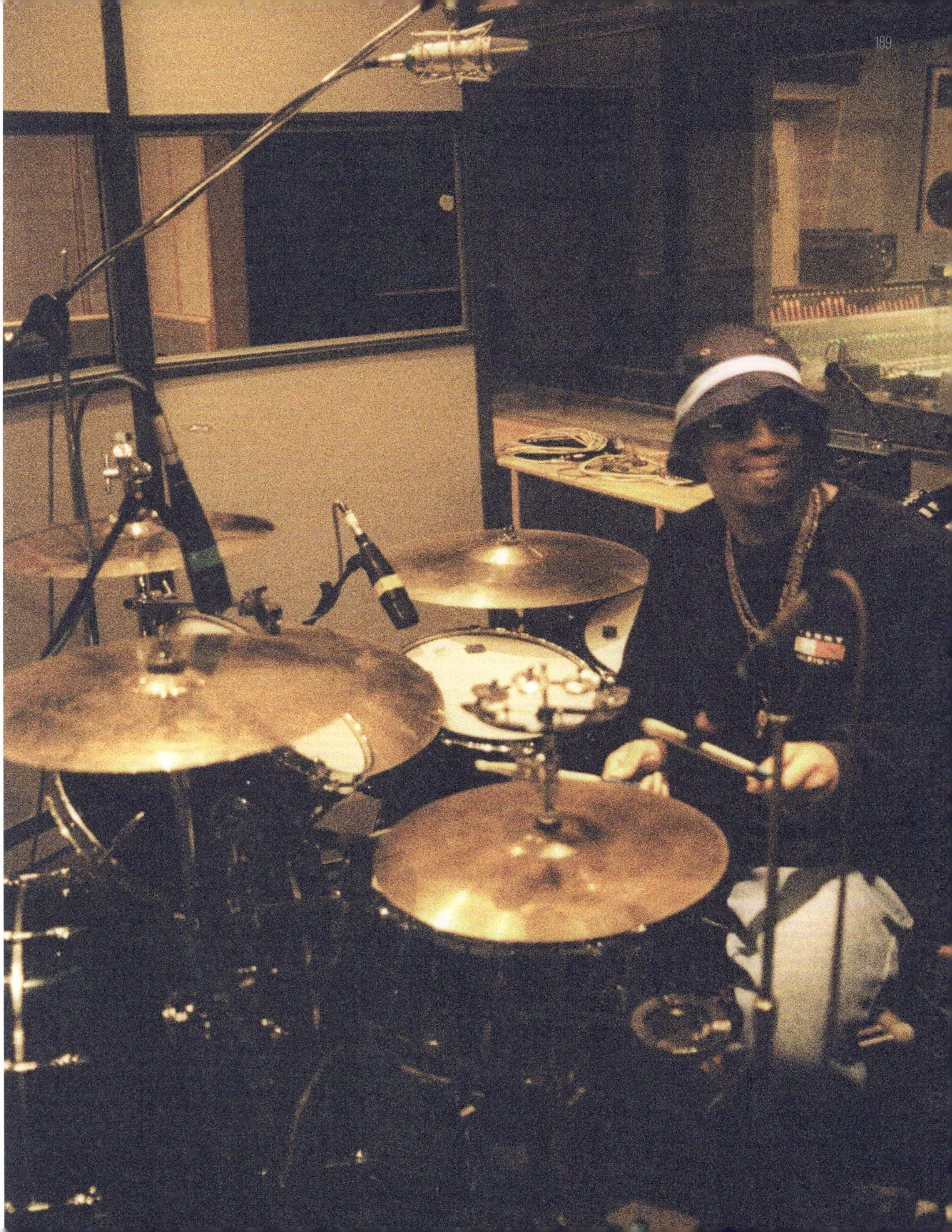

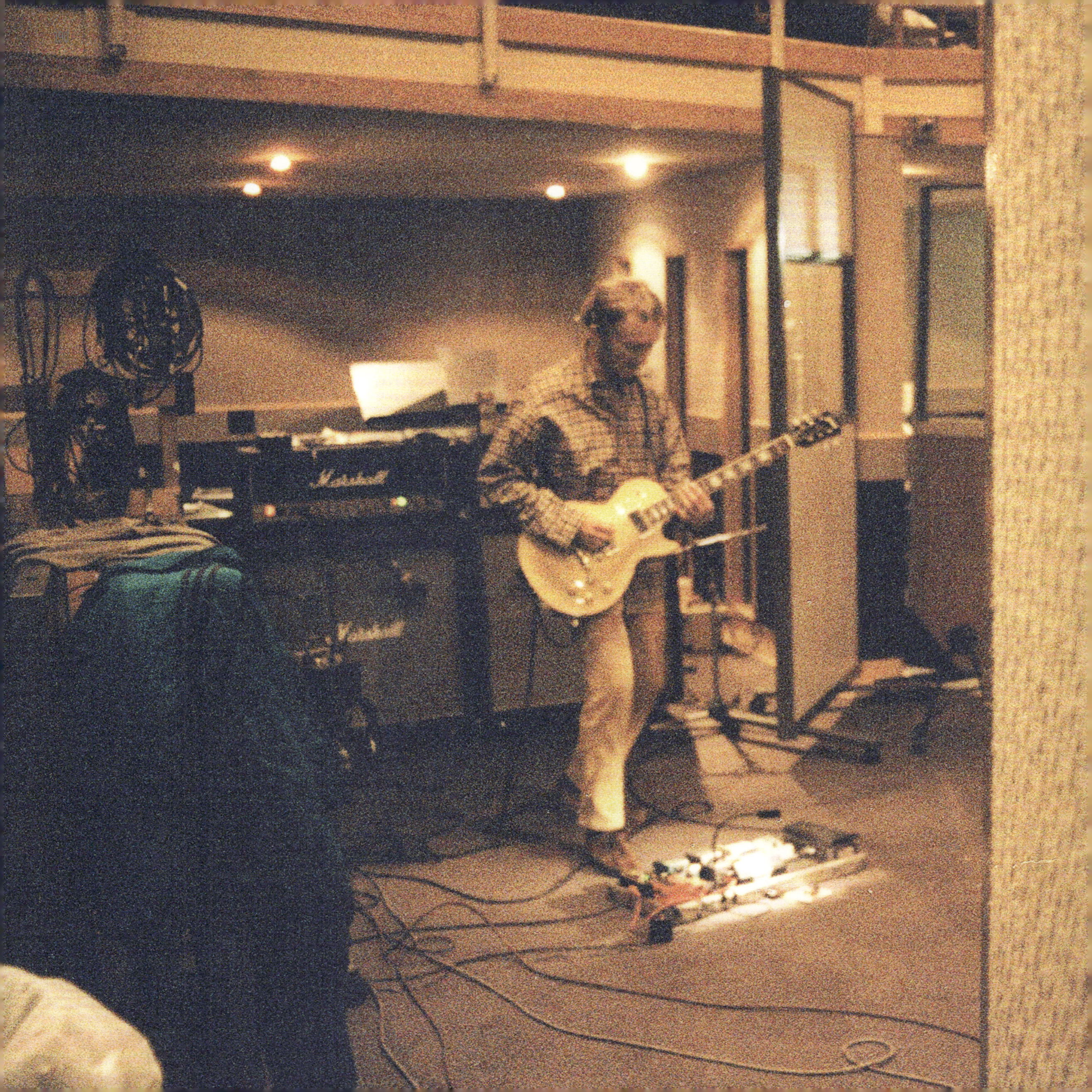
Marshall
Marshall

191

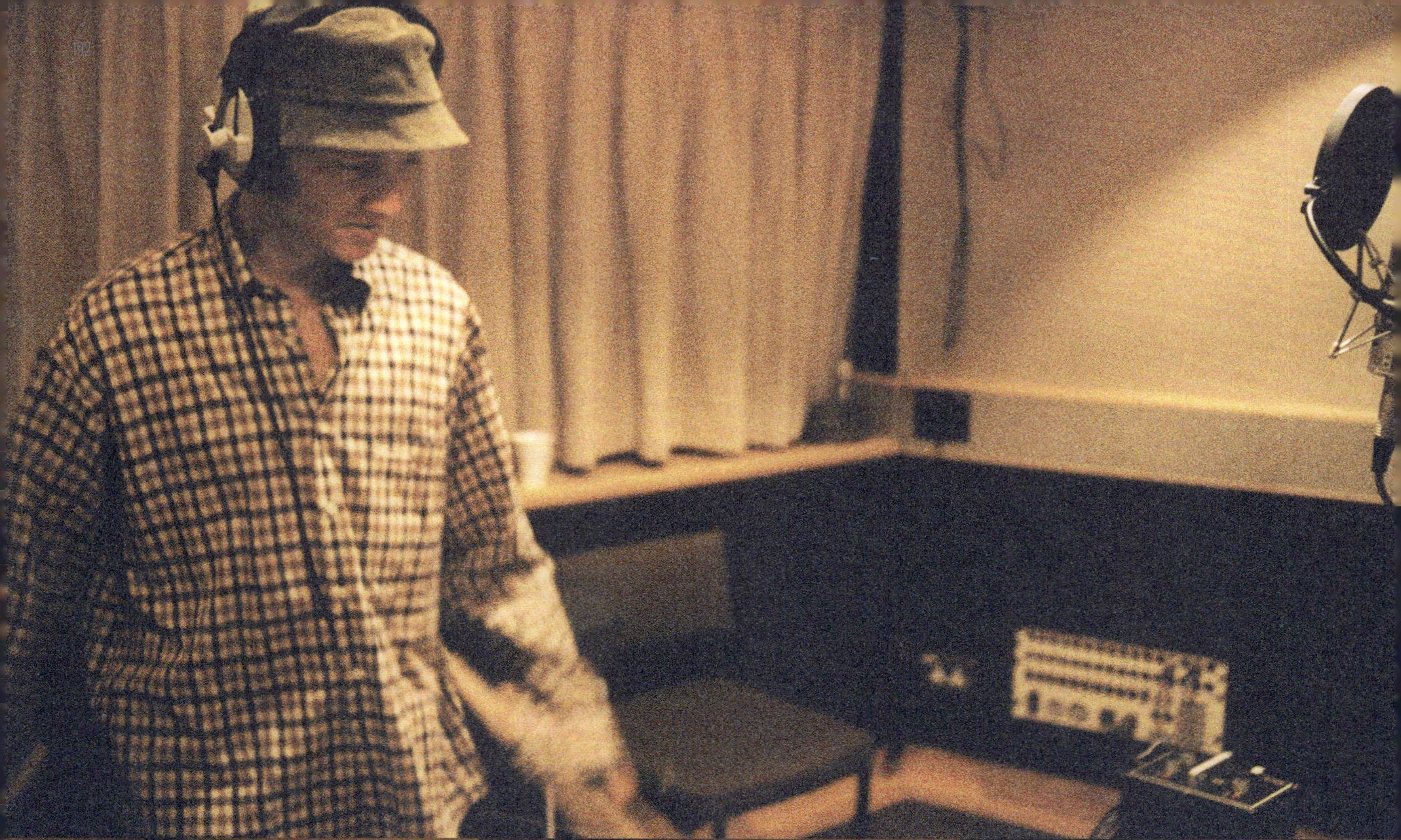

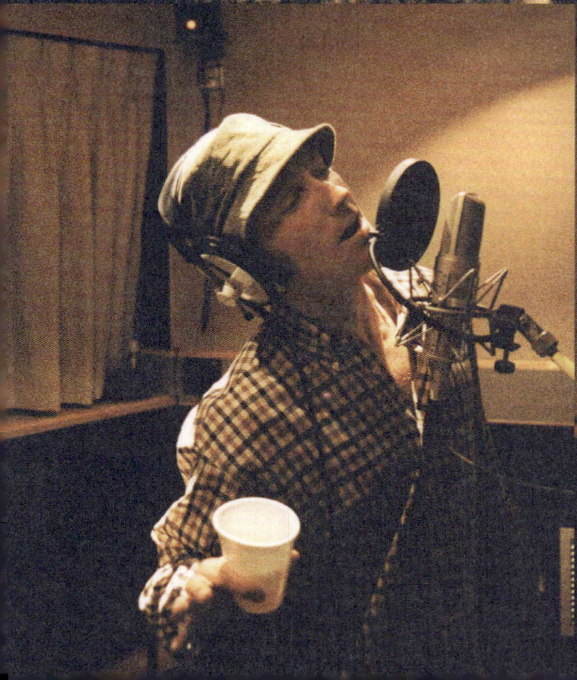

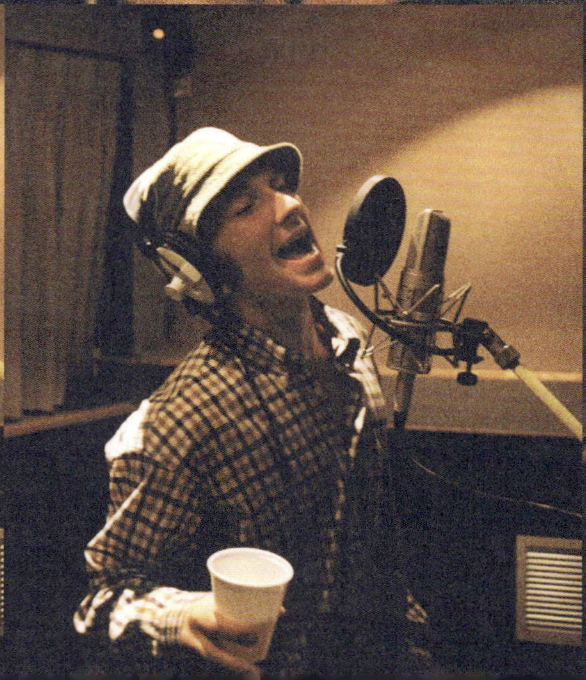

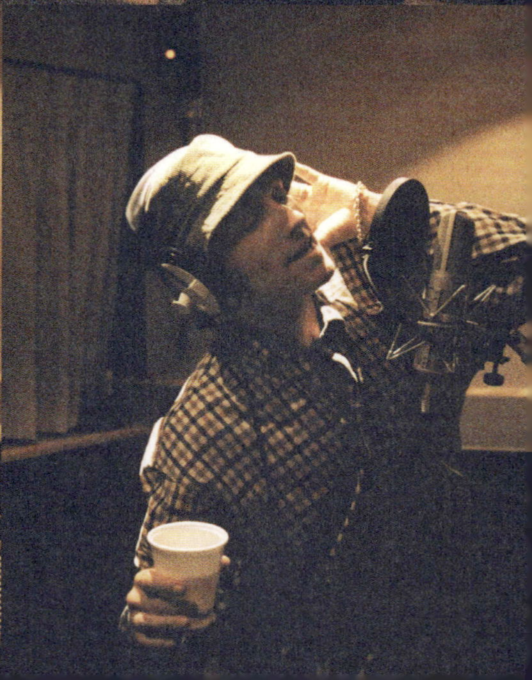

193

BBC MAIDA VALE STUDIOS (BEFORE THE SMOKING BAN...).

195

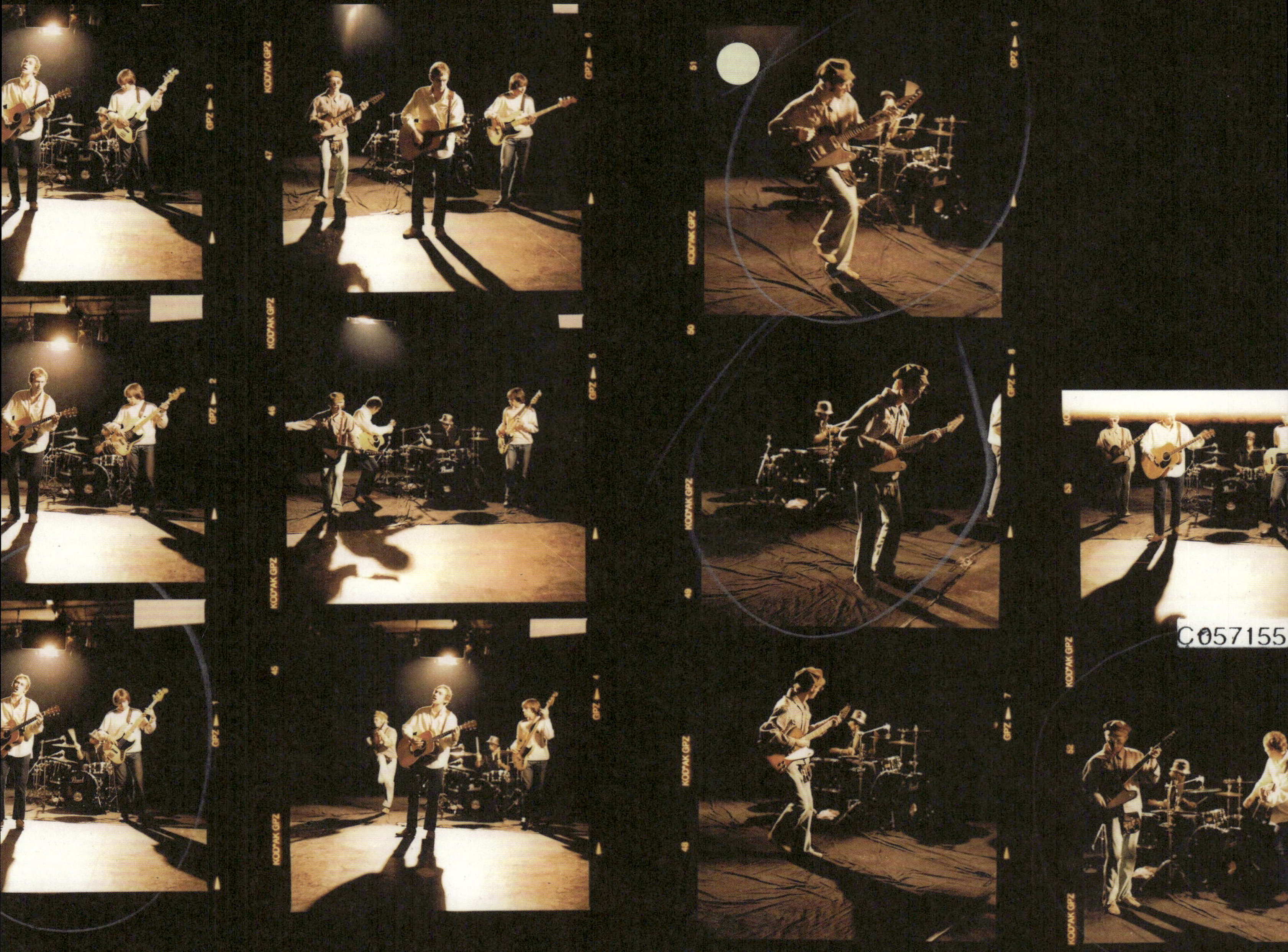
KODAK GPZ
C057155

TRAVELLERS TUNE, GALWAY, IRELAND.

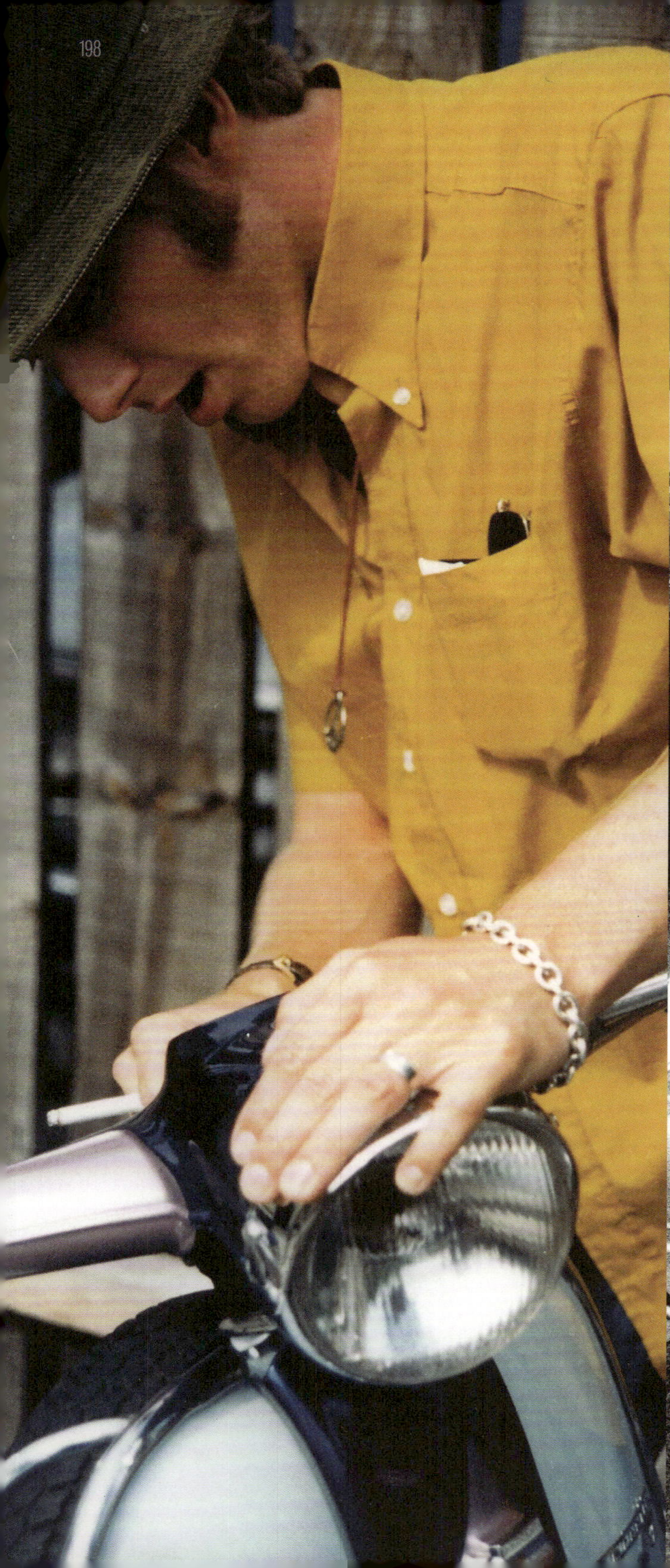

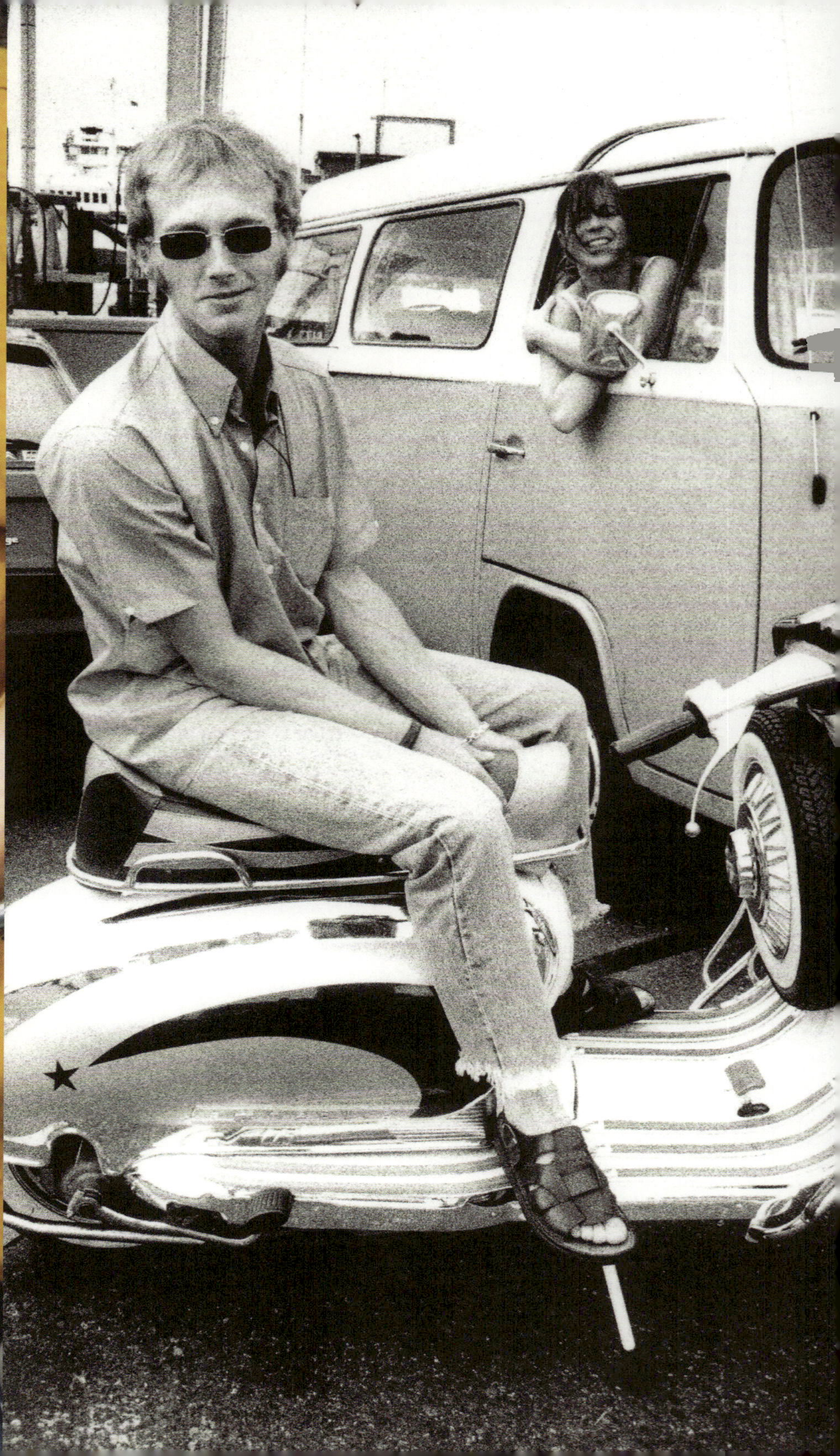

199

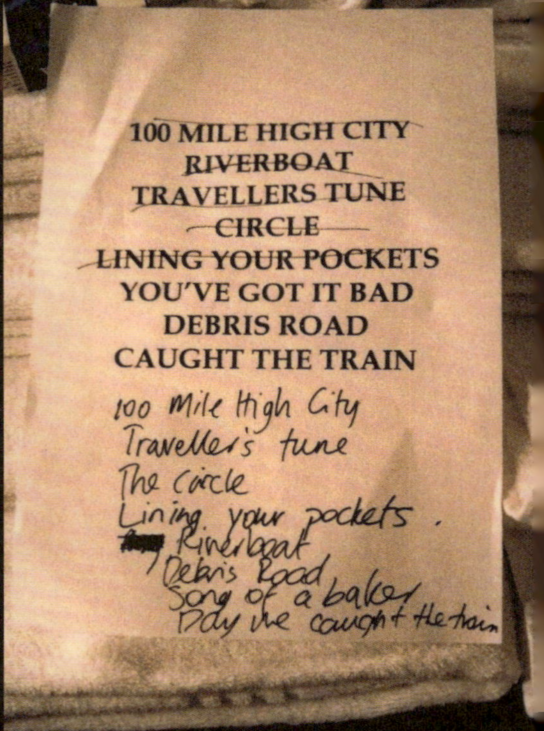
100 MILE HIGH CITY
RIVERBOAT
TRAVELLERS TUNE
CIRCLE
LINING YOUR POCKETS
YOU'VE GOT IT BAD
DEBRIS ROAD
CAUGHT THE TRAIN
100 Mile High City
Traveller's tune
The circle
Lining your pockets.
Riverboat
Debris Road
Song of a baker
Day we caught the train

oasis

BEST SECURITY TEAM IN EUROPE.

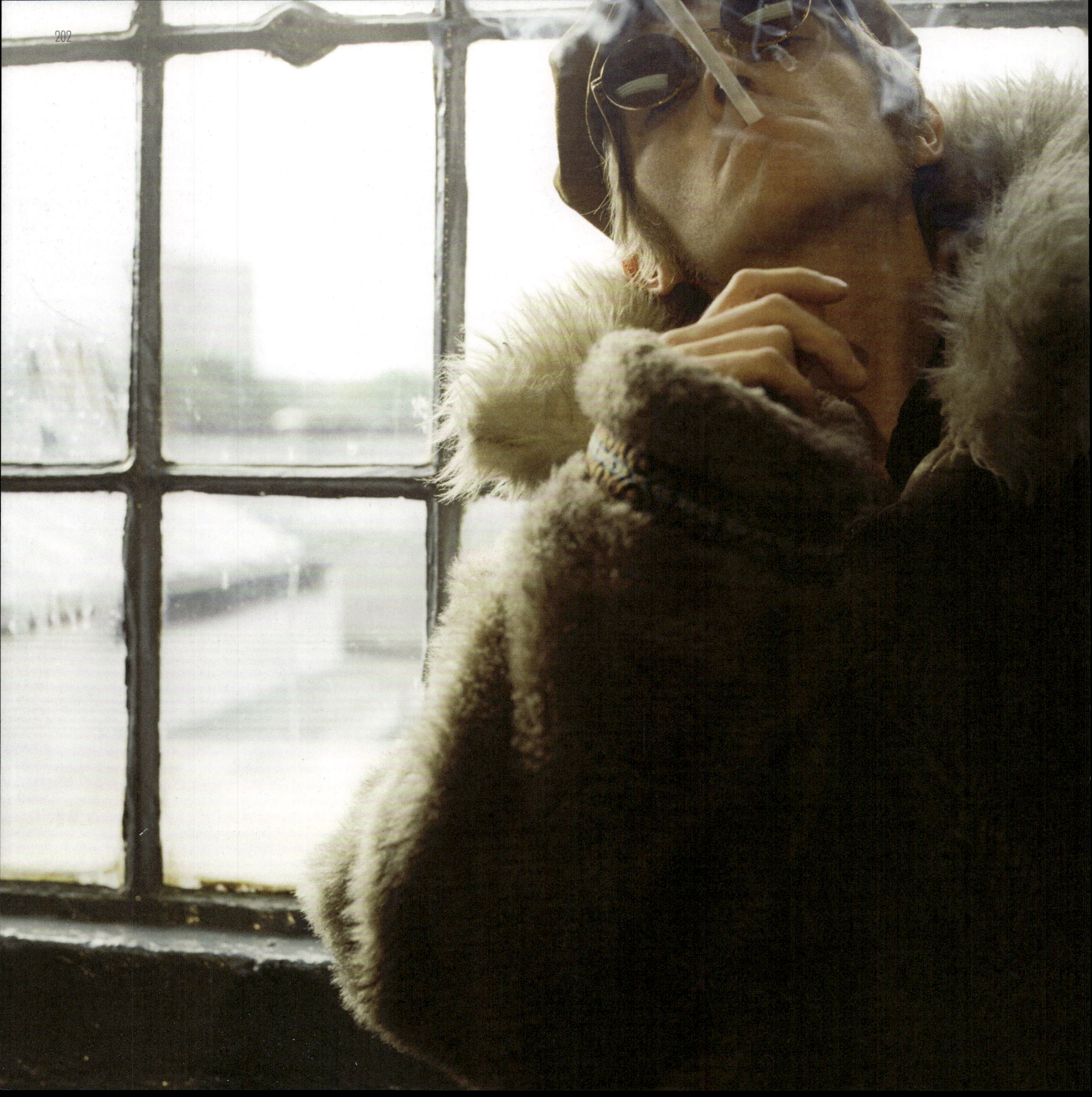

203

TO BE AT THE RECORDING OF FIRE & SKILL, WITH NOEL & LIAM, STEVE WHITE, DAMON AND STEVE WITH PAUL WAS A REAL PRIVILEGE. A SUPER GROUP. THESE ARE SOME OF MY FAVOURITE PICTURES OF THE PERIOD. **TONY BRIGGS**

IT WAS A GREAT TIME. IT WAS AT THE TIME OF THE BRIT-POP THING; THAT WAS BEGINNING TO GATHER SPEED, THAT PERIOD BETWEEN 1990 AND 1996 WAS JUST WORK, WORK, WORK AND WE WERE ALL REALLY ENJOYING IT. IT WAS A SOLID TIME AND WE WERE ALL HAPPY. THERE WAS LOTS OF GREAT MUSIC AND THERE WASN'T MUCH BULL-SHIT GOING ON AND EVERYONE WAS GETTING ON. **STEVE WHITE**

205

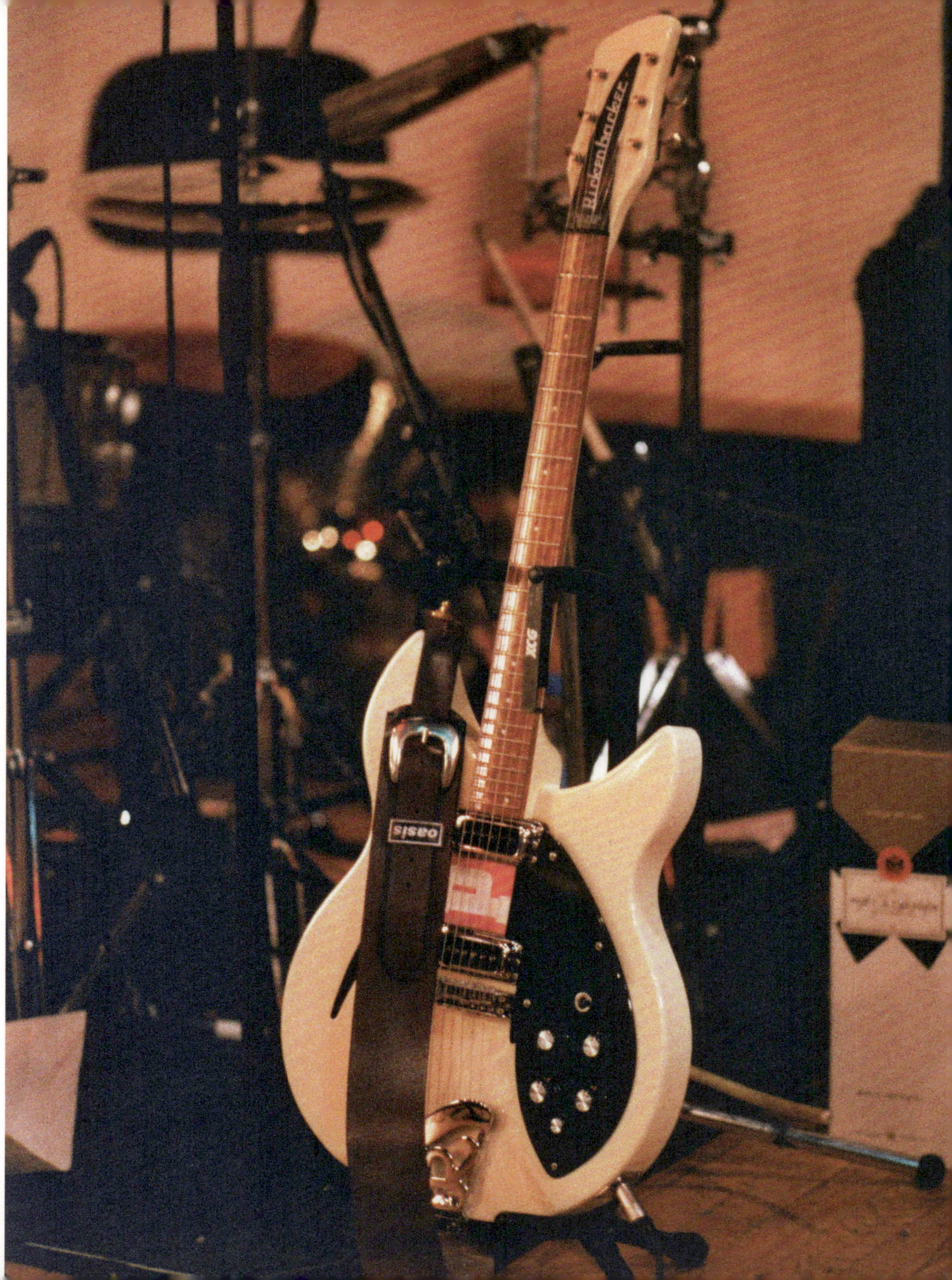
Rickenbacker
oasis

207

208

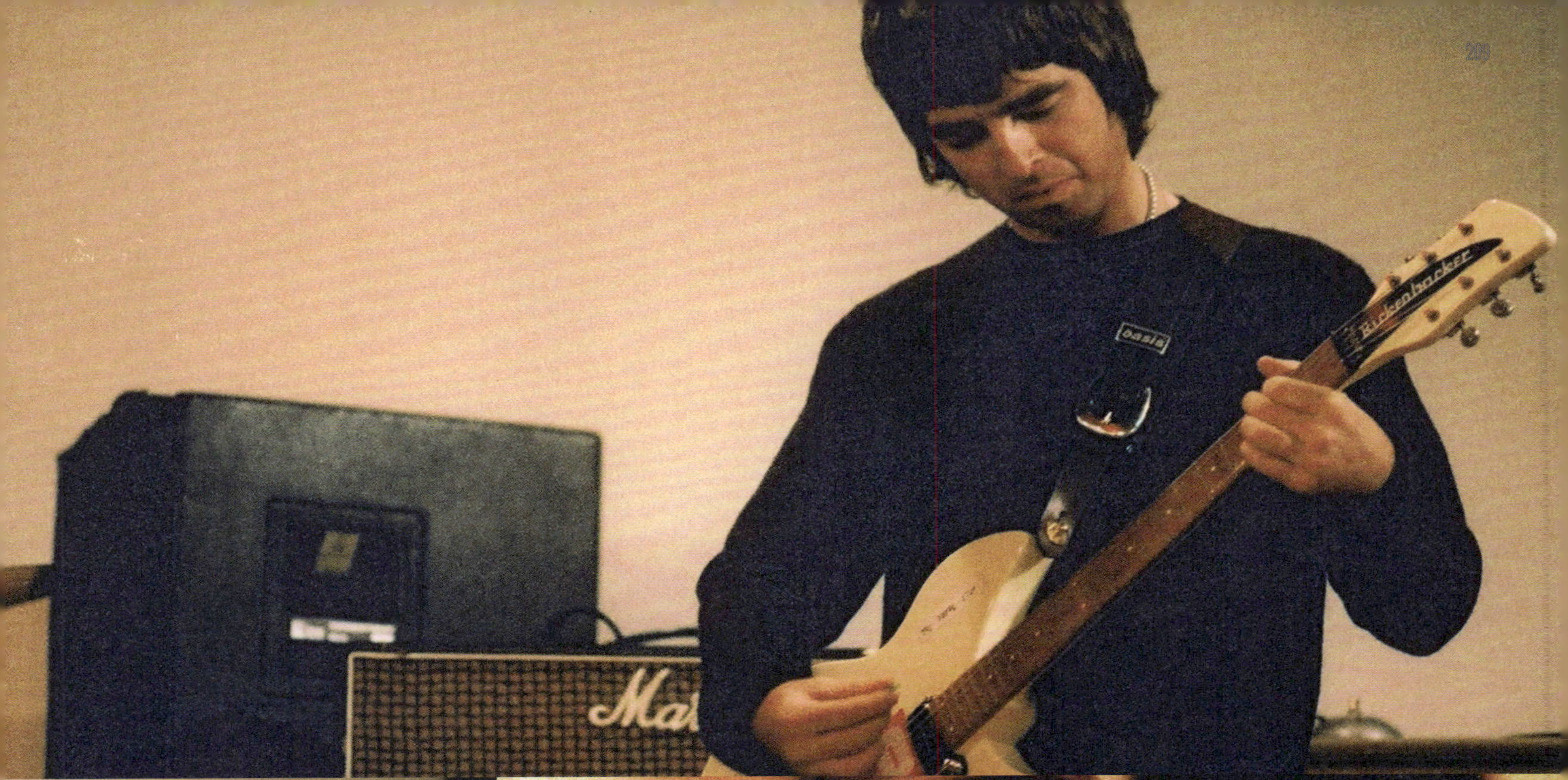
oasis
Rickenbacker

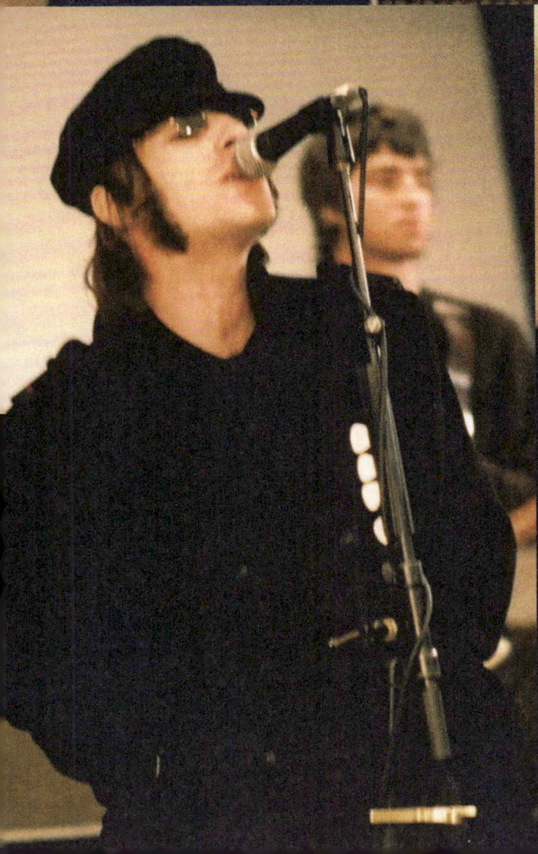

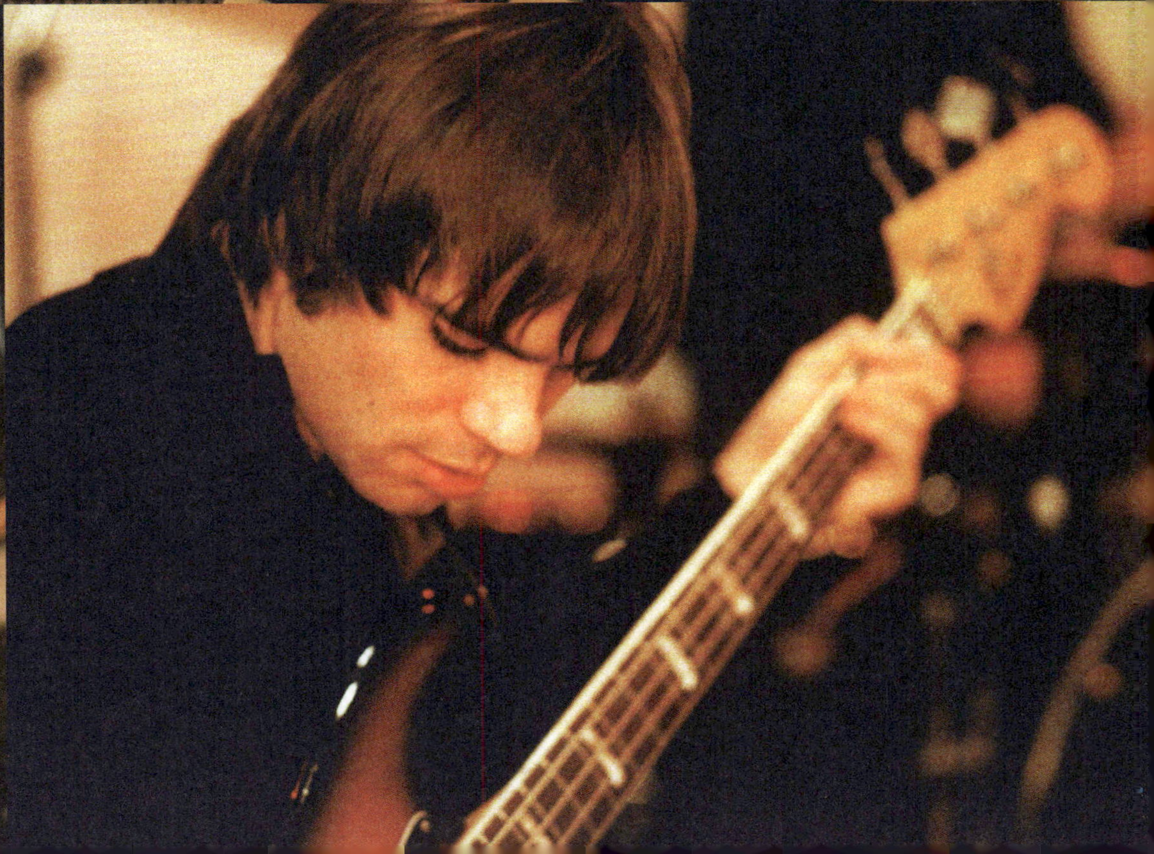

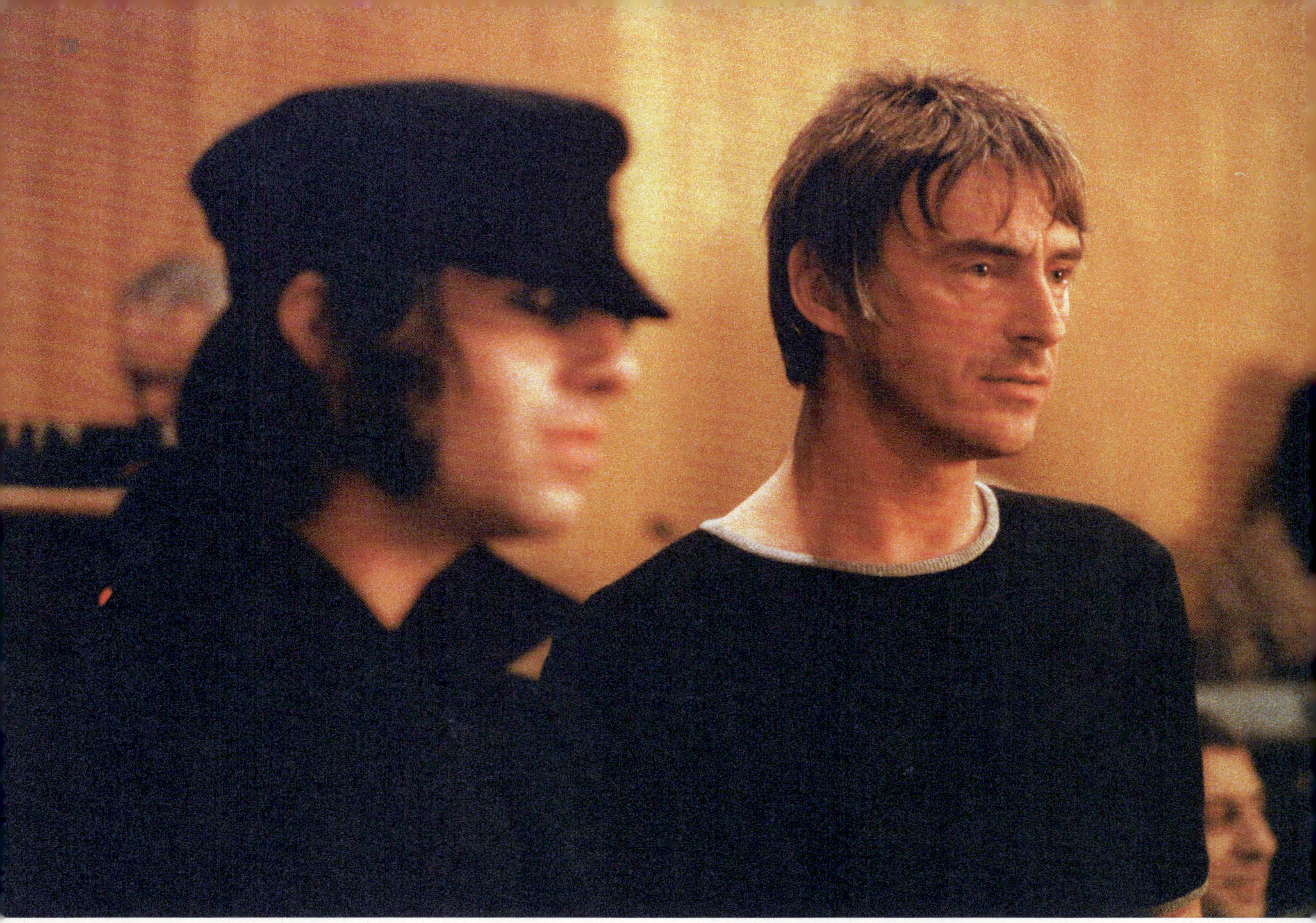

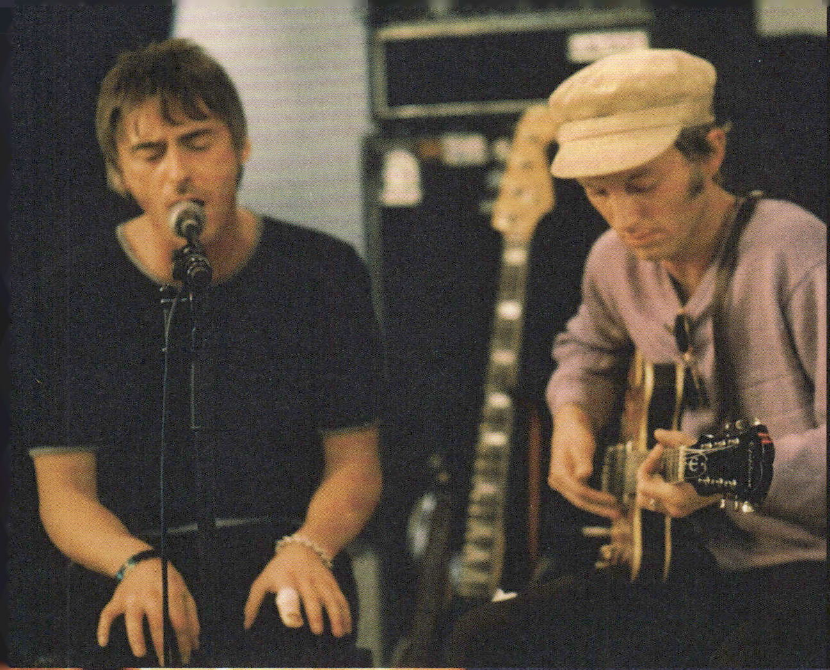

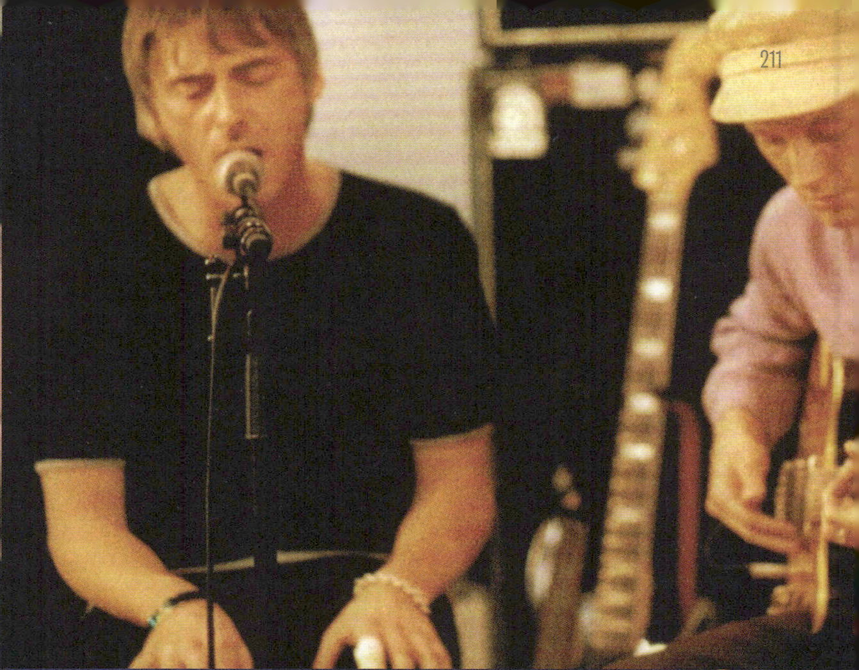

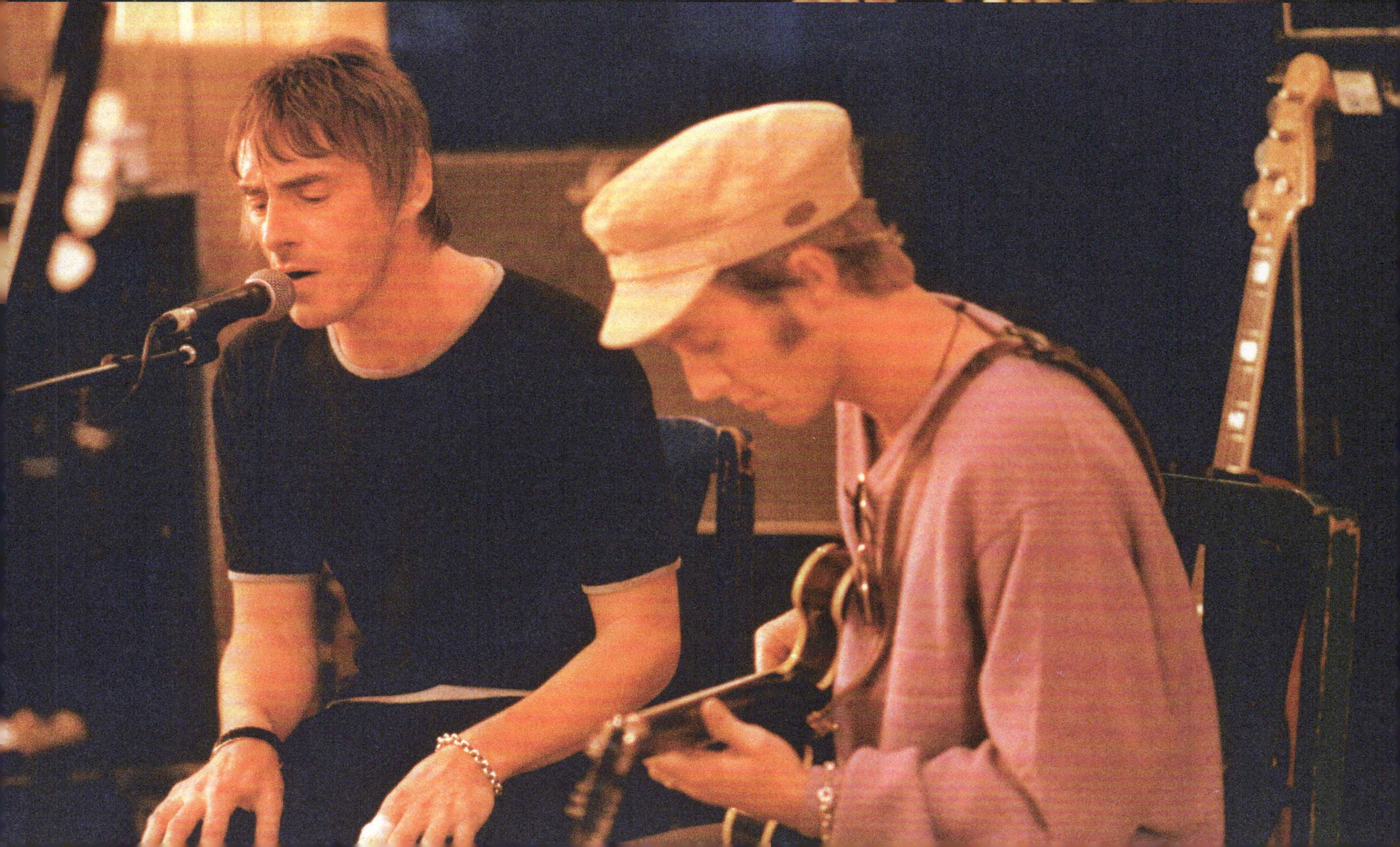

212

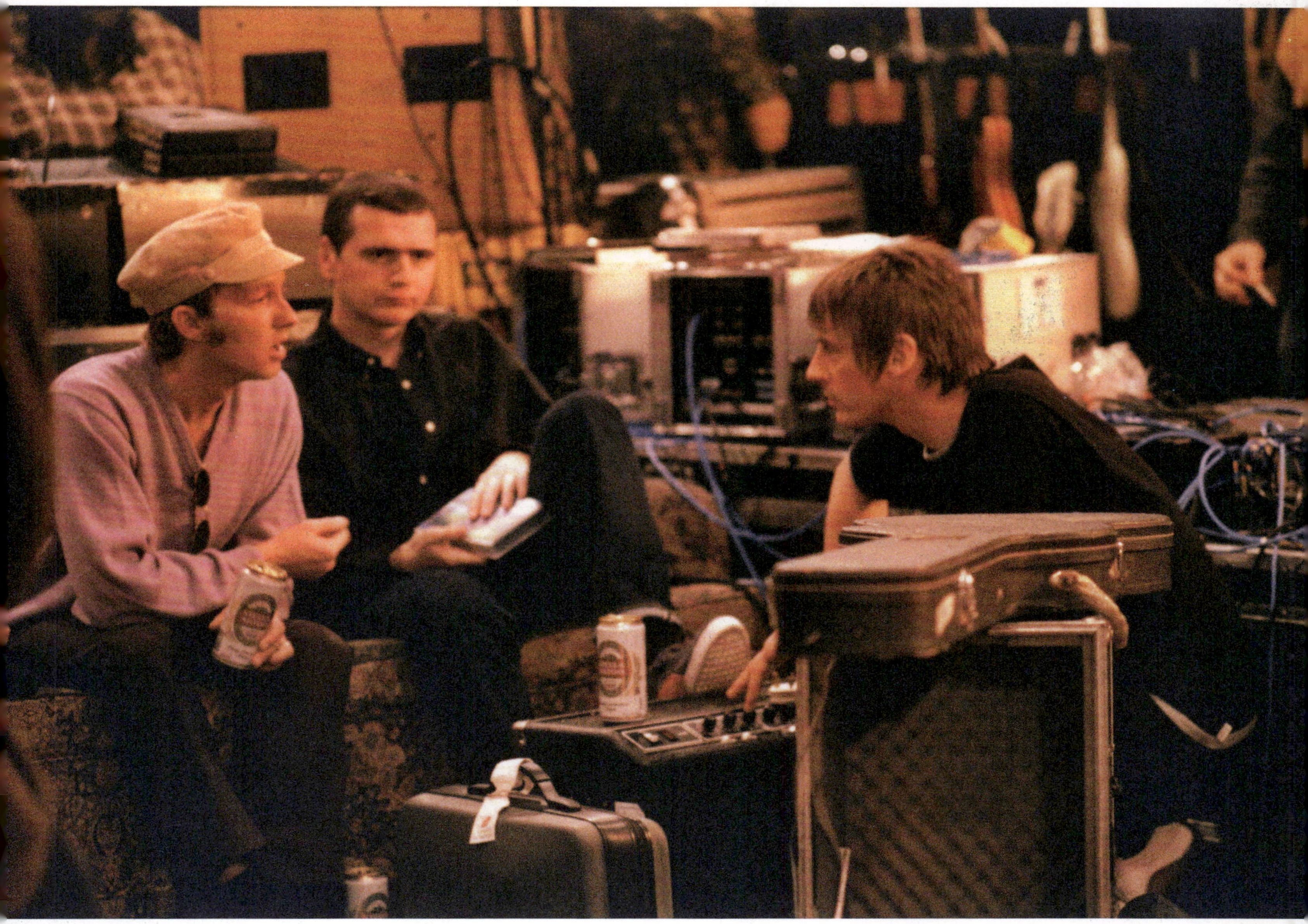

LIAM RECORDED HIS VERSION OF CARNATION WITH STEVE WHITE ON DRUMS, NOEL AND STEVE ON GUITAR, DAMON ON BASS AND PAUL ON PIANO (WITH A BROKEN FINGER). THEN NOEL RECORDED HIS VERSION OF TO BE SOMEONE. **TONY BRIGGS**

215

216

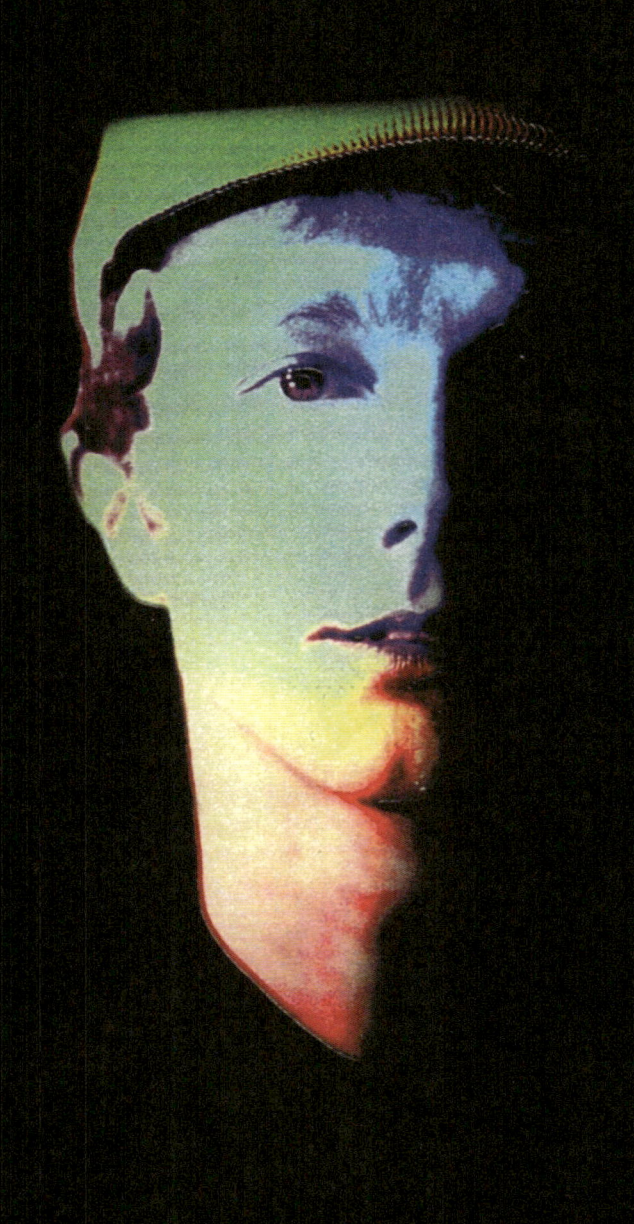

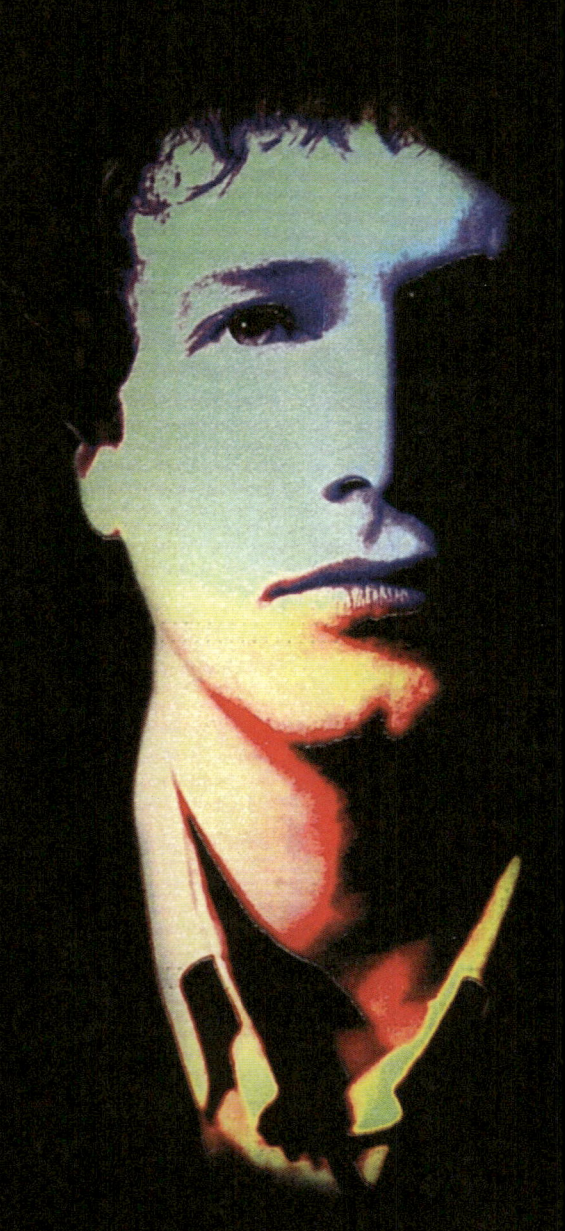

SLEEVE ARTWORK FOR PROFIT IN PEACE (UNUSED).

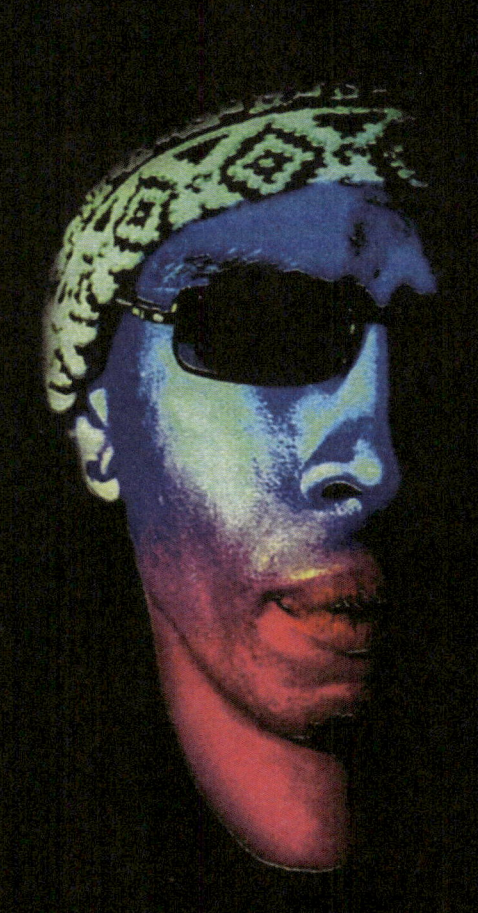

TIMELINE

1995

NOVEMBER	(11)	First and second session
DECEMBER	(12)	Weller & Noel at Reading Hexagon

1996

JANUARY	(1)	Leamington Spa studio
FEBRUARY	(2)	Moseley Shoals cover session
MARCH	(3)	Medals still life
APRIL	(4)	Beechy Head
MAY	(5)	
JUNE	(6)	Custard Factory Circle sleeve shoot
JULY	(7)	
AUGUST	(8)	
SEPTEMBER	(9)	Custard Factory Matt Cook session
OCTOBER	(10)	
NOVEMBER	(11)	
DECEMBER	(12)	

1997

JANUARY	(1)	
FEBRUARY	(2)	Royal Albert Hall 17th (Gez out)
MARCH	(3)	Moseley studio session 1 /B-Sides out
APRIL	(4)	session 2 & HMHC sleeve shots
MAY	(5)	Madrid Festival/HMHC video
JUNE	(6)	Travellers Sleeve ideas & Glastonbury
JULY	(7)	T Park / Marching sleeve/Tones birthday
AUGUST	(8)	Travellers Video & Steve's wedding
SEPTEMBER	(9)	Radio 1 / Oasis tour / album out
OCTOBER	(10)	Better Day Video
NOVEMBER	(11)	Coopers video
DECEMBER	(12)	B/thing studio b/w

1998

JANUARY	(1)	B/thing video
FEBRUARY	(2)	Carlisle / Brighton / Newcastle / Glasgow
MARCH	(3)	
APRIL	(4)	Moseley studio sessions
MAY	(5)	Matt Voss
JUNE	(6)	More studio sessions
JULY	(7)	Daily Star split-up story
AUGUST	(8)	Stirling Castle
SEPTEMBER	(9)	Flaming Cork Festival
OCTOBER	(10)	Fire and Skill, GLR Gig and 1st new album pics
NOVEMBER	(11)	Race Horse
DECEMBER	(12)	New album 2

1999

JANUARY	(1)	New press pics 1
FEBRUARY	(2)	New press pics 2 & group rehearsal shots
MARCH	(3)	RA Hall 2, sax pics and last studio rehearsal session's

DISCOGRAPGHY

ALBUMS

Ocean Colour Scene	April 1992 (Fontana)
Moseley Shoals	April 1996 (MCA)
Marchin' Already	September 1997 (Island)
One From The Modern	September 1998 (Island)
Mechanical Wonder	April 2001 (Island)
North Atlantic Drift	July 2003 (Sanctuary)
A Hyperactive Workout For The Flying Squad	March 2005 (Sanctuary)
On The Leyline	April 2007 (Moseley Shoals)
Saturday	February 2010 (Cooking Vinyl)
Painting	February 2013 (Cooking Vinyl)
B-sides, Seasides & Freerides	April 1997
Songs From The Front Row	November 2001
Live On The Riverboat	December 2002
Anthology	September 2003
Live One For The Road	September 2004
Live Acoustic At The Jam House	May 2006
Live At Birmingham Academy	December 2007
The BBC Sessions	February 2007
The Collection	August 2007

SINGLES

Suburban Love Songs EP	1989
One Of Those Days	1990
Sway	September 1990
Yesterday Today	March 1991
Sway (Reissue)	February 1992
Giving It All Away	April 1992
Do Yourself A Favour EP	May 1992
The Riverboat Song	February 1996
You've Got It Bad	March 1996
The Day We Caught The Train	June 1996
The Circle	September 1996
Hundred Mile High City	June 1997
Travellers Tune	August 1997
Better Day	November 1997
It's A Beautiful Thing	February 1998
Profit in Peace	August 1999
So Low	November 1999
July	June 2000
Up On The Downside	March 2001
Mechanical Wonder	July 2001
Crazy Lowdown Ways	November 2001
I Just Need Myself	June 2003
Make A Deal	August 2003
Golden Gate Bridge	December 2003
Free My Name	March 2005
This Day Should Last Forever	June 2005
I Told You So	April 2007
I Just Got Over You	July 2007
Go To Sea	November 2007
Magic Carpet Days	January 2010
Saturday	May 2010

OCS GEOGRAPHY ACROSS 1996 AND 1997

JANUARY 1996

Wed 24	Weybridge	The Hand & Spear
Thu 25	Colchester	Arts Centre
Sat 27	Warwick	University
Sun 28	Guilford	University
Mon 29	Sheffield	University
Wed 31	Egham	Royal Holloway College

FEBRUARY

Sat 03	Sunderland	University (Manor Quay)
Sun 04	Preston	Adelphi
Wed 07	Bournemouth	Old Fire Station
Thu 08	Portsmouth	Portsmouth University
Sat 10	Nottingham	Connection
Sun 11	Blackwood	Miners Institute
Mon 12	Exeter	The Cavern
Wed 14	Stoke On Trent	The Stage
Thu 15	Hull	Blue Lamp
Fri 16	Middlesbrough	Arena

MARCH

Fri 01	Ayr	Jonesy's
Sat 02	Alloa	Funhouse
Sun 03	Cumbernauld	Sax Venue
Tues 05	Aberdeen	Cafe Drummond
Wed 06	Dundee	Fat Sam's
Thu 07	East Kilbride	Batcave
Sat 09	Perth	Twa Tam's
Sun 10	Greenock	Rico's
Thu 14	Portsmouth	University
Mon 18	Cambridge	Junction
Wed 20	Blackwood	Miner's Institute
Sat 23	Wolverhampton	Wulfrun Hall
Wed 27	Stoke	The Stage
Thu 28	Scunthorpe	Baths Hall
Sat 30	Gloucester	Guildhall Arts Court

APRIL

Sat 27	Manchester	Maine Road
Sun 28	Manchester	Maine Road
Mon 29	Glasgow	The Garage

MAY

Wed 01	Newcastle	Riverside
Wed 08	London	Camden Electric Ballroom
Thu 09	London	Camden Electric Ballroom
Sat 11	Barcelona, Spain	Zeleste
Sun 12	Madrid, Spain	The Revolver Club

JUNE

No Events

JULY

Mon 01	Munich	Substanz
Wed 03	Cologne	Apollo Club
Thu 04	Hamburg	Marx
Sat 06	Kristiansand, Norway	Quart Festival

AUGUST

Sun 04	Loch Lomond	Ballach Country Park
Sat 10	Stevenage	Knebworth Park

SEPTEMBER

Fri 13	London	Wembley Arena

OCTOBER

Wed 02	Milton Keynes	Sanctuary
Thu 03	Bradford	St. Georges Hall
Fri 04	Doncaster	Dome
Sun 06	Norwich	UEA
Mon 07	Ipswich	The Regent
Tue 08	Nottingham	Rock City
Thu 10	Hanley	Victoria Halls
Fri 11	Gloucester	Leisure Centre
Sat 12	Reading	Hexagon
Mon 14	Exeter	University
Tue 15	Southampton	Guildhall
Wed 16	Brighton	Event
Sat 19	Newport	The Centre
Sun 20	Manchester	Apollo
Tue 22	Leicester	De Montfort Hall
Wed 23	Derby	Assembly Rooms
Thu 24	York	Barbican
Sat 26	Glasgow	Barrowlands
Sun 27	Glasgow	Barrowlands
Mon 28	Newcastle	Mayfair
Thu 31	Liverpool	Royal Court

NOVEMBER

Fri 01	Blackpool	Tower Ballroom
Sun 03	London	Hammersmith Le Palais
Mon 04	London	Hammersmith Le Palais
Tue 05	London	Hammersmith Le Palais
Thu 07	Birmingham	Aston Villa Leisure Centre
Fri 08	Birmingham	Aston Villa Leisure Centre
Mon 11	Landover, MD	USAir Arena
Tue 12	Worchester, MA	The Centrum
Thu 14	Worchester, MA	The Centrum
Fri 15	Uniondale, NY	Nassau Coliseum
Sun 17	Philadelphia, PA	CoreStates Center
Mon 18	Philadelphia, PA	CoreStates Center
Tue 19	East Rutherford, NJ	Continental Air Arena
Fri 22	New York, NY	Mercury Lounge
Sat 23	Cambridge, MA	T.T. Bear's
Tue 26	Toronto, ON	Opera House
Wed 27	Detroit, MI	The Shelter
Fri 29	Chicago, IL	The Metro
Sat 30	St. Louis, MO	The Side Door

DECEMBER

Tue 03	Seattle, WA	The Crocodile
Wed 04	Vancouver, BC	Town Pump
Fri 06	San Francisco, CA	Bottom on the Hill
Sat 07	San Francisco, CA	Slims
Sun 08	San Diego, CA	The Casbah
Tue 10	Los Angeles, CA	Whiskey A Go-Go
Sun 15	Tokyo, Japan	Club Quattro
Mon 16	Tokyo, Japan	The Garden Hall
Tue 17	Tokyo, Japan	The Garden Hall
Thu 19	Tokyo, Japan	Liquid Room
Fri 20	Osaka	Bayside Jenny
Tue 31	Edinburgh	The Mound

JANUARY 1997

No Events

FEBRUARY

Fri 14	Dublin	Olympia Theatre
Sat 15	Dublin	Olympia Theatre
Mon 17	London	Royal Albert Hall

MARCH

Thu 06	Stockholm	Gino
Sat 08	Copenhagen	Pumpehuset
Mon 10	Hamburg	Logo
Tue 11	Berlin	Loft
Thu 13	Nuremburg	Hirsch
Fri 14	Munich	Strom
Sun 16	Cologne	Luxor
Mon 17	Frankfurt	Batschkapp
Tue 18	Stuttgart	Roehre

APRIL

| Wed 23 | Birmingham | Faculty & Firkin |

MAY

Thu 22	Stockholm	Electric Garden
Sun 25	Bremen	Moments
Mon 26	Essen	Zeche Carl
Wed 28	Muenster	Odeon
Thu 29	Halle	Easy Schorre

JUNE

Sun 01	Southampton	The Common
Fri 20	Belfast	Botanic Gardens
Sat 28	Pilton, Somerset	Glastonbury Festival

JULY

Sun 13	Balado, Perthshire	T in the Park Festival
Fri 18	Dublin, Ireland	Olympia
Sat 19	Galway, Ireland	Big Day Out
Sun 20	Birmingham	Songwriters' Cafe
Fri 25	Karlsruhe, Germany	Karlruhe Festival
Tue 29	Birmingham	Aston Villa Leisure Centre

AUGUST

| Mon 25 | Birmingham | NEC |

SEPTEMBER

| Tue 9 | Stockholm | Globen |

OCTOBER

Tue 07	Glasgow	Barrowlands
Wed 08	Glasgow	Barrowlands
Thu 09	Glasgow	Barrowlands
Sat 11	London	Brixton Academy
Sun 12	London	Brixton Academy
Wed 15	Manchester	The Apollo
Thu 16	Manchester	The Apollo
Mon 27	Ebisu, Tokyo	Garden Hall
Tue 28	Ebisu, Tokyo	Garden Hall
Wed 29	Ebisu, Tokyo	Garden Hall

NOVEMBER

Wed 05	Hanover	Capitol Club
Wed 12	Bielefeld	Hechelei
Sun 16	Berlin	The Loft
Tue 18	Frankfurt	Batschkapp
Wed 19	Stuttgart	Longhorn
Sat 22	Munich	Colosseum
Sun 23	Milan	Magazzini Generali
Tue 25	Madrid	Aqualung Club
Thu 27	Valencia	
Sat 29	Bilboa	

DECEMBER

Thu 11	Groningen, Netherlands	The Centre
Fri 12	Cologne	Live Music Hall
Mon 15	Hamburg	Markthalle
Tue 16	Amsterdam	De Melkweg

TONY BRIGGS

Sunderland born and bred, moved to London in 1985. A prolific photographer and director who worked exclusively with Ocean Colour Scene from 1995 to 1999 shooting all of Moseley Shoals and Marchin Already, from Riverboat Song to Its a Beautiful Thing and Directed the promos for the remixed Hundred mile High City, Better Day, Beautiful Thing and the long form videos Travellers Tunes and Salute to Scotland.

IAN SNOWBALL

Born and dragged up in Kent to the sounds of The Jam, Northern Soul and the best of the 60's. Soon to be recognised as a cult pulp fiction writer. First book's Long Hot Summer and Once Upon a Tribe were published in 2011. Followed by His novel In the Blood, then The Jam Thick as Thieves and Oasis Supersonic, From Ronnie's to Ravers and Nightshift.

peace – equilibrium – harmony
= Modernism
contemporary

Al + Tony

I'm trapped to London (shithole).

I ♥ U 4 the photos

bad to rag-cbt –

Word

Steve

THANKS AND DEDICATIONS

Snowy would like to thank the two blondes in his life Josie (the day we caught the train) and Loz (it's a beautiful thing), Tony for doing the book with me, Damon for stepping up, my two OCS sidekicks Bazza and Dan, all at Countdown: Ian, Paul, Mark and Donna and all the contributors who made Soul Driver possible.

Tony would like to thank Damon Minchella, Billy McCartney, Gerard Saint, Wez Gibbons, Paul Fish, Pete Kelsey, Ted Cummings, Matt Cook, Jaynie Bye, Dom Delaney, Gareth Robertson, Mark, Ian and Paul at Countdown and all of our sponsors and contributors. And of course Alice for her never ending support and patience.

Countdown Publishing would like to thank Mark Hooper, Gary Williamson, Paul Jacobs, Andrea Jonasson, Luke Harris, Eddie PIller, Alan (the biker) Jones, Johanna Christie, Joseph, Hannah and Mary Hallam, Ana and Emily Hallam, Hannah and Georgia Slavin, Ollie and Isabel Roche, Joanne Smith, David Edwards, Andrew Stevenson, Poppy and Annabel Prime, Kirsty Walker, Anna Picton and Krystle Coe, Maddy and Hollie, Lucie Coe, Charlie Jefferies, all at Merc, our friends are Sherrys. Remembering Ilan Ostrove and Simon Bullock

* Taken from Moseley Shoals and Marchin' Already Sleeve notes, MCA Universal Music.